LDAP Programming, Management
and Integration

D0764530

LDAP Programming, Management and Integration

CLAYTON DONLEY

MANNING

Greenwich
(74° w. long.)

For online information and ordering of this and other Manning books,
go to www.manning.com. The publisher offers discounts on this book
when ordered in quantity. For more information, please contact:

Special Sales Department
Manning Publications Co.
209 Bruce Park Avenue   Fax: (203) 661-9018
Greenwich, CT 06830   email: orders@manning.com

©2003 by Manning Publications Co. All rights reserved.

No part of this publication may be reproduced, stored in a retrieval system, or transmitted,
in any form or by means electronic, mechanical, photocopying, or otherwise, without prior
written permission of the publisher.

Many of the designations used by manufacturers and sellers to distinguish their products are
claimed as trademarks. Where those designations appear in the book, and Manning
Publications was aware of a trademark claim, the designations have been printed in initial
caps or all caps.

⊗ Recognizing the importance of preserving what has been written, it is Manning's policy to have the
books we publish printed on acid-free paper, and we exert our best efforts to that end.

Manning Publications Co.   Copyeditor: Tiffany Taylor
209 Bruce Park Avenue   Typesetter: Dottie Marsico
Greenwich, CT 06830   Cover designer: Leslie Haimes

ISBN 1-930110-40-5
Printed in the United States of America
1 2 3 4 5 6 7 8 9 10 – VHG – 06 05 04 03

contents

preface

This book will help you understand and use the most important directory services—those based on the leading industry standards—without having to read the many esoteric standards documents available on the Web. I am tempted to start the book with a motivating example from my experience to explain why directory services are so important and why you should read this book from cover to cover, but I will resist. There is no need to tell a story from my experience, because I can tell a story from *your* experience. Every single one of you has had experience with directory services, whether you know it or not.

Did you log in to a computer today? When the computer checked your password, it was probably using a directory service.

Do you use a personalized start page, such as Netscape Netcenter? If so, your preferences and login information were found in a directory service and used to customize your experience.

Have you ever looked up the email addresses of long-lost friends on the Internet, or located the telephone number of the woman in receiving who can track down your lost package? Both of these tasks are also common uses for directories.

However, you don't need to learn how to type someone's name into a search engine or enter your password. What you *do* need to learn, and what this book will teach you, is how to apply the standards that make directory services accessible over computer networks ranging from the Internet to your corporate intranet to business partners' extranets.

We won't stop there. The most pressing issue in the area of directory services today is simply that there are so many of them. Every application written in the last 30 years seems to have come with its own proprietary directory. Operating systems also have directories. Most of these directories don't care about each other or even acknowledge the others' existence. This book will help you get these existing directories to work well with new, important standards-based directory services.

Finally, what good is a data repository without useful applications? If you are an application developer trying to get your existing applications to work with Lightweight Directory Access Protocol (LDAP), Directory Services Markup Language (DSML), and other directory standards, this book not only will help you get a handle on important application program interfaces (APIs), but also will deliver an understanding of the best strategies for using these applications to derive important application benefits.

WHO AM I, AND WHAT'S MY MOTIVATION?

Many of the people picking up this book may know my reputation as a long-time developer in the directory space. My background in this area includes writing the first comprehensive Perl module for accessing directory services via LDAP, as well as writing software for getting applications such as Apache, the Squid proxy server, and Cyrus mail servers to check passwords against servers supporting LDAP.

My recent work in this area has included the development of complete Java server software for providing data via the LDAP protocol. The server, originally a part-time open source project, is now the cornerstone of a virtual directory and proxy service product offering from OctetString. However, this book is vendor neutral; all major LDAP vendors are discussed to some extent in the first chapter.

Like many of you, I stumbled onto LDAP by accident. In 1993, I was employed as part of Motorola's Cellular Infrastructure Group in Arlington Heights, Illinois. Along with a small group of other colleagues, I cofounded one of Motorola's first web-based intranets.

Unlike today, when most major web sites are dynamic and filled to the brim with personalized content and real-time access to databases and important applications, there were few web-based applications in those days. Sensing the potential use of this new technology, yet realizing that this grass-roots project would not receive funding if we couldn't adequately expose business information, many team members proceeded to develop applications, such as card catalogs for engineering documents and similar things.

I decided that my small project would be an email directory. As the only person on this project from the IT organization, I was aware of a service provided by corporate mainframes that presented information culled from human resources and local area network (LAN) administrators over a simple protocol called WHOIS.

Using WHOIS, you could open a simple network connection to the server (which in this case resided on a mainframe) and type the data to be used for searching. The search results were returned as free-form text. My application did nothing more than read this text, parse it, and write it out as HTML that could be displayed graphically by a web browser.

It was an instant hit.

I became known at Motorola Cellular as the "directory" guy, and was instantly pushed onto most of the projects that dealt with directories. At the time, these projects primarily related to email. Email is an important use of directories—after all, if you cannot locate the address of people with whom you need to communicate, a large email infrastructure doesn't do much good. However, I began to realize that this directory wasn't just a way to look up information; it was a key storage point for identity information—the only network-accessible place in the company where a person's email address, login ID, department, name, and manager were linked together. I realized that smart applications could use this information to identify users throughout the company and authorize them based on criteria, such as their department. Those applications could also provide customized presentations based on that same information.

I also knew that as good as this idea was, it would be hard to execute given the limitations of WHOIS, unless we customized each application. At this time, I came into contact with X.500.

Like WHOIS, X.500 is a standard for a kind of directory service. Unlike WHOIS, X.500 is anything but simple. It is a detailed set of standards definitions that seems to describe everything within a 10-mile radius of directory services, including client access, real security, server-to-server communications, and similar areas. Also unlike WHOIS, X.500 comes from the OSI networking world, which was left in the dust in the wake of the Internet explosion and the mass adoption of loosely networked systems built around standards such as TCP/IP.

Nearly every book or article written about LDAP talks about X.500 being perfect except for that dastardly OSI protocol stack, which makes deployment on desktop-class hardware difficult. (Although there is truth to this reasoning, the real reason most X.500 directory projects didn't take off is that getting the right data into the directory and keeping it up-to-date was difficult—after all, garbage in, garbage out. Similarly, few applications were X.500 aware, partly due to its complexity.) This difficulty spawned LDAP, which was meant to replace X.500's Directory Access Protocol (DAP) as a client implementation.

After making the move from X.500 to LDAP for the same published reasons everyone else did, the lack of integration tools and directory-enabled applications was obvious. So, I created things like Net::LDAPapi and PerLDAP to glue together information from different sources into the directory. Not long afterward, I wrote the code that allowed users to be identified and authorized to many services, such as web, proxy, and mail.

Today many applications are directory-enabled—so many that these applications drive most new directory deployments, rather than the other way around. People looking at deploying and accessing directories are faced with many difficult choices in design and execution. My goal for this book is to help simplify this complex technology in a way that accelerates your projects and improves your end results.

LESSONS LEARNED, AND THIS BOOK'S FOCUS

Since discovering LDAP, I've spent nearly every day looking to develop solutions to these types of problems. Much of the time, the solution is centered on creating enterprise directory services. I've learned a few things about creating successful directory services. The most critical are:

- Access is access.
- Configuration is trivial; management is complex.

Although these may seem like insanely simple lessons, let me explain.

Access is access

Certain methods of access may be more efficient or provide more underlying functionality, but at the end of the day, it is only important that the directory service can share information in a way that clients and applications can use. Today, that standard for sharing information in directory services is LDAP. Therefore, we use LDAP as the primary access protocol throughout this book.

However, many of the more advanced techniques described in parts 2 and 3 of this book will work just as well with another means of access. In fact, part 3 describes the use of Directory Services Markup Language (DSML), which you can use to represent directory services information as XML.

Configuration is trivial; management is complex

This is not to say that your mother should be installing and configuring your directory servers. It is merely an indication of the relative complexity of configuration versus management.

I cannot stress enough that unless the directory is running in a stand-alone environment where it is the only source of data, there will be effort in getting information into and out of the directory. Unless you understand and make this effort up front, the data in the directory will either be stale and useless or require yet another manual administrative process to keep it up to date.

New technology is coming out that removes some of the technical barriers to splicing information into authoritative directories. However, such technology does not remove the internal political roadblocks and the need for up-front planning that is required in nearly all meaningful directory service deployments.

acknowledgments

Creating a quality technology book involves a great deal of effort from many talented and passionate individuals. There is simply no way to thank all of those involved enough for their efforts in making this book as good as it could possibly be.

I must start by thanking my wife Linda for her support in this endeavor. Without her patience and strong support, this book certainly would never have been completed. A few weeks before the book went to press, we received the special delivery of our son Ethan, who was certainly an inspiration as the book's development came to a close.

Too many people to name looked at bits and pieces of this book. Some of the people who looked through early drafts were Kurt Zeilenga of the OpenLDAP project, La Monte Yaroll of Motorola, Booker Bense of Stanford, Jay Leiserson and Richard Goodwin of IBM, Jauder Ho of KPMG, Ranjan Bagchi, Juan Carlos Gomez and Raul Cuza. Nathan Owen of IBM and Phil Hunt of OctetString also offered some very helpful feedback on several key sections later in the development cycle.

Extra special thanks go to Booker Bense, who did a detailed final review of the entire text and made a number of quality suggestions that I feel contributed to the technical accuracy and readability of the book. Don Bowen of Sun was also especially helpful in his review of key sections of the book as it neared completion.

Many people at Manning Publications were incredible throughout the process. Marjan Bace and Mary Piergies were on top of this project with their full attention and enthusiasm from the start. Lianna Wlasiuk was phenomenal as a development editor and offered many significant ideas that vastly improved the final content of the book. Tiffany Taylor did a fantastic job of editing the text and removing all of the embarrassing errors that I left behind. Dottie Marsico had the Herculean task of making sense of a vast number of graphics in a myriad formats, among other things. Syd Brown came up with the book's wonderful design, and Leslie Haimes did a great job putting together a captivating cover. Ted Kennedy did a masterful job of staying on top of the entire review process.

Finally, a special thanks to everyone I've emailed or spoken with over the years about this technology. These discussions helped shape much of the thinking that went into this book. So much was learned from sharing information with the users of the LDAP-related technology I've developed. This learning and interaction was truly a reward for any effort on my part.

about this book

Part 1 of the book has five chapters:

- Chapter 1 introduces core LDAP concepts, with the understanding that you may have little or no past exposure to the protocol.

- Chapter 2 introduces LDAP's information model and schema. Information in an LDAP-enabled directory is presented in a simple and uniform way that you should understand before proceeding. This chapter covers object classes, attribute types, and schema standards.

- Chapter 3 offers information about LDAP namespace and naming standards. Because all entries in LDAP are uniquely named, it's important for you to understand the information in this chapter.

- Chapter 4 provides an overview of LDAP search criteria. Because searching is the most commonly used and most complex LDAP operation from a client perspective, we spend considerable time introducing and explaining filters, scope, and search bases.

- Chapter 5 introduces the LDAP Data Interchange Format (LDIF) and the Directory Services Markup Language (DSML), an XML standard for representing directory information, and shows how these standards can be used to easily store and share directory information.

Part 2 is as follows:

- We begin exploring LDAP management in chapter 6. This chapter introduces the Net::LDAP module, which lets you use Perl to access and manage an LDAP-enabled directory.

- In chapter 7, we discuss administrative techniques. Examples include a web-based tool that you can use to manage individual entries.

- Chapter 8 offers insights into synchronization and migration. No data exists in a vacuum, so this chapter provides guidance about some of the ways data in other directories and databases can be leveraged in an LDAP environment.

- Chapter 9 explains how to monitor and manage information about the LDAP server. Examples include schema retrieval scripts and tools for generating synthetic transactions that can be used to check server availability.

- Chapter 10 expands on our previous discussion of DSML. Many examples are provided, in Perl, including ones for generating DSML and transforming it to HTML using XSLT.

Part 3 comprises the book's final three chapters:

- In chapter 11, we begin discussing the best methods for directory-enabling your applications. This chapter offers an introduction to the Java Naming and Directory Interface (JNDI), an API for accessing directory services based on many standards, including LDAP.

- In chapter 12, we refocus on DSML in an application context. Examples are given that relate DSML to other technologies, such as web services and SOAP. An exploration of DSML version 2 operations is also provided.

- Security ranks with messaging as a critical area for directory integration. For that reason, we spend chapter 13 going over authentication, authorization, digital certificate storage, and LDAP security issues in general.

The book ends with two appendixes:

- Appendix A provides a compilation of standard schemas from Request for Comments (RFCs), Internet Drafts, and other sources that you should consider prior to the creation of new schemas. The LDAP schema is discussed in chapter 2.

- PerLDAP is a popular alternative to the Net::LDAP module discussed in part 2. Appendix B offers an overview of PerLDAP and translation of many of the examples in part 2.

WHO SHOULD READ THIS BOOK

This book is written for network and system administrators, as well as application developers. Little or no past LDAP exposure is required.

Part 1 of this book uses command-line tools to demonstrate LDAP features. Part 2 provides examples in Perl that can be used unmodified in many cases or as the basis for more advanced tools.

Finally, part 3 of the book is focused on application development issues with examples in Java. Although less directly useful to system and network administrators, it covers many important aspects of directory-enabled application development.

AUTHOR ONLINE

When you purchase *LDAP Programming, Management and Integration* you gain free access to a private web forum run by Manning Publications where you can make comments about the book, ask technical questions, and receive help from the author and from other users. To access the forum and subscribe to it, point your web browser to www.manning.com/donley. This page provides information on how to get on the forum once you are registered, what kind of help is available, and the rules of conduct on the forum.

Manning's commitment to our readers is to provide a venue where a meaningful dialogue between individual readers and between readers and the author can take place. It is not a commitment to any specific amount of participation on the part of the author, whose contribution to the AO remains voluntary (and unpaid). We suggest you try asking the author some challenging questions lest his interest stray!

The Author Online forum and the archives of previous discussions will be accessible from the publisher's web site as long as the book is in print.

SOURCE CODE

Source code for all examples presented in *LDAP Programming, Management and Integration* is available for download from www.manning.com/donley.

Code conventions

Courier typeface is used for code examples. **Bold Courier** typeface is used in some code examples to highlight important or changed sections. Certain references to code in text, such as functions, properties, and methods, also appear in Courier typeface. Code annotations accompany some segments of code.

getting started

Throughout this book, examples are provided wherever possible. This section details where to get the tools you will need to use the examples.

DIRECTORY SERVERS

A directory server supporting LDAP is required to run these examples. The examples should work with almost any LDAP-enabled directory server, except where noted prior to the example.

This book is about getting the most from directory services, not installing and configuring all the directories on the market. Following are pointers to some of the more common directory servers available at the time of publication. Additionally, we include basic instructions for obtaining a special LDAP server that has been preconfigured to work with the examples in this book.

Directory server vendors

The LDAPZone (http://www.ldapzone.com) web site is a good place to begin when you're looking for answers to many directory issues. It has active community pages and links to other sites related to LDAP. It also has links to the most popular LDAP server implementations.

Among the servers currently listed are

- Novell eDirectory
- iPlanet Directory Server
- Oracle Internet Directory
- Critical Path InJoin Directory Server
- Microsoft Active Directory
- IBM SecureWay Directory
- Open Source OpenLDAP Directory
- Data Connection Directory
- OctetString Virtual Directory Engine

Each of these vendors provides a server that is directly LDAP accessible, with solid documentation for installation and configuration.

Basic configuration parameters

The examples in this book assume the server will be listening on TCP port 389, which is the standard LDAP port. This is usually easily configurable within the server, although certain implementations (such as Microsoft Active Directory) cannot be configured to listen on a different port.

The root of the directory tree used in the examples is `dc=manning,dc=com`. This will be acceptable to most implementations, but some older servers may not be aware of dc-style naming. If that is the case, substituting `o=manning,c=us` or any other name for the root in configuration and examples should be acceptable. You can find more information about naming and directory trees in chapter 3.

Most of the examples in this book use standard schemas related to people and groups that can be found in virtually all LDAP implementations. If an example produces an error related to a schema violation, you may need to add the schema being referenced by that example. Different directories have different files and configuration options for adding new schemas.

COMMAND-LINE TOOLS

In part 1 of the book, no programming languages are used. Instead, we use commonly available LDAP tools to demonstrate key components of LDAP, such as information model, entry naming, and search filters. These tools come with many operating systems, such as Solaris and some Linux variants. They are also distributed with many directory server products.

You can determine if the tools are available by attempting to run commands such as `ldapmodify` and `ldapsearch`. If these commands exist, they should be suitable for the examples in this book.

The source code to these tools can be found in at least two places:

- The OpenLDAP project (www.openldap.org)
- The Mozilla Directory project (www.mozilla.org/directory/)

Both of these versions are suitable for use with the examples in this book.

If you prefer to download precompiled versions of these tools, you can most easily obtain them as part of the iPlanet Directory Software Development Kit (SDK). This kit is available at http://www.iplanet.com/downloads/developer/.

LDAP PERL MODULES

Part 2 of this book, which focuses on directory management, uses the Perl language to populate, synchronize, and otherwise manage information in directories. These examples require a modern version of Perl (at least 5.005 is required, but 5.6 or higher is recommended) and the Perl-LDAP module. This is not to be confused with PerLDAP, which is the module previously released by Netscape and the author of this book. Although both modules do the same job, Perl-LDAP is becoming more widely used; and, because it is completely written in Perl, it is portable to any platform where Perl is available.

The Perl-LDAP module is written and maintained by Graham Barr and can be found at perl-ldap.sourceforge.net along with detailed installation instructions.

Active State Perl users can use these commands to install the necessary module automatically:

```
C:\ >ppm
PPM interactive shell (2.1.6) - type 'help' for available commands.
PPM> install perl-ldap
```

Users of other versions of Perl can access the module on the Comprehensive Perl Archive Network (CPAN) (http://www.cpan.org).

JAVA

Java is used extensively throughout part 3 of this book. We use core Java functionality found in J2SE as well as extensions for communicating with LDAP and parsing XML/DSML.

Java LDAP Access

There are two primary ways to access LDAP in Java:

- *Java Naming and Directory Interface (JNDI)*—You can use this generalized interface to access LDAP and non-LDAP directory and naming services.

- *Netscape Java SDK*—This set of Java classes was created specifically to talk to directory servers via the LDAP protocol.

This book uses JNDI. JNDI comes standard as part of Java development kits and runtimes at or above the 1.3 version. It is available for download at java.sun.com for earlier Java development kits.

DSML/XML

The examples in chapter 12 use both JNDI and the Java API for XML (JAXP). The JNDI examples that read DSML files require the DSML provider for JNDI. This provider is a preview technology on java.sun.com at the time of publication. The JAXP reference implementation from Sun is included with Java 1.4 and available for earlier Java releases from Sun's Java site at http://java.sun.com/.

about the cover illustration

The figure on the cover of *LDAP Programming, Management and Integration* is called an "Aga de los Genizaros," an officer in the Turkish infantry. The illustration is taken from a Spanish compendium of regional dress customs first published in Madrid in 1799. The title page of the Spanish volume states:

Coleccion general de los Trages que usan actualmente todas las Nacionas del Mundo des-ubierto, dibujados y grabados con la mayor exactitud por R.M.V.A.R. Obra muy util y en special para los que tienen la del viajero universal

which we translate, as literally as possible, thus:

General Collection of Costumes currently used in the Nations of the Known World, designed and printed with great exactitude by R.M.V.A.R. This work is very useful especially for those who hold themselves to be universal travelers.

Although nothing is known of the designers, engravers, and workers who colored this illustration by hand, the "exactitude" of their execution is evident in this drawing. It is just one of many figures in this colorful collection. Their diversity speaks vividly of the uniqueness and individuality of the world's towns and regions just 200 years ago. This was a time when the dress codes of two regions separated by a few dozen miles identified people uniquely as belonging to one or the other. The collection brings to life a sense of isolation and distance of that period and of every other historic period except our own hyperkinetic present. Dress codes have changed since then and the diversity by region, so rich at the time, has faded away. It is now often hard to tell the inhabitant of one continent from another. Perhaps, trying to view it optimistically, we have traded a cultural and visual diversity for a more varied personal life. Or a more varied and interesting intellectual and technical life.

We at Manning celebrate the inventiveness, the initiative, and the fun of the computer business with book covers based on the rich diversity of regional life of two centuries ago brought back to life by the pictures from this collection.

Fundamental LDAP concepts

The Lightweight Directory Access Protocol (LDAP) has emerged as the standard for accessing directory services over networks. In this first part of the book, we will look at everything you need to know about LDAP.

Chapter 1 begins with an exploration of the many uses and benefits of LDAP, as well as its origin. From there we move on to an overview of current directory management and interoperability issues. At the end of chapter 1, we glance at the available and emerging tools that allow for easier integration between different data sources.

Information is exchanged between LDAP clients and servers using containers called *entries*. These containers are formed based on a particular information model that we discuss in chapter 2.

Entries in a directory are given unique, hierarchical names in an LDAP directory. In chapter 3, we look at how these names are formed, naming issues, and best practices.

Chapter 4 covers LDAP search criteria. The focus here is on simplifying the some-times complicated combination of search filters, scopes, and bases that make up an LDAP search request.

You will get your first look at Directory Services Markup Language (DSML), the latest standard for representing directory information and operations in XML, in chapter 5. Chapter 5 also formally introduces the LDAP Data Interchange Format (LDIF), which is a commonly used format for sharing and storing directory information.

C H A P T E R 1

Introduction to LDAP

In this chapter, we introduce the Lightweight Directory Access Protocol (LDAP) and attempt to answer the following questions:

- What is LDAP? Who needs it? How is it used?

- What are directory services? Where do they fit in the grand scheme of things? Which ones exist? What is their relation to LDAP?

- What are common issues in planning and deploying directory services?

- Where do metadirectories, provisioning tools, and virtual directories fit with LDAP?

- What standards organizations and industry consortia are responsible for further development of directory services and LDAP standards?

1.1 WHAT LDAP IS

LDAP is a standard that computers and networked devices can use to access common information over a network. The ability to provide network access to data in itself does not make LDAP stand out from dozens of other protocols defined for data access, such as Hypertext Transfer Protocol (HTTP). As you will see in this chapter and those following, a number of features and vendor efforts make LDAP very well-suited for access and updates to many types of common information.

For example, information about employees might be stored in a directory so that people and applications can locate their contact information. Such contact information might include email addresses and fax numbers, or even additional data that unambiguously identifies employees' attempts to access enterprise applications.

1.1.1 Directory services and directory servers

A *directory* is simply a collection of information. For example, the telephone book is a directory used by virtually everyone to find telephone numbers.

Directory services provide access to the information in a directory. A simple directory service that most people use from time to time is the directory assistance offered by most telephone companies. By dialing a telephone number, anyone can receive instant access to information in the telephone directory.

In the computer world, directories exist everywhere. The Unix password file can be considered a directory of computer accounts. The Domain Name Service (DNS) acts as a directory service providing information about network hosts.

Computer applications often have their own directories. The Apache web server can store usernames and passwords in a data file, which is thus a directory of users. Customer information stored in a database can also be considered directory information if it is of a common nature with applications outside a single program or system.

Directory servers are applications that primarily act as directory services, providing information from a directory to other applications or end users. This functionality is most applicable in client/server environments, where the service may be located remotely from the calling application or system. For example, on Unix or Linux computers running the Network Information Service (NIS), the ypserv program can be considered a directory server.

1.1.2 LDAP and directory services

LDAP provides client-server access to directories over a computer network and is therefore a directory service. In addition to offering the ability to search and read information, it defines a way to add, update, and delete information in a directory.

Two general types of directory server software implement the LDAP standards:

- Stand-alone LDAP servers
- LDAP gateway servers

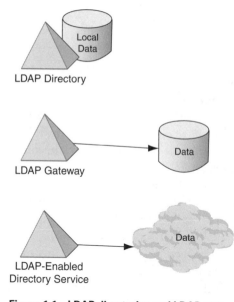

Figure 1.1 LDAP directories and LDAP gateways are different types of products that provide LDAP-enabled directory services.

Stand-alone LDAP servers focus exclusively on LDAP as their only access mechanism; their proprietary internal data stores are tuned for LDAP access. These are typically what people mean when they use the words *LDAP server*.

Instead of being tied to a local data store, LDAP gateway servers translate between LDAP and some other native network protocol or application program interface (API) to provide access to directory information that is more directly available via other means. One example is the original use of LDAP: to gateway to other directory services supporting the X.500 standards. Another more modern example of such an LDAP gateway is a server that provides LDAP access to information residing in Oracle database tables.

Figure 1.1 illustrates the two types of services that can be used to provide LDAP-enabled directory services.

The examples throughout this book will not address one type of server over the other—the idea behind LDAP is that it shouldn't matter where the end data is stored, as long as the client and server can use LDAP to communicate that information in a standard way understood by both sides.

In addition, we will focus primarily on accessing and managing information and services through the LDAP protocol. Each directory server product is installed and configured differently, usually in ways that are well-documented in product manuals. It would be of little use to duplicate such information, because installation and configuration of the software is relatively trivial.

1.1.3   Other directory services

LDAP is not alone in providing computerized directory services. It is also not the first or even the most completely defined directory service.

Other directory services that have been popular in the past, and that are still in use in many organizations, include those based on standards such as X.500, WHOIS, NIS, PH/QI, and various proprietary directories from companies such as Novell, Banyan, and others.

X.500 is a set of standards that originated in the late 1980s, with significant updates as late as 2001. The standards are extensive and cover everything from access to replication. In many respects, X.500 is more mature as a protocol than LDAP, including such technologies as multimaster replication and access control, but its relative complexity has made it less popular for access. However, it is still very popular, and a number of vendors sell servers that support these standards. These vendors tend to focus on X.500-based protocols for interoperability between servers, while exposing the data using an LDAP gateway.

WHOIS was an early attempt at a simple protocol for Internet-accessible white pages. The services supporting this protocol took a simple string and returned free-form text in response. A WHOIS server could be written on most operating systems in a short amount of time, but lack of standard data representation made it difficult to do anything but display the results as they arrived. Unfortunately, this limitation makes programmatic use of the resulting data in non–white pages applications very difficult.

NIS, originally called Yellow Pages (YP), was Sun's remote procedure call (RPC)-based operating system directory. Most Unix-based servers support some variant of this protocol. With a relatively simple replication model and access protocol, as well as the ability to discover servers on a local network, its creation was necessary due to the growth in client-server computing where users might exist on a number of servers. However, it was not well-suited for wide area networks (WANs) offered little in the way of security, and was not easily extensible for storing additional information in existing maps.

PH/QI was very popular at about the time HTTP became widely used. It was a multipurpose client-server directory service developed by Paul Pomes at the University of Illinois at Urbana-Champaign (UIUC). It was especially popular at universities in North America and was used to store not only white pages information, but also information that could be used for security, such as logins and credentials. One of the earliest applications to take advantage of the Common Gateway Interface (CGI) that shipped with the original National Center for Supercomputing Applications (NCSA) HTTP server was a gateway that presented an HTML interface to a PH server. Some mail applications, such as Eudora, were also able to perform PH queries for address books. LDAP's acceptance in the industry curtailed any serious move to PH/QI; in addition, the service was somewhat limited. The protocol was relatively simple and text-based; it was easy to access programmatically but designed to run on a central server, limiting its scalability and scope.

Banyan was an early leader in MS-DOS/Windows operating system directories, but it didn't fare well as Microsoft and Novell became more directory-aware. Banyan eventually changed its name to ePresence and is currently one of the larger integrators focused on directory services.

Novell based the proprietary directory service for its Netware Network Operating System (NOS) on the X.500 standards. Netware's directory has long been regarded as one of the more solid operating system directories, and Novell has a long history of directory integration in its products. As LDAP picked up steam, Novell separated the NOS from the directory and created eDirectory; it is now a popular LDAP-enabled directory service with the broadest platform support of any directory services vendor's product.

1.2 WHAT LDAP IS NOT

LDAP is an access protocol that shares data using a particular information model. The data to which it provides access may reside in a database, in memory, or just about anywhere else the LDAP server may access. It is important that the data be presented to an LDAP client in a way that conforms to LDAP's information model.

LDAP is being used for an increasing number of applications. Most of these applications are appropriate—but some aren't. To get a better idea what LDAP should and shouldn't be used for, we begin this section with an overview of LDAP limitations that make it a bad choice for certain types of applications.

LDAP is not:

- A general replacement for relational databases
- A file system for very large objects
- Optimal for very dynamic objects
- Useful without applications

1.2.1 LDAP is not a relational database

LDAP is not a relational database and does not provide protocol-level support for relational integrity, transactions, or other features found in an RDBMS. Applications that require rollback when any one of multiple operations fails cannot be implemented with the current version of LDAP, although some vendors implement such functionality when managing their underlying datafiles. LDAP breaks a number of database normalization rules. For example, 1NR states that fields with repeating values must be placed into separate tables; instead, LDAP supports multi-valued data fields.

Some LDAP server vendors proclaim that directories are somehow faster than relational databases. In some cases, this is true. In other cases, databases are both faster and more scalable. Nothing inherent in the LDAP protocol makes it in any way faster than other data access mechanisms, such as Open Database Connectivity (ODBC). Everything depends on how the underlying data store is tuned.

LDAP lacks features found in relational databases even in cases where LDAP sits on top of a relational data store, as is true with Oracle and IBM directory server products. The LDAP protocol currently has no standard for transmitting the type of information necessary to take advantage of the powerful relational and transactional capabilities present in the underlying data store.

1.2.2 LDAP is not a file system for very large objects

LDAP provides a hierarchical way of naming information that looks remarkably like that found in most file systems. Many people see this aspect of LDAP as an indication that it might be a great way to centrally store files to make them accessible over a network.

In fact, LDAP is not a great way to do network file sharing. Although it allows information (including binary data) to be transmitted and stored, it does not have the locking, seeking, and advanced features found in most modern file-sharing protocols. Figure 1.2 shows some of the disadvantages of using LDAP in this manner.

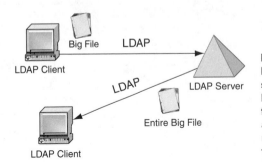

Figure 1.2
LDAP is not a network file system. Here you see that if you stored a large file using LDAP, clients would need to read the entire file via LDAP rather than page through the applicable sections. If either client died in midtransfer, it would need to start again from scratch.

The Network File System (NFS) and similar file-sharing protocols have this advanced functionality and are well-tested and accepted for use on local intranets. Web protocols such as the HTTP and File Transfer Protocol (FTP) are more appropriate when you're providing Internet access to data on local file systems.

In a similar vein, LDAP is often only marginally useful to store serialized objects, large structured documents (such as XML), and similar types of data in the directory. Because the LDAP server may not know how to parse these blobs of data, it will not be able to search on attributes within them.

For example, if you store XML documents in the directory, you will not be able to search for all XML documents in the directory that implement a particular document type unless you also store the document's type in the directory. Such a process involves duplicating information already stored in the XML document.

Without storing this metadata, the XML document is an opaque object that can only be stored and retrieved in full. By contrast, a good file-based XML parser has the ability to seek through parts of the XML document and retrieve or manipulate only those sections that are pertinent to the current operation. This situation may be changing as LDAP vendors become increasingly XML savvy and begin supporting such functionality as XPath searching.

Note that because the LDAP protocol is separate from the data to which it provides access, it is possible for a particular LDAP server to be extended to handle particular types of objects more intelligently. For example, the server might include an XML parser that indexes XML documents for easier search and retrieval with LDAP. We'll explore this process briefly in the context of attribute syntax and matching rules in chapter 2.

1.2.3　LDAP is not optimal for very dynamic objects

Generally speaking, LDAP is not the place to store very dynamic information. For example, there are a number of reasons it would be unwise to write extensive audit logs to an LDAP entry each time a user accesses a system.

First, most LDAP servers optimize for search performance at considerable cost in write performance. Updating a single attribute in some LDAP environments generally takes a longer time than comparable updates to a well-designed database.

Second, even with high write performance, LDAP as a protocol does not have facilities to ensure that a set of transactions will happen in the right order. This complicates even the simplest updates to dynamic information involving multiple applications or threads. Even a simple counter can get corrupted when two applications try to update it simultaneously.

Finally, even if a particular server supports tuning for updates and adds proprietary protocol extensions to support better locking that allows for better multiapplication updates, using these special features may avoid a major benefit of LDAP. This benefit is the ability of application developers to use LDAP without having to take note of the server implementation being used.

1.2.4　LDAP is not useful without applications

LDAP lacks an SQL-like general reporting language of the kind found with most general-purpose databases. Such reporting languages can often be used to generate sophisticated reports from a database. Because directories are used for more generally useful information, such as account information usable by many applications, this lack of report generation support is insignificant.

Lack of generalized report generation makes it even more important that LDAP directories be built around the notion that applications will be using them. In addition, it's important that LDAP directory services be designed and deployed with full cooperation from the application developers who will use the service.

Although it lacks a general report-generation language, LDAP offers a number of powerful APIs. Many of these APIs are based on well-documented industry standards whose wide acceptance has been one of the strongest drivers of early LDAP adoption. Unlike databases, directories using LDAP have a wire protocol that can be used without using special vendor drivers, making directories important for information that can benefit many applications that otherwise have nothing in common.

Thanks to the ease with which these APIs can be used, a large number of applications now provide native support for LDAP where it makes sense. You can find some of these LDAP-enabled applications, such as those providing shared address book or white pages functionality, on the Internet and in nearly all modern email and web browser software.

LDAP is now mature technology used by a wide variety of applications for many critical purposes. These applications include everything from authentication, authorization, and management of application and operating system users to routing of billions of email messages around the world. New applications are developed every day that ensure that LDAP's importance will continue to grow.

1.3   CURRENT APPLICATIONS

As we just discussed, successful directory services depend on application support. In this section we begin to examine the types of applications that normally leverage LDAP-enabled directories.

1.3.1   White pages

One of the first uses of enterprise directories was to provide electronic shared address books, called *white pages* (see figure 1.3). LDAP has long been used to provide access to information that enables white pages functionality. In fact, white pages applications are the most widely deployed and visible LDAP-enabled applications.

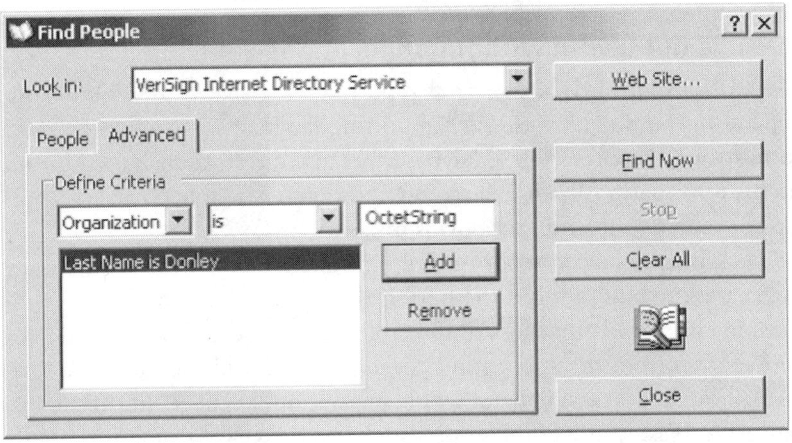

Figure 1.3   This screen from the Outlook Express email client is an example of a white pages application.

Both Netscape and Internet Explorer have built-in support for searching LDAP directories and presenting the results in the form of an address book. Most email applications released in the past few years provide this same functionality, although some still support their own proprietary standards to remain compatible with legacy workgroup-oriented directories. Figure 1.4 shows how such a client might talk to a directory to retrieve this information.

A quick chat with most corporate intranet webmasters would reveal that the most frequently accessed application on an intranet is usually a corporate contact database. Everyone from the mailroom clerk to the CEO needs to be able to locate their peers;

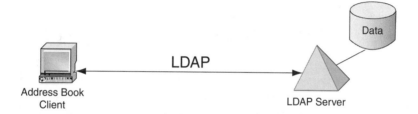

Figure 1.4 An address book client talks directly to an LDAP server.

therefore, it is the simplest application available to demonstrate the power and simplicity provided by directory access.

Web-based white pages applications are useful for extending LDAP information to points beyond an intranet environment when firewalls or a lack of installed clients prevent pure LDAP communication. Figure 1.5 shows how a web server might act as a gateway for white pages requests from an end-user's web browser.

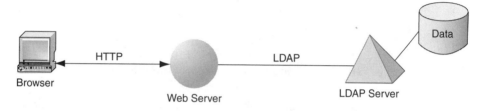

Figure 1.5 The same directory shown in figure 1.4, with a web application rather than the end-user's client communicating via LDAP

Most people already have an LDAP-enabled browser or email client, or can access white pages via a web interface. This simplifies deployment and allows for more widespread access.

In fact, creating an application that can search for information in LDAP is not particularly difficult. The following is a full code listing in Java using the Java Naming and Directory Interface (JNDIJ) for a program that can search for information in an LDAP-enabled directory service:

```java
import javax.naming.directory.*;
import javax.naming.*;
import java.util.Vector;
import java.util.Enumeration;
import java.util.Properties;

public class SearchLDAP {

    public static void main(String[] args) {
        String base = "";
        String filter = "(objectclass=*)";
```

```
Properties env = new Properties();
env.put(DirContext.INITIAL_CONTEXT_FACTORY,
        "com.sun.jndi.ldap.LdapCtxFactory");
env.put(DirContext.PROVIDER_URL,"ldap://localhost:389");

try {
    DirContext dc = new InitialDirContext(env);

    SearchControls sc = new SearchControls();
    sc.setSearchScope(SearchControls.OBJECT_SCOPE);

    NamingEnumeration ne = null;
    ne = dc.search(base, filter, sc);

    while (ne.hasMore()) {
        SearchResult sr = (SearchResult) ne.next();
        System.out.println(sr.toString()+"\n");
        dc.close();
    }
} catch (NamingException nex) {
    System.err.println("Error: " + nex.getMessage());
}
```

The results of this code are not pretty, but they show how easy it is to tie LDAP into a new or existing application for white pages or other lookup functionality.

Another benefit of using a web-based white pages application is that whereas most browsers and email clients enable LDAP searches, a web-based application can offer a point of self-administration for contact information. Information such as phone numbers and mailing addresses can be managed using a simple interface that is integrated with the search tools. This approach makes it easy for someone to change his or her information quickly when necessary.

1.3.2 Authentication and authorization

It is virtually impossible to discuss user access and system security today without LDAP being part of the conversation. Although it isn't as visible to the casual user, LDAP is emerging as the de facto way to access the identity information and credentials needed to support authentication. *Authentication* is the process of validating the identity of a user (or any other object, such as an application).

This process allows identity information to be managed and distributed much more easily than via traditional means. Information stored in an LDAP-enabled data store can be segmented for simpler management while presenting a unified view to applications and authentication services.

Using LDAP also has the benefit of reusing identity information. This approach offers a significant advantage over authentication processes that use an operating system or proprietary mechanism. For example, using LDAP allows both Unix- and

Windows-based servers running a particular application to authenticate users in the same manner and from the same repository. In effect, application development time is reduced, authentication code is relatively static between platforms, and the administrative cost of managing two identity repositories is removed. Figure 1.6 shows how an application might use LDAP to authenticate a user.

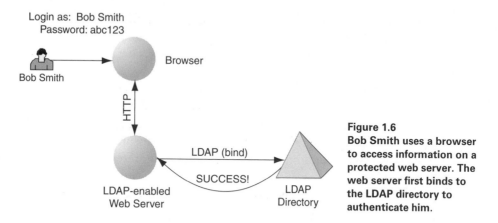

Figure 1.6
Bob Smith uses a browser to access information on a protected web server. The web server first binds to the LDAP directory to authenticate him.

After authenticating, it is possible to use other available information about the authenticated user (such as department, company, age, and so on) to determine whether he or she is authorized to perform a particular action on resources within a particular computing environment or application.

We will cover the use of LDAP as an authentication and authorization resource in chapter 13. This discussion will include more sophisticated authentication mechanisms, single sign-on issues, and many other related security concerns.

1.3.3 Personalization

Once a person has been identified through authentication, it is useful to personalize the user's experience based on their identity and preferences. In some cases, personalization may simply mean placing the current user's name at the top of a web page. A more sophisticated use might be to pull the customer's location information from the directory to prepopulate an order form.

In a complex web environment with a variety of features, LDAP-enabled directories are a useful place to store information about users' preferences. For example, you might allow users to choose a particular product line as their primary interest when a site covers a large number of products.

Capturing this information and enabling access to it via LDAP allows a variety of applications to customize users' experiences based on their interests. Doing so offers an important benefit: personalized content can be consistent between multiple applications.

LDAP has been gaining wide acceptance as a place to store and retrieve personalization information in enterprise applications. For example, most enterprise portals support LDAP as a means of obtaining the information needed for personalization.

1.3.4 Roaming profiles

Closely related in many respects to personalization, but focused more on operational preferences than content preferences, is the concept of *roaming profiles*. Roaming profiles allow users to authenticate to an application on any machine and get an identical environment. You do so by storing considerable individual configuration options in a directory.

In addition to enabling roaming, directory-based security also offers the potential to lock down certain configuration items or create organizational or group defaults. In environments with less-sophisticated users, doing so makes it possible to update user configurations without a system administrator needing to make a trip to each cubicle or spend time on the phone walking a user through complicated steps within an application.

Few stand-alone applications provide roaming profiles. Part of the reason is that most applications vary widely in their configuration. Thus each application may require additional information in the directory server to enable storage of that application's configuration values.

This requirement showcases a common conflict between application developers, who often want to change schema to meet their applications' needs, and system administrators, who realize that changes in schema require a great deal of administrative effort. The challenge is deciding where to draw the line between generally useful information that belongs in a directory and application specific information that belongs elsewhere. We will discuss this conflict further in chapter 2.

1.3.5 Public Key Infrastructure

Traditional authentication and encryption systems use secret keys. Generally speaking, a secret key system requires both ends of a communication to know a secret password that will be used to hide the communication. The right secret password produces a legible message, which both protects the message in transit and proves that the message must have been written by the other party, because they were the only other ones with knowledge of the secret. This approach works well as long as the secret isn't compromised and you communicate with few enough people that you can remember a shared secret with each one.

Public key technology changes all this and makes the process more scalable. In this system, two keys are produced. One key, called the *private key*, is still secret. However, unlike the secret key in a shared-secret system, the private key is never shared with anyone. Instead, a second key called the *public key* is distributed. A public key can be placed in a digitally signed container called a *digital certificate*. Such certificates are commonly used to distribute public keys.

A successful deployment of public key infrastructure is highly dependent on a well-designed directory services infrastructure. An LDAP-enabled directory answers the question of where to store and locate digital certificates. Centrally storing digital certificates in a directory allows people and applications to find certificates on demand for business partners and peers with whom they need to communicate securely.

In addition to helping you locate certificates for encryption, directories let you find a list of certificates that have been revoked prior to their expiration time. These *certificate revocation lists* (CRLs) are commonly stored in LDAP-enabled directories.

This book is not specifically about Public Key Infrastructure (PKI), but PKI is one common application that uses directories. We discuss the use of directories with PKI in much more detail in chapter 13.

1.3.6 Message delivery

On the Internet, messages are routed based on the fully qualified host name to the right of the at sign (@). Such routing is typically done by using the DNS to identify the IP address associated with the human-readable fully qualified host name.

Once a message has been routed to the correct machine, it is delivered on that machine based on the username to the left of the @. Many mail systems now support the use of LDAP to determine how to deliver a message.

The delivery process can include advanced operations, such as locating the exact mail drop for the user in a cluster of mail servers. However, the most common usage is for allowing full-name email aliases and implementing email lists.

As mentioned in section 1.3.3, directories can help you target mailings based on information associated with identities. In an LDAP directory, users are often placed together in groups, either as a list of users or as a dynamic specification (such as all users in department A). These groups can be used for authorization, personalization, and even mailing lists.

We discuss group schemas in chapter 2. Examples of managing groups appear in chapter 7.

1.4 BRIEF HISTORY

The previous section makes it obvious that there are a wide variety of uses for LDAP-enabled directory services. Many of these uses first came about with earlier standards—particularly X.500, which we mentioned briefly earlier in this chapter. In this section we will take a quick look at how LDAP came to its latest incarnation.

1.4.1 X.500 and DAP

LDAP is a TCP/IP-based client/server directory access protocol originally based on a subset of the X.500 Directory Access Protocol (DAP). X.500 is a comprehensive set of standards from the ITU Telecommunication Standardization Sector (ITU-T) that describes all aspects of a global directory service. X.500, like many standards, has gone through many revisions; work is still in progress to update it further. As shown in figure 1.7, a client originally talked to an X.500 server using the DAP protocol.

Designed to be the standard directory service for the Open Systems Interconnection (OSI) world, X.500's fortune has risen and fallen over the years, but it still has a substantial following. Early on, X.500 was accepted by many large information technology (IT) organizations as the direction for global directory services. Although early products had their problems, they also showed a great deal of promise. Many large companies and universities implemented pilot projects, usually involving the hosting of white pages.

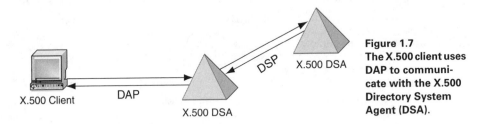

Figure 1.7
The X.500 client uses DAP to communicate with the X.500 Directory System Agent (DSA).

One big issue arose very quickly with X.500: the fact that its access protocol required an OSI protocol stack and complex binary encoding of structures represented in a language called Abstract Syntax Notation One (ASN.1). Most desktop computers at the time were ill equipped to deal with DAP.

As Internet Protocol (IP) became the dominant networking standard, DAP's OSI origins made it less attractive. Many of the organizations piloting X.500 directories had already adopted IP and were looking for a protocol with less baggage for client access. Even worse, X.500's complexity and the lack of freely available standards documents or easy-to-use APIs made it difficult to develop clients without paying fees to the ITU-T.

As we've stated since the beginning of this chapter, even the best directory is useless when applications are not available to take advantage of it. Several white pages applications were available, but an electronic phone book is often not enough to justify the expense of collecting and cleansing all the information necessary to make a directory truly useful.

1.4.2 A new standard is born

In 1991, after a few false starts with other potential standards, LDAP was brought forth as a lightweight means for accessing the DAP-enabled directories of the X.500 world. The first set of standards, LDAPv2, were eventually defined and accepted by the Internet Engineering Task Force (IETF), an important standards body responsible for many important Internet standards, as RFCs 1777 and 1778.

These standards provided basic authentication, search, and compare operations, as well as additional operations for changing the directory. From the start, LDAP made

Figure 1.8 The X.500 client goes away, replaced by an LDAP client talking to an LDAP server. Here, the LDAP server acts as a gateway between LDAP-aware clients and DAP-aware X.500 DSAs.

X.500 more accessible, as intended. Figure 1.8 shows an X.500 server being accessed by an LDAP gateway service that is forwarding requests from an LDAP client.

Almost as important as the protocol itself was the release of a standard API and the production of a client development kit. For the first time, it was possible to access these servers programmatically without wandering knee-deep into an arcane protocol.

1.4.3   LDAP goes solo

As time went by, some people began to wonder what made X.500 so special in the first place. The University of Michigan, which had developed the reference implementation of LDAP, released a stand-alone server called Slapd that would allow the LDAP server to present data from a local data store rather than simply act as a gateway to an X.500 server.

Slapd was followed by a second service called Slurpd, which read the changes from one server and replicated those changes via the LDAP protocol to other Slapd servers. Figure 1.9 shows a typical stand-alone LDAP environment.

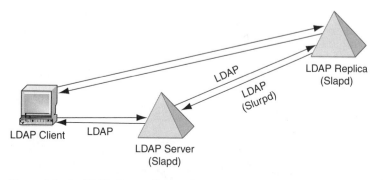

Figure 1.9 An LDAP client talks to a Slapd server. X.500 is no longer involved.

At this point, Netscape hired most of the original developers from the University of Michigan Slapd server to develop the Netscape Directory Server. Netscape, which was riding high with an incredible share of the Internet browser market, decided that networks would require directories and that LDAP, not X.500, should be the standard. Nearly 40 other companies announced support at that time, bringing LDAP the focus and support it needed to become the de facto standard for directory services.

1.4.4 LDAPv3

LDAP may have gained acceptance as a stand-alone service, but it was far from complete. Due primarily to its reliance on X.500 servers to provide the server-to-server communications, access control, and other functionality, LDAP was still only a skeleton of a full directory service by the mid-1990s.

Many interested parties pushed forward with the development of the next generation of the LDAP standards. In December 1996, the new version was published as RFCs 2251 to 2256. These new specifications covered items including the protocol itself, mandatory and optional schema, and LDAP URLs. A set of standard authentication mechanisms and a standard for session encryption were added to the list of core specifications in 2000. Figure 1.10 shows the core specifications that make up the LDAP standard.

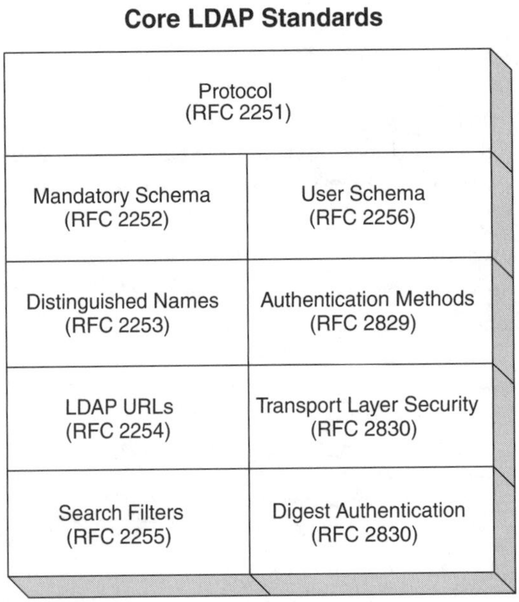

Core LDAP Standards

Protocol (RFC 2251)	
Mandatory Schema (RFC 2252)	User Schema (RFC 2256)
Distinguished Names (RFC 2253)	Authentication Methods (RFC 2829)
LDAP URLs (RFC 2254)	Transport Layer Security (RFC 2830)
Search Filters (RFC 2255)	Digest Authentication (RFC 2830)

Figure 1.10
The IETF has been the primary standards body for most of the existing LDAPv3 specifications. This figure shows a list of published RFCs that are considered the core LDAP standards.

1.5 LDAP REVISIONS AND OTHER STANDARDS

LDAPv3 was considered a great leap forward in several key areas, but it takes more than a protocol to make a directory service successful. It is now up to several standards bodies and industry consortia to enhance the LDAP core specifications and build a framework that allows directories from different vendors to interoperate, or at least share some of the most crucial information in a standard way, and play a more pivotal role in e-business. Figure 1.11 shows some of the many standards bodies and industry consortia that shape directory standards and define best practices in deployment and management.

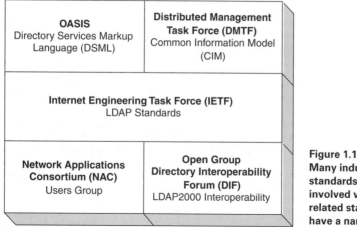

Figure 1.11
Many industry consortia and standards bodies are involved with LDAP and related standards, but most have a narrow focus.

1.5.1 Replication and access control

Version 3 of the LDAP protocol was greatly improved from version 2, but lacked two important items: replication and access control. The IETF has created workgroups to deliver these missing pieces and others, as shown in figure 1.12.

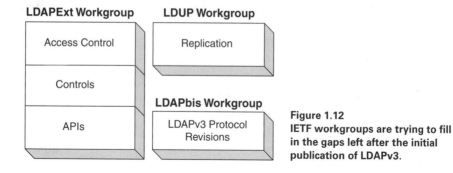

Figure 1.12
IETF workgroups are trying to fill in the gaps left after the initial publication of LDAPv3.

Lack of a standard replication process has since become an interoperability nightmare as each LDAP server vendor implemented its own proprietary solution. Many products use simple LDAP protocol operations to distribute data as shown in figure 1.13. However, even those solutions using the LDAP protocol sometimes require proprietary controls or attributes.

Many parties recognized that replication was critical to obtaining scalability, redundancy, and other important benefits. To resolve this issue, the Lightweight Directory Update Protocol (LDUP) working group was created within the IETF. At the time of this writing, the group has completed draft documents detailing requirements, a model for meeting those requirements, conflict resolution processes, and a protocol specification. The use of replication is discussed further in chapter 6.

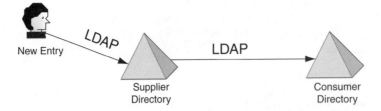

Figure 1.13 Supplier-to-consumer replication exists in some products using the LDAP protocol. Unfortunately, most need to use proprietary attributes or controls to get around current limitations in the specifications.

In addition to the supplier-consumer model of replication available in most existing directory servers, LDUP was chartered with allowing for multiple directory masters for the same information, which is shown in figure 1.14. It also documents a process for resolving conflicts that may arise when different and potentially conflicting changes are made independently to the same entry on each master. In addition, LDUP defines a protocol that can be used for both supplier-initiated and consumer-initiated replication.

Security was further along in some respects. The Simple Authentication and Security Layer (SASL), originally developed for the Internet Mail Access Protocol (IMAP), was added as a core LDAP standard early on as a way to negotiate an appropriate type of client and/or server authentication and even session encryption.

Developing a standard for access control has proven to be much more time consuming and has produced fewer results. As shown in figure 1.15, such a standard will allow a server to determine if an authenticated entity should be able to read or update a particular entry or an entire portion of the directory.

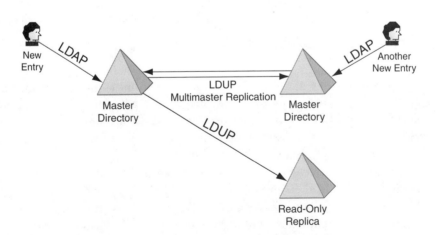

Figure 1.14 Multimaster replication will allow changes to the same directory tree in multiple directories.

Figure 1.15   LDAP access control standards will include a mechanism for determining in advance whether an operation will be permitted.

The task of creating such a standard fell into the hands of the LDAP extensions (LDAPEXT) workgroup within the IETF. This workgroup was formed to handle any extensions needed to the LDAPv3 standards outside of replication. As this book is being written, most activities of the LDAPEXT workgroup have been moved to individual submissions and will likely become an informational RFC rather than a full standard. Some aspects of access control may be pursued as part of the interoperability requirements for replication.

To understand why access control might be bundled with the replication workgroup, think about the fact that any replication of information outside a vendor's products will render that data insecure—other vendors will not know the access control rules of the source data. Any practical solution for replication is dependent on a standard for access control. We will look at access control further in chapter 13 when we discuss directory security in more detail.

1.5.2   Directory Enabled Networking

As computer networks evolve to support more variety and depth of services, the complexity of network management increases accordingly. Most network devices, including routers and switches, have traditionally been configured using command-line shells. Although this configuration enables relatively consistent management of a single device, it does nothing to simplify the coordination of configurations across large numbers of devices. Such coordination is critical when you're enabling guaranteed quality of service and other offerings that span multiple devices.

Directory Enabled Networking (DEN) provides a way for devices to configure themselves based on information in a directory. Originally an initiative from Microsoft and Cisco, DEN is now part of the CIM defined by the DMTF.

CIM is a set of object-oriented, implementation-neutral schemas that represents logical and physical attributes of hardware and software. The DMTF, rather than being protocol architects like the IETF, focused primarily on creating common object definitions that allow two CIM-aware applications to store and use information consistently.

Contrary to popular belief, CIM and DEN are not LDAP-specific information models, but are instead "meta" models that can be specialized for a number of environments, of which LDAP is one. XML is an example of another way that CIM objects can be represented.

Momentum behind DEN as the killer application that would drive directories has died down to an extent over the last few years, and most of the work around directories has moved to identity management solutions. In this book, we will not focus on DEN as a specific application due to the current lack of software and hardware that can truly exploit this technology.

1.5.3 XML and directories

The eXtensible Markup Language (XML) is an industry standard language used to define structured documents. It offers a set of common tags for defining data about data, or *metadata*. This metadata can be used to describe particular document types. Instances of documents implementing these types can then be shared and used by XML-aware applications.

DSML is an XML document type that can be used to create structured documents representing information in a directory service. This information represented in DSML can include both directory entries and schema information. DSMLv2 extends the specification to cover the representation of directory operations. Documents conforming to these standards can be exchanged using non-directory protocols like HTTP, as shown in figure 1.16. Many new services that support DSML are becoming available from both large vendors (Sun and Microsoft) and startups.

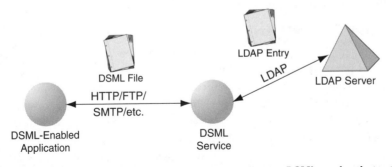

Figure 1.16   Here a DSML-enabled application talks to a DSML service that acts as an intermediary between an LDAP server and the DSML-enabled application.

DSML is most useful in applications that are already XML enabled. These include most modern application servers. DSML is especially useful in cases where direct access to the directory would normally not be permitted. For example, consider a situation in which a firewall is blocking all traffic except HTTP. To get around this limitation, a DSML encoding of a directory entry can be transmitted over the HTTP protocol for interpretation and presentation. Such a situation is shown in figure 1.17.

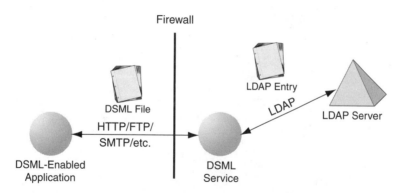

Figure 1.17   DSML is useful for sharing directory information across firewalls that might limit direct access to directories.

Emerging standards like Simple Object Access Protocol (SOAP) make it clear that LDAP will not be the only standard for sharing directory information in the future.

1.6   DIRECTORY MANAGEMENT

Despite the importance of having well-defined standards, it is rarely the reason for a directory services–related project to fail. Rather, the biggest headache with most new directory deployments is proper management of information in the directory. In the days when enterprise directories were used primarily for storing white pages information, it was often adequate to simply import information into the directory periodically from other, more authoritative data sources. Due to the lack of sophisticated management tools, there wasn't much choice.

Today, directory management tools for users and groups are much more sophisticated. In addition to giving a central administrator the ability to change information about objects in a directory, these tools typically allow for delegation of administrative duties and even user self-management, where appropriate.

This ability to distribute administration works well in intranet and Internet environments, but it is especially critical in *extranet* environments where multiple organizations are working together, potentially using the same applications and data. In such environments, the segmentation of administration and access is very important (see figure 1.18).

For example, a car manufacturer with just-in-time manufacturing facilities needs to give its business partners access to certain systems in its extranet. Access to applications on the extranet is controlled based on identities in each of its distributors and component suppliers. Tracking by identity offers audit trails, which will deter a random individual from anonymously ordering unauthorized parts.

The problem is, in addition to the employees at the company, such an extranet environment including suppliers and distributors may include hundreds of thousands,

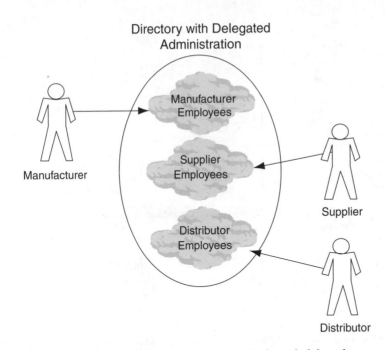

Figure 1.18 Directories can be segmented such that administration can be delegated to business partners. Such separation may be logical rather than physical.

if not millions, of users. Trying to manage all these users centrally would be an incredible effort.

By segmenting users by company and other means, you can push administration of identities to primary contacts within each of the business partners, thereby reducing administrative overhead. Aside from reducing administration costs, this approach also ensures better accuracy by pushing identity management closer to the identities being managed.

Information that is not related to identities and groups can still be difficult to manage with off-the-shelf products. This is the case primarily because little attention has been paid to other advanced uses of directories, such as DEN, which require management of more exotic information.

In chapter 7, we will look at managing all types of directory entries, complete with example applications to reduce manual data entry and allow some degree of user self-management.

1.7 DIRECTORY INTEGRATION

Many organizations spend months designing the schema, entry naming, and other related aspects of an enterprise directory service without considering the need for integration with existing information repositories. What usually results is a well-designed, standards-based directory service that contains stale information and is nearly useless.

Meanwhile, legacy data stores that contain mission-critical information continue to thrive because they contain fresh information, although in a way that is often inconvenient to access from new applications and nearly impossible to access from off-the-shelf applications without substantial custom development. Figure 1.19 shows how this typical scenario plays out.

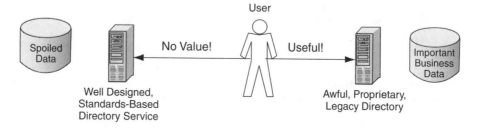

Figure 1.19 Data in legacy systems is nearly always more useful than data in poorly integrated new systems.

By designing and implementing an appropriate level of directory integration between legacy data stores and the new directory service, you can dramatically increase the value of the new directory (see figure 1.20).

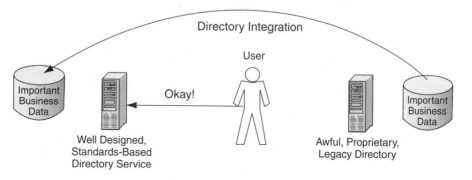

Figure 1.20 Some level of directory integration is important in increasing the value of applications using new directory services.

Directory integration is far more complicated than simply synchronizing everything from a legacy data store into a newly created directory. It demands that you evaluate the needs of applications that depend on both new and legacy data stores. In many cases, both new and legacy applications that utilize the respective data stores. Very often, these applications need access to some set of the same information.

Without any directory integration, it is often difficult to get more than a small group of pioneers to quickly adopt the new applications. A new application may have substantially better functionality, but without the proper data it will be difficult to move the masses that use the legacy applications to the new environment. This issue is demonstrated in figure 1.21.

Figure 1.21   **It is difficult to move the masses to new applications based around a standards-based directory when important information still resides only in a legacy directory.**

By using integration techniques, such as synchronization, you can create a high degree of interoperability between the two environments. This approach, shown in figure 1.22, provides the necessary data flow between the two directories, offering a relatively easy migration path to the new environment. It also ensures that the information in both environments is consistent.

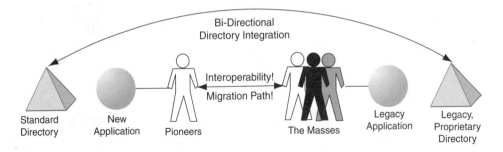

Figure 1.22   **Synchronization is often necessary to offer a migration path from legacy to new applications or interoperability where legacy applications will not be migrated.**

Consolidating these two environments can vastly simplify management. For example, you may find a way for a Unix-based system to use the same directory as your white pages application to store password information.

However, not every connected data store is a candidate for consolidation. Take, for example, a human resources application that relies on a set of database tables to store information. It may not make sense from an application functionality perspective for that particular application's data store to be consolidated into an enterprise directory. Some of the information may fit better in relational databases for the reasons we stated in section 1.2.1, whereas other information may not be a good

CHAPTER 1   INTRODUCTION TO LDAP

candidate for synchronization because of privacy concerns. So, instead of attempting to directly replicate everything from human resources into the directory, you need a form of intelligent synchronization.

In the area of identity management, directory integration almost always seems like a great idea in theory. For example, the management of users' computer accounts in a particular organization from hire to fire demonstrates the value of synchronization and other advanced integration technology.

Today, it is often necessary to touch multiple data repositories to commit a single change uniformly to all the places that store information about a person. These changes are usually performed by different application and system administrators. In more mature environments, changes may be synchronized with scripts to facilitate this process. When administrators do not coordinate their changes, or if an automated synchronization script fails, the data repositories are no longer synchronized, and at least one of the repositories will contain stale data.

If this stale data is simply a telephone number, the impact is probably minimal. However, if an account must be deleted or suspended due to an employee's termination, the data repository with stale data is at risk from the terminated employee. If the stale data resides in an enterprise directory that is used for authenticating and authorizing users to all non-legacy systems and applications, this one failed change can potentially put the organization's entire intranet at risk. Proper directory integration is key to reducing these types of risks. For this reason, it is important to spend an adequate amount of time planning for integration.

A general integration planning process entails identifying which data elements exist in each existing data source, selecting those that should be shared, and mapping between the source and destination schema (see figure 1.23).

This process and ways of implementing it are described in detail in chapter 7.

1.7.1 Integration via metadirectories

We cannot emphasize enough that the consolidation of all data repositories into a single enterprise directory within even the smallest of organizations is not likely to happen in our lifetimes. Even if it were possible to rewrite every legacy application to use a single standard, different directory and database software is better for different tasks. As shown in figure 1.24, this leads to many different environments within an organization that have different variations of the same user.

In the past few years, a new breed of applications called *metadirectories* has come to market to remove some of the burden associated with directory integration. Although it may sound like yet another directory, a metadirectory is really a sophisticated directory integration toolkit.

You can use metadirectories to connect and join information between data sources, including directories, databases, and files. The connection process usually involves identifying changes in each data source. Such a connection may be real-time monitoring of changes using a direct access method into the connected data store, an occa-

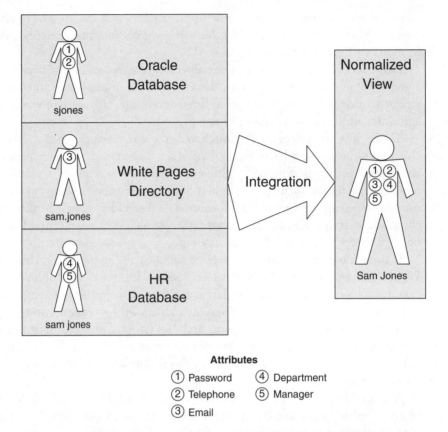

Attributes

① Password ④ Department

② Telephone ⑤ Manager

③ Email

Figure 1.23 Multiple data repositories typically store information about a person. Deciding which attributes come from where and mapping them to a normalized schema is an important part of any directory integration process. Note that the word *normalized* here should not be confused with database normalization rules.

sional scan of a file-based list of changes, or a review of a full export from the connected data store.

The join process is much more complicated and usually involves several steps. Its most important job is determining that an object in one data source is the same as an object in a second data source. This aggregation of information from multiple data sources is one of the most important features of a metadirectory and the heart of the join process. Other tasks performed by a metadirectory may include unification or mapping of schema and object names, filtering unwanted information, and custom processing and transformation of data. Figure 1.25 shows a relatively logical view of how a metadirectory might work to provide a linkage between key enterprise information repositories.

With careful planning, you can create an environment in which users can be created at a single point. Then, the metadirectory service will instantiate a subset of the

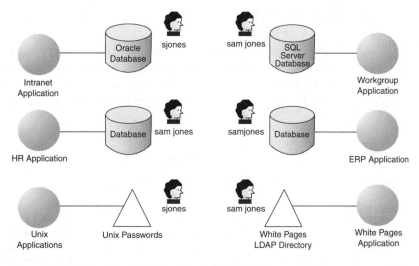

Figure 1.24   Different applications have different data repository requirements. It is not likely that a single data store could accommodate all of them.

users' information in other connected data stores automatically, or with very little manual intervention. The actual point of instantiation may be managed by another type of software that handles the workflow needed by this process. Such software is called *provisioning software*.

For example, if PeopleSoft, white pages, and an Oracle database all use a telephone number, you would like that telephone number to be entered once and propagated to the other data stores. Metadirectories must also handle environments where

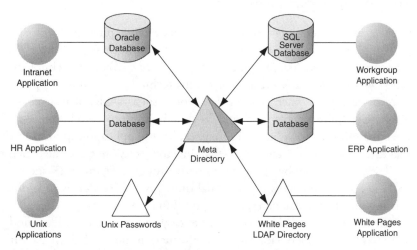

Figure 1.25   Metadirectories provide advanced integration capabilities between different types of data stores.

both Oracle and PeopleSoft would be able to master new changes depending on business rules.

Metadirectories are also proving to be popular in extranet environments where two or more organizations have their own directories and want to share a portion of them with business partners or vendors. Figure 1.26 shows an extranet environment where the addition of Joe Distributor might be propagated to the manufacturer using metadirectory technology.

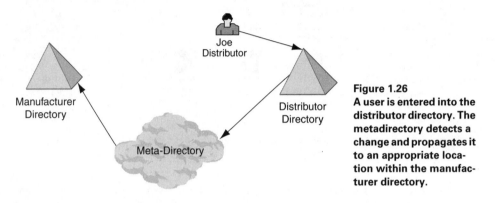

Figure 1.26
A user is entered into the distributor directory. The metadirectory detects a change and propagates it to an appropriate location within the manufacturer directory.

It is beyond the scope of this book to offer an in-depth look at metadirectory products. However, directory integration is critical, and some of the functionality provided by metadirectory products can be performed with a general scripting language. We discuss such techniques in detail in chapter 6.

1.8 INTEGRATION AND FEDERATION VIA VIRTUAL DIRECTORY TECHNOLOGY

Usually, metadirectories involve the creation of a new, physical directory, the contents of which are based on an aggregation of multiple information sources. One emerging alternative to metadirectory technology is *virtual directory* technology, sometimes called *directory federation* technology. This technology attempts to provide real-time directory access to other types of data stores, such as relational databases and memory-based application components. To visualize this process a bit more easily, think of the virtual directory as a kind of proxy server: the application speaks LDAP to the virtual directory software, and the virtual directory software grabs the data directly from the legacy data store by speaking its native tongue. Figure 1.27 shows a directory-enabled application accessing a virtual directory service that is providing data from existing directories, databases, and application components.

Virtual directory technology is not as easy as it may sound. Each underlying data store has its own query language and information model. The virtual directory must find ways to optimize queries and map between LDAP and non-directory information models.

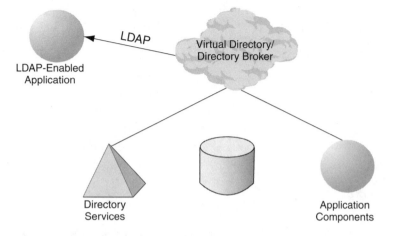

Figure 1.27 Virtual directories (sometimes called directory federators) accept directory requests and transform them into requests for potentially non-directory information.

At this time, virtual directory technology is in its infancy, as metadirectories were a few years ago. However, it is emerging as another useful tool for providing a unified view of information to LDAP-enabled applications. It is the only way to view information in many kinds of existing repositories using directory protocols in real time.

1.9 WHY THIS BOOK?

People who have worked with directories know that installing and configuring most directory server software is generally the easiest part of a directory deployment. Writing simple applications to query the directory and use the results is also quite easy, once you understand the basics. Trouble begins to brew when it becomes necessary to keep the information in the directory up to date through both front-end data management and back-end integration with other data sources. This book focuses on making your directory deployments more successful through advanced application and interdirectory integration.

Consider that every element of data stored in a directory must be placed into the directory at some point. You can leverage the data that already exists in other repositories, someone can enter it into the directory through an administrative interface, or the data can be generated by an application. In many environments, all these tasks may need to happen to create a suitable directory service. Figure 1.28 shows some of these different techniques for moving information into the directory.

For new and experienced directory service managers charged with deploying or managing a directory service, these management and integration issues are clearly the biggest challenge. Not having the right information, or having stale versions data, dilutes the value of the directory to all applications that leverage it.

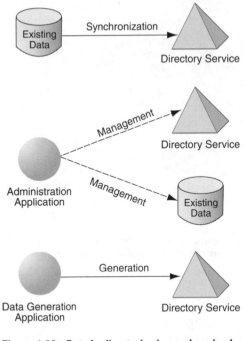

Directory management involves having the right tools and tying in the right information from other, often authoritative, sources of data. In this book, we'll focus on practical solutions to common directory management problems. We will look at Perl code for administration interfaces, directory synchronization, and directory migration. The entire second part of the book is devoted to this topic.

Directory-enabled applications let you use all the information you've been collecting in directories. After all, why collect data if it nobody wants to use it? We'll look at ways to leverage LDAP in a variety of application environments with source code in Java. You'll find that such application integration is key to having a useful and important directory that people want to keep current.

Figure 1.28 Data in directories is synchronized with existing data stores, managed through administration applications, and/or generated in some way.

With the information in this book, you'll have information flowing through your directories with much less perspiration. Servers that support the LDAP standard can provide a wide variety of functionality to a properly enabled application. This book aims to help you manage your LDAP directories and enable your applications, both new and existing, to support these directories.

1.10 SUMMARY

The LDAP standard for accessing directory services is important to software developers and system administrators. It can be used through LDAP-enabled applications and various APIs.

A number of different directory services have come into existence in the past few decades; LDAP was derived from another popular standard called X.500. These directory services provide everything from white pages to application security.

Management and application integration are the two biggest issues people tend to encounter when deploying directory services. You can address these issues many ways, as the second and third parts of this book explain.

The IETF has been the driving force behind the core LDAP specifications and many enhancements. Its most important current work is related to replication and access control. Other industry consortia and standards bodies are important in developing LDAP server and application interoperability guidelines, as well as standards that represent data from the LDAP information model in XML.

Metadirectories provide synchronized integration between multiple data repositories, and virtual directories provide real-time integration between applications and existing data via directory protocols. Provisioning tools allow for manual management of the information in directories. Each of these types of tools plays an important role in a well-rounded directory service.

In the remainder of part 1, we will focus on the LDAP standards in more detail, and discuss how to use LDAP tools to communicate with a directory server.

CHAPTER 2

Understanding the LDAP information model

In chapter 1, we took a general look at LDAP. In this chapter, we look in more depth at the way LDAP represents information. LDAP's information model is very important because every piece of data exchanged between an LDAP client and server uses it.

Questions that will be answered in this chapter include:

- How is information stored in LDAP? What is an information model? Why is it important, and how does it simplify application development?

- Where is LDAP's information model defined?

- What is the LDAP schema? What makes up the schema?

- What is an entry? How do entries compare to rows in a database? How does the schema affect entries?

- What are object classes? What are attribute types? How are object classes in LDAP different from classes in a programming language? What is inheritance, and how does it affect an object class's definition?

- How are attributes different from fields in a database? How are attributes different from variables in a programming language?

34

2.1 INFORMATION MODEL OVERVIEW

LDAP information is represented in a specific logical form. The model used is not relational, nor is it completely object oriented. It is therefore important that we spend some time discussing the information model that LDAP uses.

In a nutshell:

- Information in LDAP is logically represented as entries.
- Entries belong to one or more object classes.
- Each object class is defined by a set of attributes.
- An attribute consists of a type and one or more values.
- Object class and attribute type definitions make up the schema.

Having a standard information model means that a client does not need to worry whether the server it is communicating with is providing data from state-of-the-art fiber-channel-connected disk arrays or a ticker-tape machine connected to a spool of toilet paper encoded with Braille dots. The server's physical data access mechanism is simply not important to the LDAP-enabled client.

Many vendors approach LDAP with the goal of making it their primary directory protocol, rather than just an add-on that lets people access their proprietary data stores. Other vendors tend to focus on LDAP as an available external interface while using proprietary protocols to manage interactions within their own environments. Thanks to the extensibility of LDAP's standard information model, it is possible to do things either way without substantially affecting the way applications need to behave.

2.1.1 Entries

When LDAP clients and servers share information, they use *entries*. Entries are basic elements of an LDAP server. Searches return a set of matching entries, but modifications can affect only one entry at a time.

Entries can be created by any LDAP-enabled client, imported using tools in most servers, and in some cases generated by an LDAP-enabled application based on externally available information or user input from non-LDAP data in other repositories. At the moment, we will concern ourselves primarily with the structure of entries, rather than their creation. An example entry with three attributes and a name might look like:

```
dn: cn=Ethan Daniel,o=manning,c=us
objectClass: person
cn: Ethan Daniel
sn: Daniel
```

Figure 2.1 shows a logical view of the composition of an individual entry. Every entry follows this simple pattern. In the previous entry, the first line is the distinguished name, and the following lines show attributes.

Distinguished Name		
Attribute	Value	
Attribute	Value	Value
Attribute	Value	

Figure 2.1
An LDAP entry containing attribute types and values

2.1.2   Attributes

Entries are made up of smaller units of data called *attributes*. Like fields in a data-base, these attributes contain key/value pairs that describe a particular entry. The key portion of the attribute is called the *attribute type*, and the value or values are called *attribute values*. Figure 2.2 shows a simple entry that demonstrates the struc-ture just described.

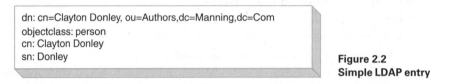

```
dn: cn=Clayton Donley, ou=Authors,dc=Manning,dc=Com
objectclass: person
cn: Clayton Donley
sn: Donley
```

Figure 2.2
Simple LDAP entry

In the figure, you see a list of attributes. The attribute type is the part before the colon (:). A value follows each type. In one case, a key is associated with more than one value.

The dn attribute in this example is really not an attribute at all. Rather, it is the entry's distinguished name. This name is unique across the directory and is a useful way of referencing an individual entry. For now, think of the distinguished name as the primary key for the entry.

Take note of the objectClass attribute. As we will discuss in section 2.4, this is a special attribute that helps you determine which attributes must (or may) be stored in a particular entry.

2.1.3   LDAP entries vs. database records

Although LDAP entries may seem similar to database records in that both contain a set of type/value pairs, there are a number of critical differences. For example, infor-mation cannot be joined from multiple entries. Such functionality is trivial with a relational database using an SQL statement similar to the following:

```
select table1.description,table2.price
       from table1,table2 where name='abc'
```

This line in an RDBMS would return a row of data containing values from two tables. LDAP offers nothing similar, so the task of combining information from mul-tiple entries is left to software.

Likewise, a single LDAP operation cannot affect multiple entries. Thus LDAP has no equivalent to the following SQL statement, which updates all the rows in a particular table:

```
update table2 set price = price * .80
```

2.2   WORKING WITH LDAP SCHEMA

The schema supported by an LDAP server determines the types of information that can be stored in a particular directory. A schema consists of attribute type and object class definitions (see figure 2.3).

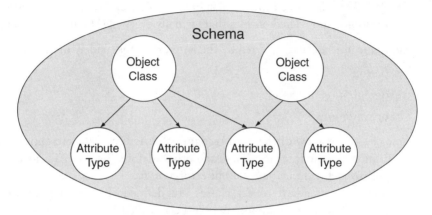

Figure 2.3   The LDAP schema comprises object class and attribute type definitions.

Most servers include some standard schemas, as we will describe in section 2.6. Virtually all servers support extending the schema to some extent; this functionality is important, but it can create problems and incompatibilities.

2.2.1   Standard LDAP schema

You now know that LDAP entries are defined by a set of attributes. We have also noted that the attribute types an entry contains are dependent on the object classes to which the entry belongs. The definition of object classes and attribute types make up an LDAP directory server's schema.

Before you begin to create schema, it is important that we discuss the standard schema. Everyone has his or her own idea about how an attribute type should be named and which attribute types should be included in a particular object class. Having schema standards ensures that although not everyone gets to use a favorite attribute type and object class names and definitions, we are all using the same names when we talk about common things. Using these standards, in turn, ensures that applications not only will work with your directory, but also will work with any other directory that supports the same standard schema. This doesn't mean you will never need to create your own object classes and attributes; it simply means that you delay your explosion of new and exciting schemas until you have first evaluated the standards for a more workable, shareable solution.

Where are these standard object classes and attribute types defined? The short answer: everywhere. The long answer is explained in the following subsections.

Internet Engineering Task Force

The IETF is responsible for releasing the core LDAP specifications:

- RFC 2252 defines the operational schema that every LDAP server must support.
- RFC 2256 defines a number of standard object classes for people, groups, organizations, and related entities that virtually every LDAP-enabled server supports.

Among the object classes defined by the latter, the most widely used are:

- person
- organizationalPerson
- organization

These classes are a few of the most recognized structures for representing people and organizations on the Internet. These and others defined by the IETF are derived from object classes defined for the X.500 directory service.

Many more standard object classes are defined. In addition to the ones in RFC 2256, many vendors support an object class called `inetOrgPerson`, which was initially developed by Netscape and published as an Internet Draft on multiple occasions. Although it isn't an Internet standard, `inetOrgPerson` is an industry standard that is implemented by many modern LDAP servers.

> **NOTE** Microsoft Active Directory is one of the few directory servers that does not support the `inetOrgPerson` standard out of the box. It can be configured to support it. By default, Active Directory does support `organizationalPerson` and other schema defined in RFC 2256.

In addition to the schemas defined in the core LDAP standards, schemas exist in other RFC documents. Some of the older schemas are based on X.500 standards, whereas new schemas exist in areas such as policy management. Workgroups within the IETF that are not focused on directories, especially the policy-related workgroups, are also putting out new directory schemas.

Distributed Management Task Force

As we mentioned briefly in chapter 1, the DMTF has defined a number of object models that represent a wide variety of object types. These object models include those previously defined as part of the DEN initiative founded by Microsoft and Cisco.

Many of the models produced by the DMTF have since been translated into standard LDAP schema and published as Internet Drafts. They can be found online at http://www.dmtf.org.

2.3 ATTRIBUTE TYPES

Attribute types are the building blocks of LDAP entries. This section provides a foundation for understanding the composition and definition of attribute types.

2.3.1 Defining attribute types

Attribute type definitions include the following components:

- Name
- Object IDentifiers (OIDs)
- Syntax
- Matching rules
- Inheritance

Attribute type names

Attribute type names in LDAP are case-insensitive strings containing only letters, numbers, dashes (-), and semicolons (;):

By *case insensitive*, we mean that for directory servers and clients, Name is the same as NAME or nAmE. Semicolons have a special use that we will discuss later; for now, keep in mind that they're not used arbitrarily.

Character	Example
Letters	givenName
Numbers	x509Certificate
Dash (-)	test-attribute
Semicolon (;)	x509Certificate;binary

The standard practice for writing the name of attribute types is to use lowercase characters. If the attribute type name consists of more than one word, those additional words are started with an initial capital letter.

Here are some example attribute type names that demonstrate this pattern.

- displayName
- telephoneNumber
- facsimileTelephoneNumber
- mobile

Attribute type Object IDentifiers

In addition to having a name, an attribute type is also associated with an OID. This OID is a dot-separated number that is always unique.

Figure 2.4
The OID 2.5.4.41 might be used by the attribute types `name` and `mingZi`. A search performed using 2.5.4.41 as the attribute type will return matches for either attribute type.

Languages may have completely different names for a particular attribute type. By associating an attribute type name with a unique OID, you can easily map an attribute type name in one language to the corresponding type name in a native language (see figure 2.4).

Top-level OIDs are assigned in the United States by the American National Standards Institute (ANSI). Your organization may already be assigned a top-level OID. If not, you can register for a number at http://www.ansi.org.

2.3.2   Syntax definitions

If the LDAP protocol transmits all information as 8-bit strings, how are integers and other nonstring syntaxes handled? The fact that data is being transmitted or encoded in a standard way has little to do with how applications should use that data or even the nature of the data itself. Instead, the syntax of the attribute type tells you how you should handle data.

For example, the attribute type `uid` is defined as a string. Thus you shouldn't try to put the value of `uid` into an integer in your favorite programming language and expect to perform arithmetic operations.

Many different syntaxes exist in LDAP. The most basic syntaxes are those that simply contain generic strings or binary blobs. For example:

- *Directory String*—A syntax used for printable Unicode strings encoded in UTF-8 that are generally case insensitive
- *Binary*—A syntax used for nonprintable binary data

Other syntaxes can be used to identify attribute values that are either complex or generally associated with special matching rules:

- *Certificate*—A complex, binary-encoded certificate
- *Telephone Number*—A simple string representing a telephone number, where non-numeric content is usually ignored in a search

> **NOTE**   Because LDAP uses 8-bit strings for communication, it is possible for attribute values to be sent to the server without the need for special encoding, such as Base64.

Like attribute types, syntax definitions have OIDs. These OIDs are normally used when defining attribute types to prevent conflict and reduce the dependency on English syntax names. Here are the OIDs for a few LDAP syntaxes:

- *Binary*—1.3.6.1.4.1.1466.115.121.1.5
- *Certificate*—1.3.6.1.4.1.1466.115.121.1.8
- *Directory String*—1.3.6.1.4.1.1466.115.121.1.15

Finally, an attribute type can define its syntax by specifying both a syntax and a size, or *bounds*. For example, you can define a particular attribute as a string that is normally no larger than 10 characters. Some servers use this size as a hard limit, whereas others do minimal or no bounds checking. It is therefore important that applications check for possible overflows if they might cause problems.

Figure 2.5 shows three attribute types, each of which is associated with a different syntax. An example of an attribute value for each type is shown in order to give you an idea of the various types of information that can be represented within the directory. As mentioned previously, the binary-encoded information is actual binary data, not a printable encoding of that information.

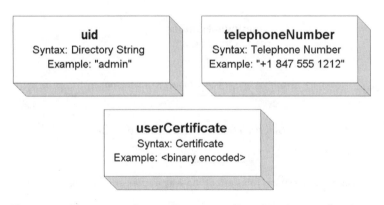

Figure 2.5 **The syntax of an attribute type affects how its associated values should be used.**

Unlike some directory servers that allow syntaxes to be added through plug-ins and other mechanisms, Active Directory supports only those syntaxes that come out of the box. This shouldn't be a limitation under most circumstances.

2.3.3 Matching rules for attributes

Although figure 2.5 may make it seem as if the syntax of a type is responsible for returning appropriate matches, it only indicates the syntax of the value stored in a particular attribute type. In fact, this is only one factor. Attribute types have associated matching rules that indicate how they should handle searches.

For example, the definition for a fictional `employeeNumber` attribute type may state that the syntax of its values consists of integers and that when you compare these values, you should use a matching rule called `integerOrderingMatch`. When comparing values for this type, the value 1000 is larger than the number 101. The `uid` attribute type specifies that the syntax of its values consists of directory strings and the matching rule to use for ordering is `caseIgnoreOrderingMatch`; in this case, the string "101" is larger than "1000" (see figure 2.6).

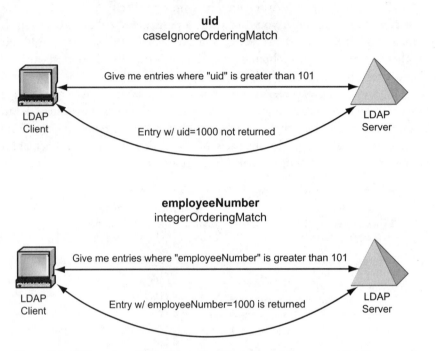

Figure 2.6   Different matching rules affect the way entries are matched in a search.

Matching rules are created to handle a number of possible assertions that may be specified in an LDAP search. An LDAP client is not allowed to specify the rule it would like the server to use in matching. Instead, the matching rule used is completely dependent on the attribute type's definition on the server. You can use four kinds of matching rules:

- *Equality*—Equality matching rules are used to determine equality between values of this attribute and the value asserted by the query. For example, `caseIgnoreMatch` will determine if a case ignore string (CIS) is exactly equal to "Joe".

- *Greater or less than*—Ordering matching rules are used to determine whether one value is equal to or greater/less than another value. Figure 2.6 shows the use of ordering match rules to determine if 1000 is greater than 101 for different attribute types.

- *Substring*—Sometimes you want to know if one value contains another. Substring matching rules allow you to do this. For example, the `caseIgnoreSubstringsMatch` matching rule determines if one string can be found within another when you ignore case.
- *Subschema*—Subschema matching rules match particular information about the schema supported by a directory. We will look at these rules further in chapter 7, when we explore manipulating schema information directly on a server.

Like other aspects of LDAP, the matching rules available for use with LDAP attributes can be extended by server vendors to provide matching of complex values. Support for a new matching rule usually entails extending the server through plug-ins or other means.

For example, if a small structured document is to be stored in an attribute, it may be desirable to create a special matching rule that knows how to parse the document's header to provide functional searching. After all, if you knew what the entire document looked like, you probably wouldn't be searching for it.

2.3.4 Support for multiple values

Attribute types in LDAP may be associated with multiple values. Here is an example of an entry with a multivalued attribute type called `givenName`:

```
objectClass: person
cn: Jonathon Johnson
sn: Johnson
givenName: Jonathon
givenName: Johny
givenName: John
```

This entry will be returned to a client that queries for any of the three values specified for `givenName`.

A common misconception among people first getting started with LDAP centers on support for multiple values. At first glance, multivalued attributes look like a great way to store things like telephone numbers and addresses (nearly everyone has more than one of each). However, this approach doesn't quite work—attribute values are returned unordered.

Because you can never count on value ordering to ensure that the first telephone number is the primary number and the second number is a backup, dependence on this ordering will send people to the wrong telephone number as often as the right one. It is therefore necessary in such cases to define separate `telephoneNumber` and `homeTelephoneNumber` attribute types; these types offer the context needed by directory-enabled applications and end users, so they can determine which number to use at which time.

Without ordering, what good are multiple attribute values? Having multiple values does simplify the process of searching multiple values in instances where order is insignificant. A good example of this involves groups. With most group implementations, you simply want to list all the members in the group. The name of each group member can easily be stored in an attribute within the group to indicate that the referenced entry is a member of this group. When the group contains multiple members, the member attribute contains multiple values (see figure 2.7). Multivalued attributes work well in this case because you don't care if someone is member number 1 or 1,000,000; you simply want to know if a particular user is listed as a member.

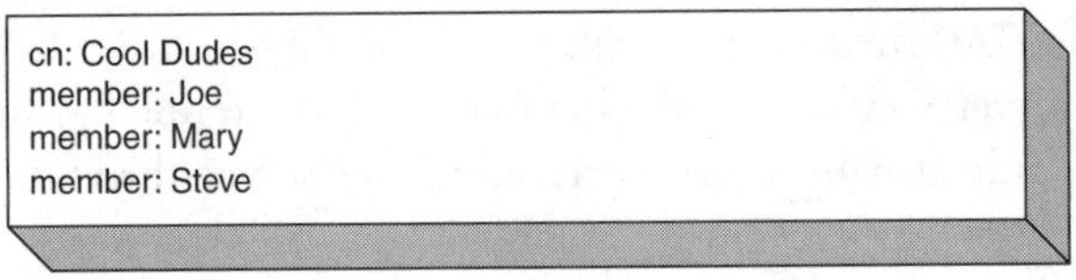

```
cn: Cool Dudes
member: Joe
member: Mary
member: Steve
```

Figure 2.7
Pseudo-entry representing a group. Here we have multiple members and can easily find out whether a given person is a member of this group.

However, using this approach you can't assume that the first person returned is the group's owner. Instead, you need to put the owner into a new attribute, perhaps associated with an attribute type called owner (see figure 2.8).

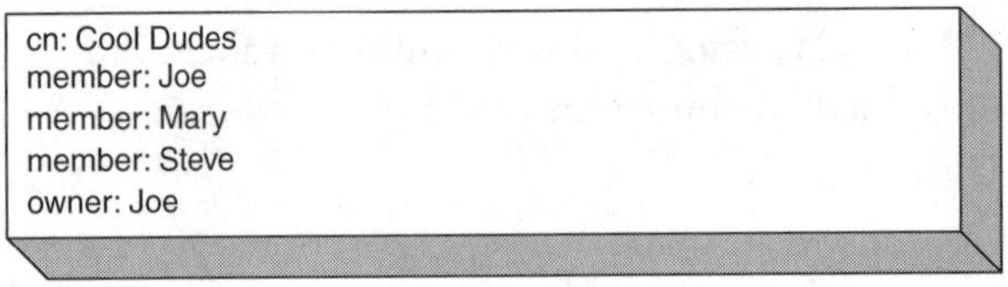

```
cn: Cool Dudes
member: Joe
member: Mary
member: Steve
owner: Joe
```

Figure 2.8
Here is our Cool Dudes group again, but this time we've included an additional attribute to represent the group's owner.

In summary, you should use multivalued attributes only in cases where ordering does not make a difference in how the value is used or displayed.

2.3.5 Inheritance

Many attribute types share common features. Rather than redefine these common features each time you create a new type, you can create a generalized attribute type with only the common elements. You can then create a specialized type that inherits all the features of the generalized type.

For example, there are many different types of names: givenName, surName, commonName, and so on. These types have many things in common: they are all case-insensitive strings, and they all use the same matching rules. Knowing this, it is possible to create a generalized attribute type called name that has only the common features we just mentioned. Figure 2.9 shows how this attribute might look.

LDAP attribute types can inherit part of their definition only from a single superior type. Thus it would not be possible to inherit from the definitions of both the name attribute type and a telephoneNumber attribute type.

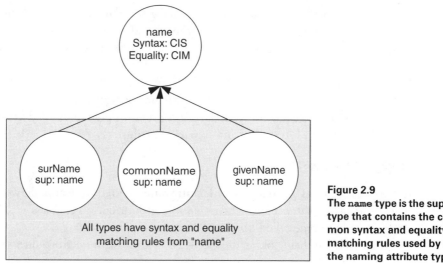

Figure 2.9
The `name` type is the superior type that contains the common syntax and equality matching rules used by all the naming attribute types.

2.3.6 User modification

Some attribute types are not designed for update by directory applications. Such attributes are often used by the server to manage internal information, while still making that internal information accessible via the LDAP protocol.

For example, an LDAP server may track modification times on an entry by storing a time stamp in an attribute. In such cases, it makes sense that only the server can change this attribute. Therefore, the `modifyTimestamp` attribute is designated as not permitting user modification.

2.3.7 Variables in Java, Perl, and C

At first glance, attributes look very similar to variables in most programming languages. Both store information, and both can usually specify a particular type or syntax for the information being stored.

Beyond this surface similarity are some major differences. First, unlike most programming languages, attributes can never point to other attributes in a way that is universally recognized. Attributes can reference another entry by containing an entry's name, but there is no way to say that one entry's attribute is a pointer to the value of a different entry such that when the "different" entry is changed, the value in the referencing entry reflects that change.

Additionally, LDAP attributes are meant for searching, so much of the information in the attribute type definition defines more about how an entry is searched than how it is stored. Even inheritance is more about determining the applicable matching rules and syntax.

A major difference between variables in object-oriented languages like Java and C++ and LDAP attributes is that a variable in these languages can be an instance of a class, rather than a simple primitive data type. Variables that are instances of a class often have both functionality (methods) and data. Even the data in these class instances is often structured in a way that would be unworkable as attribute types in LDAP.

This concept of structured data—or even simple hash-of-hash or hash-of-array structures in Perl, which has poor support for real structured types—is missing in LDAP. If an attribute has complex data, it is often simply represented as an unsearchable binary blob or broken out into separate attributes.

2.4   OBJECT CLASSES

Object classes in LDAP tell you which attributes are required and allowed to be in a particular LDAP entry. LDAP entries are placed into an object class via the use of a special attribute type called `objectClass`.

Let's take another look at the `objectClass` attribute from one of our earlier examples:

```
objectClass: organizationalPerson
objectClass: person
objectClass: top
```

The `objectClass` attribute simply gives you information about the type of entry being stored in the directory.

This example tells you that the entry belongs to three object classes: `top`, `person`, and `organizationalPerson`. In turn, knowing the object class of an entry helps you figure out what kinds of attributes you will find in it.

2.4.1   Defining object classes

Like attribute types, object classes include the following components:

- Name
- OIDs
- Inheritance

In addition to those components, an object class includes information that defines the allowable contents of entries that use that object class. Such information includes:

- Class type
- List of required attribute types
- List of allowed attribute types

Object class names

Object class names in LDAP are case-insensitive strings containing only letters, numbers, dashes (-), and semicolons (;). Traditionally, names have included only letters and numbers.

OIDs

Like attribute types, object classes are associated with unique OIDs. These dotted strings of numbers should be universally unique and have no particular meaning. Also like the OIDs associated with attribute types, the OIDs assigned to object classes should reside under a registered OID root.

2.4.2 Required and allowed attributes

The most critical aspect of an object class is the fact that it defines the contents of entries. It does so by specifying the attributes that an entry must and may contain.

For example, the `person` object class mentioned previously is defined to require the `cn` and `sn` attribute types. Entries of this class may also contain the `userPassword`, `telephoneNumber`, `seeAlso`, and `description` attribute types, but these are not required.

2.4.3 Object class inheritance

You've seen already that an LDAP object class can specialize a superior object class. This specialization is commonly referred to as *inheritance*. One object class inherits the required and allowed fields from its superior object class.

As an example, let's say you have a class called `animal` that you use to describe animal entries in the directory. This is a great class until the day you decide to add cats. Because you know that cats can have funky personalities, you figure that you should track information about the cats' personalities in their LDAP entries.

You have two options for accomplishing this. First, you can add a `personality` attribute to the `animal` class. Doing so may not make sense if the other animals you track are lacking in the personality department. Instead, you can create a new class called `cat`. Rather than list all the attributes that are allowed and required for animal entries in your new class, you simply inherit these specifications. Thus you might have definitions that look something like those shown in figure 2.10.

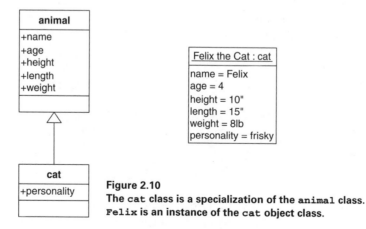

Figure 2.10
The `cat` class is a specialization of the `animal` class.
`Felix` is an instance of the `cat` object class.

Now, when you create a new `cat` entry, you will be required to specify the cat's name and age just as if you were creating a new `animal` entry. However, you are now allowed to add a `personality` attribute in addition to the attributes allowed for `animals`.

The best thing about inheritance is that you can still use these new `cat` entries as if they were `animal` entries in all your existing applications that know how to deal with `animals`. After all, if you simply need to extract the name and age of the `animal`, you probably couldn't care less whether that entry has an additional `personality` attribute.

On the flip side of this equation, just because a cat is an animal doesn't mean that an animal is a cat. So, you shouldn't be looking for `animal` entries if you expect to receive attributes types and values that are specific to `cat` entries, such as `personality`.

2.4.4 Multiple object class memberships

```
objectclass: cat
objectclass: protectedObject
name: Felix
age: 4
height: 10"
length: 15"
weight: 8lb
personality: frisky
public: true
```

Figure 2.11   Pseudo-entry of a cat that is also a `protectedObject`

An LDAP object class can have only a single superior object class, meaning that multiple inheritance is unsupported. Interestingly enough, an entry can be a member of multiple object classes, even if those object classes are not related. For example, an entry can be both a `cat` and a `protectedObject`. Defined as such, the entry will have the required and allowed attributes from the union of both object class definitions.

If you define `protectedObject` to have an attribute called `public`, an entry that implements this class and the `cat` class might look something like figure 2.11.

In this case, you might be using the `public` attribute for all your entries to decide whether they should be displayed in a search. This behavior has nothing to do with the fact that `Felix` is simply a `cat`.

2.4.5 Object class types

All object classes are not created equal. There are three different types of object classes:

- Abstract
- Structural
- Auxiliary

Abstract object classes

An object class that is defined to be abstract is never the primary object class for an entry. Rather, it contains a list of required and allowed attribute types that are common to a variety of other object classes. An abstract object class can be used as the superclass for other types of object classes.

The `top` object class is an example of an abstract object class. It is defined to require the `objectClass` attribute. Every LDAP object class ultimately extends the `top` object class; therefore, every entry must contain an `objectClass` attribute:

`top` object class

Description	The root object class
Type	Abstract
OID	2.5.6.0
Required	`objectClass`
Allowed	`dITStructureRules, nameForms, ditContentRules, objectClasses, attributeTypes, matchingRules, matchingRuleUse`
Defined	RFC 2256

Structural object classes

Structural object classes are the bread and butter of LDAP. Every LDAP entry belongs to exactly one structural object class.

An example of a structural object class is `organizationalPerson`. It extends the `person` object class, which is also a structural object class. Thus an `organizationalPerson` is a `person`, but a `person` is not an `organizationalPerson`:

`organizationalPerson` object class

Description	A person belonging to an organization
Type	Structural
Superior	`person`
OID	2.5.6.7
Required	`sn, cn`
Allowed	`userPassword, telephoneNumber, seeAlso, description`
Defined	RFC 2256

Auxiliary object classes

Auxiliary object classes are used for things that can add secondary data elements to an entry. Our earlier example of the `cat` that is a `protectedObject` clearly demonstrates this concept. You can have an auxiliary object class called `protectedObject` that you can add to any type of entry to add values; however, adding this class would not fundamentally change the purpose of those entries in such a way that they no longer represent their structural class.

Additionally, it does not make sense to use an auxiliary object class without a structural object class. For example, `protectedObject` by itself is meaningless, because the attributes it defines are useful only in adding value to the core entry defined by its structural object class.

The following definition of `strongAuthenticationUser` is an example of an auxiliary object class:

strongAuthenticationUser object class

Description	A user that is associated with a digital certificate that can be used for strong authentication
Type	Auxiliary
Superior	Top
OID	2.5.6.15
Required	userCertificate
Allowed	serialNumber, seeAlso, owner, ou, o, l, description
Defined	RFC 2256

You can form auxiliary object classes without adding required or allowed attributes. Thus the object class can be associated with an entry such that the entry can be differentiated from others solely on the basis of object class information

Active Directory binds auxiliary classes to structural classes at initialization. This binding presents a number of limitations when compared to many other directories. Most importantly, auxiliary classes cannot contain new required attributes. In addition, searches cannot be performed to return all the entries that implement an auxiliary class.

2.4.6   LDAP object classes and Java or C++ classes

There are significant differences between LDAP object classes and classes in object-oriented programming languages like Java or C++. The most obvious difference is that these languages have the concept of a class having both data and methods. The methods are a means of performing actions within the language. These actions may range from simply setting and getting information in an instance of that class to performing complex business logic.

LDAP object classes have no such concept and are used only for data. Object class definitions merely list the attribute types that can be stored in a particular entry. Even inheritance in LDAP is a matter of inheriting the list of allowable attribute types, rather than the more complex inheritance supported by object-oriented programming languages.

Finally, LDAP is made for searching data, so concepts like public, protected, and private data are not relevant. These concepts relate primarily to access between objects or classes, but LDAP has no concept within the server of relationships between objects or classes.

2.5 USING OBJECT MODELING TO DESIGN *LDAP* SCHEMA

Object modeling is commonly used when designing classes and interrelationships that will be implemented in object-oriented programming languages. It allows you to ensure that the classes you create are reusable and extensible. For example, you might begin by defining a class for people, but by using modeling, discover that you actually have three different types of people with some common information and some specialized information between classes.

Because LDAP supports many object-oriented concepts, you can use some object modeling techniques to design new directory object classes prior to their creation within a particular server. This section uses Unified Modeling Language (UML) to present a basic overview of object modeling as it pertains to modeling directory information.

2.5.1 Modeling classes

At its most basic level, a class in UML consists of a name, a list of attributes, and a list of methods. UML attributes can have varying levels of visibility outside the class. Because LDAP classes do not have methods and cannot have private attributes for uses in those methods, you will model your classes with only names and public attributes.

Each attribute is assigned a particular syntax, such as String or Integer. Additionally, you can assign whether the attribute will occur zero or more times (allowed) or one or more times (required).

Figure 2.12 shows a simple class definition for a monitor. In it, we have defined a number of attributes, including `size` and `brand`.

Monitor
size : String
supportedResolution : String
brand : String
model : String
connector : String
scanRate : Integer

Figure 2.12 UML class definition for a monitor

2.5.2 Modeling relationships

Relationship modeling helps you understand how different classes relate to one another in a way that can improve overall directory design. This section describes basic relationship modeling in UML with an eye on its relevance to directory design.

Associations and aggregations

Relationships tend to be either weak or strong. In a weak relationship, the two classes have few dependencies. An example might be `Person` and `Computer`. A person might be assigned a computer, but removing a computer does not remove a person; nor is the reverse true.

Associations are one type of relationship that classes may have with one another. The diagram in figure 2.13 shows a `Computer` class and how it is related to other classes, such as `Printer`, `Monitor`, and `Keyboard`. You could also show an association between the computer and a person who uses it.

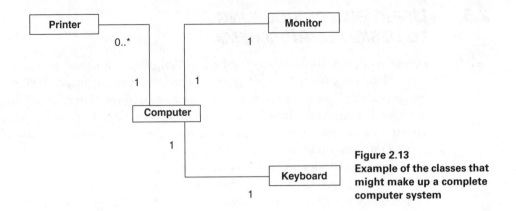

Figure 2.13
Example of the classes that might make up a complete computer system

Stronger relationships, sometimes called *composition associations* or *aggregation*, have stronger dependencies. For example, a laptop is composed of an integrated keyboard and display. Removing the laptop object should also remove its associated keyboard and display. On the other hand, a basic computer has a weaker relationship with its keyboard and monitor. Figure 2.14 shows an example of a composition association that defines the components of a laptop.

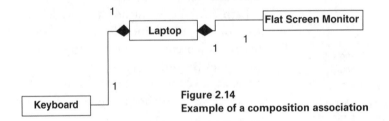

Figure 2.14
Example of a composition association

Although associations and aggregations may be difficult to translate explicitly into directory design elements, they can help determine placement of entries within the directory tree or in final definition of object classes. For example, if printers are always related to a single computer, it may make sense to place printers below computers in the directory hierarchy or to add an attribute to computers that can point to the printers associated with it.

Shown in the previous figures, but not explained, is the concept of *multiplicity*, which is an important element in association and aggregation relationships. Figures 2.13 and 2.14 show some relationships that are one-to-one and some that are one-to-many. You indicate these relationships by putting a number at each end that says how many relationships exist in each direction. For example, in figure 2.14, a one-to-one relationship exists between a laptop and a keyboard. Similarly, in figure 2.13, a printer may have only one computer, but that a computer may have zero or more printers (0..*). If you were defining network printers, you might have a many-to-many relationship instead, where printers could be associated with many computers just as computers could be associated with many printers. Thus the number of relationships between two classes can play an important part in designing all aspects of the directory.

Inheritance relationships

Many classes are related in that they are specific or general types of other classes. Specialization and generalization are ways of expressing inheritance relationships.

Figure 2.15 shows how Flat Screen Monitor and CRT Monitor classes specialize, or inherit from, the Monitor class. The arrow points to the more general class.

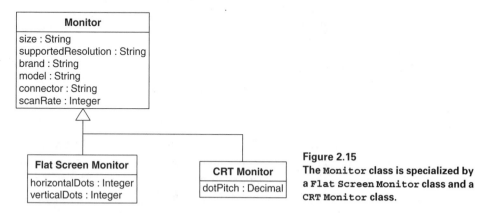

Figure 2.15
The Monitor class is specialized by a Flat Screen Monitor class and a CRT Monitor class.

Unlike associations and aggregations, inheritance relationships can be directly translated into directory design elements using LDAP's support for inheritance. For example, you can define the flatScreenMonitor object class in LDAP to have a superior class of monitor. The monitor class itself might even be defined as abstract if you expect that all monitors will fall into one of the subclasses.

2.5.3 Modeling object instances

Once you've defined classes and the inheritance hierarchy, you can model instances of objects based on the classes defined. Figure 2.16 shows an instantiation of the Flat Screen Monitor class defined in the model in the previous section.

```
              myLaptop : Flat Screen Monitor
size : String = 14"
supportedResolution : String = 1024x768, 800x600, 640x480
brand : String = Dell
model : String = Inspiron 3800 Internal
connector : String = Internal
scanRate : Integer = 60
horizontalDots : Integer = 1024
verticalDots : Integer = 768
```

Figure 2.16
An instance of the Flat Screen Monitor class includes attributes from that class, including those inherited from the Monitor class.

Although it's easy to think of an object instance as an entry (and in some cases it may be), an entry can include multiple object instances if it includes both structural and auxiliary classes. However, it is quite possible that an LDAP entry equivalent to the object instance in figure 2.16 might look like this:

```
dn: cn=myLaptop,cn=Ethan Daniel,dc=manning,dc=com
objectClass: top
objectClass: monitor
objectClass: flatScreenMonitor
cn: myLaptop
size: 14"
supportedResolution: 1024x768
supportedResolution: 800x600
supportedResolution: 640x480
brand: Dell
model: Inspiron 3800 Internal
connector: Internal
scanRate: 60
horizontalDots: 1024
verticalDots: 768
```

Notice that this LDAP entry lists three class memberships. Most directory servers will automatically add superclasses to an entry so that an entry can easily be searched by any object class that it may be a member of through explicit specification or inheritance. The added attribute called cn is assigned the instance name.

2.6 SUMMARY

In this chapter, you learned that information is stored in LDAP using entries, which are in turn made up of attributes. You now understand why LDAP's information model and particularly standard schema make it easier for a wide variety of applications to use the directory.

We looked at how entries compare to rows in a relational database, including differences between LDAP's pseudo-object-oriented model and the relational model. We also covered object classes and attribute types, with an understanding of how they compare with similar concepts in other areas. Finally, we discussed how object classes and attribute types can be modeled, while maintaining a focus on reusing existing standard attributes.

In chapter 3, we'll move from looking at the contents of entries to the naming and positioning of entries within the directory.

C H A P T E R   3

Exploring the LDAP namespace

We discussed in chapter 2 how LDAP-enabled directories use a consistent information model to represent information in the directory. Although the information model is concerned with the representation of individual objects, it does not cover how those objects relate to one another.

In this chapter, we will discuss how these individual objects, or *entries*, are positioned in a hierarchy that plays an important role in deciding how data in that directory will be secured, distributed, and managed. In turn, this hierarchy determines the naming conventions of the LDAP entries.

By the end of the chapter, you will understand the answers to the following important questions:

- What is a namespace? What does LDAP's namespace look like? How is a hierarchical tree different than a flat structure?

- What is a directory tree, and why is it sometimes called a DIT? How can the tree be used to relate data? Distinguish it?

- What is a distinguished name? What components does it consist of? How is it written?

- What is the advantage of a flat tree over a deep tree? Why is a deep tree sometimes more important?

- What factors should be used to determine the relative distinguished name (RDN)?

- Should distinguished names be meaningful or unchanging unique identifiers?

- What is a Globally/Universally Unique ID (GUID/UUID)? When are these IDs useful in LDAP? How are they generated?

3.1 WHAT IS A NAMESPACE?

Directory entries require names. For example, an entry in LDAP might be called `uid=csmith,dc=manning,dc=com` or an entry in DNS might be called www.manning.com. A directory server's *namespace* refers to the names permitted and used within a particular group of connected and potentially connected directories. This namespace is usually defined at initial configuration of an LDAP-enabled server by a system administrator.

The structure and contents of a name in the namespace can be meaningful or meaningless. For example, the name given to the `csmith` entry is clearly meaningful, whereas a sequential or generated number that is unrelated to the actual contents of an entry may be meaningless outside the directory.

Namespace as used here is somewhat different than the namespace used in the XML world. In LDAP, a server has a particular namespace; in XML, the namespace is primarily used to qualify the tags used in elements to avoid naming collisions. However, certain types of directory namespaces are designed to avoid naming collisions. For example, if there are two people named Carole Johnson in an organization, the use of a unique identifier rather than a full name in the namespace design prevents two entries from being generated with the same name.

LDAP requires that each name in the namespace be unique. However, now that directories are being linked more frequently, it is often necessary for people who design and deploy directories to design and use a directory namespace that not only works in a stand-alone manner, but also can be connected to other directories without having names collide. In fact, some of the earliest pilot projects related to LDAP's predecessor, X.500, involved creating a global namespace in which any company could participate and share directory information in much the same way that companies currently use DNS to distribute host names.

Additionally, many directories are designed with people and accounts in mind; but with relatively new standards like the CIM, this approach may not be enough. Suddenly, computers, networks, applications, and other entities need a logical place within the global namespace.

3.1.1   Hierarchical namespaces

Entry names in LDAP are hierarchical: they are organized in a tree structure. Each entry is given a name relative to its position in the tree. This relative name need only be unique among entries that share the same parent entry. This is different from a flat namespace, in which the name of an entity is unrelated to any other entities in the namespace.

LDAP is not unique in having a hierarchical namespace. Let's look at a couple of examples of hierarchical namespaces. As you can see in figure 3.1, hosts on the Internet employ hierarchical names. The use of a marketing container helps you differentiate between the server named www that resides within the top level of your company and another server with the same name that resides within the marketing domain.

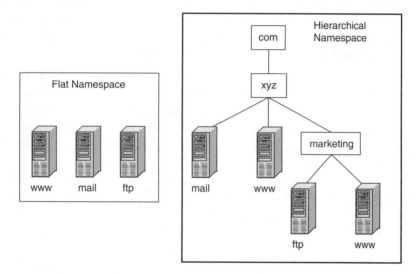

Figure 3.1   Host names on the Internet are an example of how a hierarchical namespace can help to fully qualify the names of individual entities.

A computer file system is another good example of a system with a hierarchical namespace. In this case, files are contained within folders. Fully qualified filenames are then created by stringing together the names of folders and the short filename, usually separated by a slash (/) or backslash(\). For example, if two people have files on a Linux system called .profile, those files are qualified by the name of the person's home folder. These full name for these two files might be /home/user1/.profile and /home/user2/.profile, with each file potentially having different contents.

In the directory world, this type of trees is usually referred to as the directory information tree (DIT).

DIT functions

The DIT has multiple functions:

- *The DIT allows entry names to be unique across enterprise boundaries.* Each enterprise has names within the DIT that fall under their own place in the hierarchy.

- *The DIT can be distributed.* Most directory servers allow different levels within the DIT to be placed on different servers (see figure 3.2). In many organizations where data ownership is distributed, this function allows the people closer to the data to manage their portion of a larger directory more easily.

   This approach is similar to how IT organizations around the world split the management of DNS across seemingly infinite groups of people. Such management scalability is often one of the most attractive aspects of LDAP once properly enabled applications move beyond the development phase to the deployment phase; at that point, scalable management is often an important factor in how fast an application can be rolled out.

- *The DIT facilitates security.* Security rules in most directory servers are usually relative to certain branches of the tree. In the latest Internet Drafts related to access control, an access control rule can apply to a particular entry, or to that entry plus all the entries below it in the hierarchy (see figure 3.3). This approach is similar to how access control rules work in most other commercial LDAP products.

In many modern directories, the need to add hierarchy in order to distribute directory information is much more important than the need to distribute for security

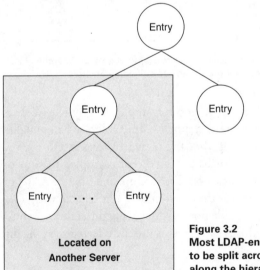

Figure 3.2
Most LDAP-enabled directory software allows entries to be split across multiple servers, but typically only along the hierarchy.

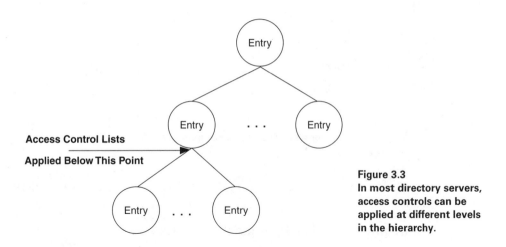

Figure 3.3
In most directory servers,
access controls can be
applied at different levels
in the hierarchy.

Access Control Lists

Applied Below This Point

reasons. This is true because in many cases, access control rules can be specified in a way that can be applied selectively within a part of the directory.

3.2 SPECIFYING DISTINGUISHED NAMES

The fully qualified name of an LDAP entry is called its *distinguished name or DN*. This distinguished name can be broken into two pieces:

- The RDN
- The base

Every LDAP operation that changes the LDAP directory uses the full distinguished name to identify the entry to affect. Similarly, operations that authenticate the user to the directory also require specification of the full distinguished name. Search operations may involve all or part of the distinguished name, as we will discuss in chapter 4.

The relative distinguished name is composed of one or more attributes from the entry. For example, if you have the cn attribute type with a value of Joan Smith in an entry, the RDN might be cn=Joan Smith (see figure 3.4).

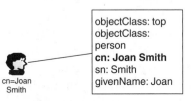

objectClass: top
objectClass:
person
cn: Joan Smith
sn: Smith
givenName: Joan

cn=Joan
Smith

**Figure 3.4   The cn attribute is
selected as the RDN for this entry.**

The base is formed by joining the names of the current entry's ancestors. You can create the base by walking up the tree from your current entry and adding the RDN of each entry in your path. Each naming component is then separated with a comma. An example of a base is dc=xyz, dc=com (see figure 3.5).

Think of the distinguished name as a way to reference an individual entry within the directory in much the same way that a primary key is used to access a particular record in a database. The concept of a distinguished name is extremely important to

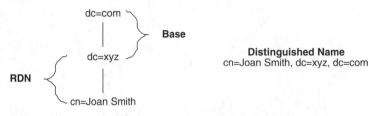

Figure 3.5 Combining the RDN with a base-naming context gives the entry a narrower context.

LDAP, so we will look a bit closer at RDNs and bases to be sure you understand these logical segments of an entry's distinguished name.

3.2.1 Choosing a relative distinguished name attribute

As we just discussed, the RDN of the entry is equal to one of the attributes in an entry. This is an important part of the standard, although some directory servers do not enforce it.

In virtually every case, the best attribute to choose is one that is unique and unchanging, even if it must be created or generated. If you want to use the same attribute as the RDN for each entry, it is important to select an attribute that everyone has. Some companies begin by using employee numbers, only to remember that the human resources (HR) department doesn't assign such numbers to nonemployees, such as contractors. Others begin with semiprivate information, such as Social Security numbers, but then realize that distinguished names are relatively public information within the directory.

Because distinguished names are rarely displayed outside the confines of the most basic LDAP browsing tools, there is no requirement that the RDN have any meaning when displayed. In fact, it is highly recommended that these identifiers have no meaning, particularly if the content of the attribute might change. For example, if you're naming organizational units, unique department names may have been assigned; but in all likelihood, those departments may change names over time. A better identifier in this case is an unchanging department code, or simply a generated unique attribute.

If the RDN attribute is binary, it will be encoded using the Base64 standard. All information in the distinguished name must be represented in the UTF-8 character set.

Common names as RDNs

Don't use a person's or organization's name as an RDN. Companies, divisions, and even people change their names all the time. The most common example in Western civilization is a woman changing her last name when she marries. If you consider that an entry's distinguished name is used as a reference to that entry in groups and other entries, you see that changing the distinguished name is an inconvenience—particularly because LDAP does not guarantee relational integrity on the server.

Generating new attributes for the RDN

If an appropriate attribute doesn't already exist, one should be created. Doing so early in a directory project rather than after a directory has been deployed will save you considerable time and headache.

There are a number of ways to do this, including:

- Sequential assignment of a numeric or alphanumeric code
- Giving users the ability to pick their own at request time
- Using an algorithm that generates UUIDs

Assigning identifiers sequentially works well in many directory environments. Because LDAP doesn't support transactions, you can't make a reliable incrementing counter using the directory itself; but with enough consideration within account or entry management tools, creating such an attribute is painless.

Giving users the ability to pick their own identifier might be right in the case where an attribute like uid will be used as both the RDN and a login ID. If you intend to display the attribute and RDN, keep in mind who is being allowed to select their own identifiers—you don't want users to choose four-letter words or other unwelcome values.

If the identifier should be unique in multiple directory environments, the best way to assign one may be to generate it using a special algorithm that focuses on making a unique value across multiple systems. An example of an appropriate algorithm is documented at http://www.opengroup.org/onlinepubs/9629399/apdxa.htm.

Nonunique attributes in the RDN

If no attributes can be guaranteed to be unique on their own, then best practice is to create or generate such a unique identifier. However, if doing so is not practical, most directories (with the exception of Microsoft Active Directory) support multiple attributes as part of the RDN. To assign multiple attributes, you put a plus sign (+) between each of the attributes that make up the RDN, as shown in figure 3.6.

cn=John Smith + ou=Sales

Figure 3.6   RDNs can contain multiple attributes if required to make the entry name unique at a particular level in the hierarchy.

Note that even though a directory supports multivalued RDNs, many applications do not display them well and using them in general tends to cause more problems than it solves. It is usually a better idea to create unique identifiers specifically for the purpose of ensuring uniqueness, if such a unique attribute doesn't already exist.

Multiple attribute values

If the chosen attribute has multiple values, you can use any of the values as the RDN value. You can do so because the RDN is separate from the actual attribute.

Although it may not seem like a big deal, having multiple values in the attribute used for the RDN is an issue. A generic LDAP-enabled application has no easy, programmatic way to decide which attribute should be used, particularly because there is no guarantee that attribute values will be in any particular order.

> **NOTE** People using Active Directory don't need to worry about using multivalued attributes as RDNs as a design alternative, because Active Directory doesn't allow you to do so.

To avoid this problem, focus on attributes that are not only unique, but single-valued. An example is `uid`.

Active Directory limitations

Microsoft Active Directory only allows `cn`, `ou`, `l`, `o`, and `dc` attributes as naming components. This limitation can be an issue for people with both Microsoft and other directories, particularly if the `cn` attribute is not unique and you want a separate unique identifier. In most directories other than Microsoft's, `cn` is a human-readable name for a person or other entity. This type of information is generally bad as an RDN in the first place.

However messy this sounds, you should note that Active Directory is a little more intelligent than many other directories about allowing for renaming of *non-leaf nodes*, which are entries that contain child entries. For these non-leaf entries, such as organizations, changing the RDN of the entry would require the distinguished names and references to all its children to be updated—not a fun ordeal with most directory products.

3.2.2 Determining the base

ou=Marketing,dc=manning,dc=com

Figure 3.7 The base of the distinguished name includes the ancestors of the current entry, separated by commas.

The base contains the RDN of each ancestor of the current entry, separated by commas. Figure 3.7 shows a simple distinguished name base. Note that the base is also a valid name for an entry.

As you will see more clearly in chapter 4, the base of the entry can play an important role in defining what results are returned from a particular search. Additionally, an entry with the name equal to the base must exist before you create an entry with that base. Thus you should not be able to create an entry called

```
cn=Jane Chen, ou=Sales, dc=manning, dc=com
```

without first creating an entry called

```
ou=Sales, dc=manning, dc=com
```

Note that in these examples, there is a space after the comma that separates each RDN component. Any amount of whitespace around the comma is ignored as part of the entry's name. The comma and any whitespace merely act as a separator. If you want to use an RDN value that ends in a space, you should escape the space by placing a backslash (\) before it; however, such cases should be few and far between.

A simple example: Mike Lee

As you just learned, the distinguished name of an entry is generated by tracing a path up the naming tree from an individual entry to the root. Each ancestor further qualifies the one below it, thus helping to distinguish it from similar entries in other parts of the tree.

An LDAP directory tree for the local zoo might look something like the diagram in figure 3.8.

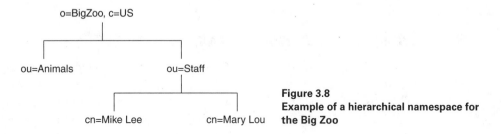

Figure 3.8
Example of a hierarchical namespace for the Big Zoo

To determine the distinguished name for Mike Lee, you climb the tree and add the names of his ancestors, separated by commas. Doing so gives you his distinguished name:

```
cn=Mike Lee, ou=Staff, o=BigZoo, c=US
```

Using higher nodes in the tree as part of the full entry name offers important contextual information that allows you to easily differentiate between different entries with otherwise indistinguishable names. For example, when you refer to his distinguished name, you are saying that it is not just any Mike Lee you are talking about, but rather the one under the `ou=Staff, o=BigZoo, c=US` branch of the directory tree (see figure 3.9).

As we noted in the previous section, each entry in the tree is always assigned an RDN composed of one or more of its attributes. Here, Mike Lee is assigned the RDN,

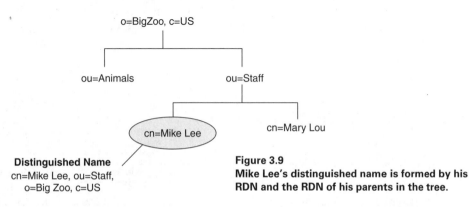

Distinguished Name
cn=Mike Lee, ou=Staff,
o=Big Zoo, c=US

Figure 3.9
Mike Lee's distinguished name is formed by his RDN and the RDN of his parents in the tree.

cn=Mike Lee, ou=Staff, o=Big Zoo, c=US

cn: Mike Lee
sn: Lee
objectClass: person

Figure 3.10   Mike's entry must contain the attribute used as his RDN.

cn=Mike Lee; you expect that his entry contains an attribute with that type and value (see figure 3.10).

As expected, the entry contains that attribute, and the entry is valid. Also notice that the attributes listed in the base are not part of the entry—this fact is important, because any attribute not in the entry will not be found in a standard search.

3.3   ASSIGNING THE ROOT NAMING CONTEXT

LDAP-enabled directory servers do not typically allow you to use arbitrary bases. Instead, a server is configured with one or more suffixes for which it will contain data. This suffix will be the entry name of the server's highest node in the directory tree.

The top level entry name supported by a particular server is sometimes referred to as the server's *root naming context*. Some servers support more than one root naming context; others do not.

These root naming contexts are usually assigned in one of two ways by the individual or individuals managing the server:

- Traditional style
- Domain component style

3.3.1   Traditional style of assigning the root name context

The traditional convention for assigning the root naming context has been to use o=company, c=country, where company is a free-form company name and country is a two-character ISO-standard country code such as US or CA. This convention was inherited from LDAP's X.500 ancestry (see figure 3.11).

The problem with using traditional root naming contexts is that few people go through the trouble of registering organization names with ANSI or other registration authorities. Thus it's easy for two groups with a similar organization name to have completely different directories starting with the same root. Because the root naming

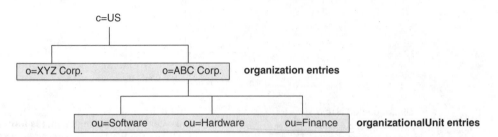

Figure 3.11   Traditional root naming contexts inherited from X.500 directory standards

context is designed to make your entry names globally unique, this ambiguity can cause problems.

3.3.2 Domain component style of assigning the root name context

More common today is the root naming context `dc=company,dc=domain`. In this instance, *company* and *domain* are two or more parts of an organization's DNS domain name. Thus abc.com might have a root naming context of `dc=abc, dc=com` as shown in figure 3.12.

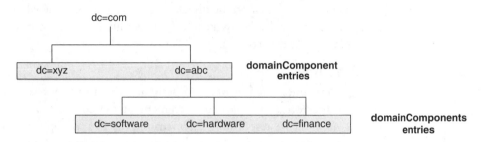

Figure 3.12   The domain component style of assigning root naming contexts is better suited for the Internet.

One drawback to using domain component (dc) style root naming contexts is that some certificate authorities (CAs) only allow traditional X.500 attributes (c, o, ou, cn, and so forth) in the subject names of the certificates they issue. We will discuss digital certificates in chapter 13, but for now it is enough to know that issues in this regard are highly dependent on the way applications using certificates plan to map those certificate names to names in the directory. As you will see, this process is critical when you're doing directory-based authorization and users authenticate using digital certificates.

> **NOTE**   Users of Microsoft Active Directory do not have a choice about the style of root naming context that will be used, because Active Directory requires the top levels of the tree to be dcs. Most other directories leave the decision to the person designing the directory. If you want to work with Active Directory, you should keep this point in mind.

3.4   SELECTING AND DESIGNING A DIRECTORY TREE

We just talked about selecting naming components. What about defining the holistic view of a particular directory tree? After all, it is sometimes difficult to know exactly what will be stored in a directory.

Because the standards do not dictate best practices for designing a hierarchical directory tree, many companies that go through the effort of deploying new directories get stuck for months designing a tree to meet the needs of their organization.

Designing a tree is difficult because different tree structures present different advantages and disadvantages in different environments.

In this section, we'll look at a variety of common directory trees used by companies today and some of the benefits and disadvantages of using each. Because directories designed for use in extranets, intranets, and the Internet have different needs, our discussion about directory trees will be based on trees that may be appropriate for each of these directory types.

In general, directory trees can be referred to as *flat* or *deep*. Flat trees are those that have little hierarchy, whereas deep trees may have considerable hierarchy. In general, it is a good design practice to keep the directory tree as flat as possible while still maintaining any level of hierarchy necessary to offer flexibility in the distribution of directory information and access control.

3.4.1 Intranet directories

In most large companies, the organization designing the directory has responsibility only for those directories in a particular segment of the company. Even corporate organizations may not be responsible for managing users and applications in some fairly autonomous business units. In small-to-midsize companies, a single organization may be responsible for managing the enterprise's directory. In almost any case, the directory being designed is expected to "leave room" for the entire company, even if the entire company will not at first be managed in the directory.

The types of trees most commonly used for intranets are:

- Organization-based
- Flat
- Geographic

Organization-based trees

Many people tasked for the first time to create an organization-based directory create a hierarchy that models the organizations in an organizational chart. For example, if the company is split into sales, operations, and engineering, the resulting tree will also be split this way. The diagram in figure 3.13 shows this type of directory tree.

This type of tree is appealing in many ways. First, IT organizations in many companies are split along organizational boundaries. These boundaries may not be along functional lines, such as sales and engineering, but they're probably along major product lines or markets.

NOTE   We'll use the branches labeled Employees, Groups, and Applications in figure 3.13 in most of the designs featured in this section, although they may be located in different positions in the directory tree. Although we use readable RDNs that include people's names in these diagrams, we do so primarily for readability—this approach is not meant to endorse the bad practice of using these types of entry names.

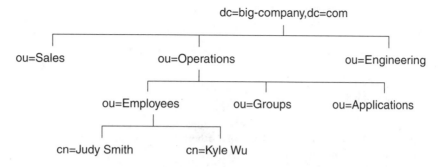

Figure 3.13 Organization-based trees are commonly selected to allow for multiple organizations within an enterprise to manage their own directory servers, while ensuring that they'll work well together.

Dividing the tree along such lines leaves room for other organizations that may not be active in the directory at the start. It also leaves room for a type of directory management called *delegated administration* that we will discuss in part 2.

However, such trees do present a problem. To understand you need to consider nonpeople LDAP entries (such as groups) that might need to point to a list of other LDAP entries. References to one entry from other entries are done using the distinguished name of the entry. If that distinguished name changes, nothing in the LDAP specification encourages referential integrity checking that will keep those pointers referencing the right entry. This situation is even more complicated if a data store outside the directory uses the distinguished name as a reference.

As anyone who has ever worked in a large company knows, people change divisions and departments all the time. If such a change has the potential to break groups and applications, then you should avoid such designs where possible.

Flat trees

We come now to the opposite side of the intranet directory design spectrum: the relatively flat directory tree. In this design, shown in figure 3.14, the Employees branch of the tree is located beneath the company's root naming context. Employees will always be employees, so it is rather unlikely that they will be moved to another part of the directory tree.

Because the tree is so flat, entries are typically added and deleted only when someone is hired or fired, not when internal events happen. Attributes within the entry can hold the additional information required to find out the division or department to which an entry belongs.

Perfect, right? Not quite. There are a few drawbacks to using such a simple namespace. The main one is that most directory server products do not allow a single branch of the tree to be split across multiple servers. Although every directory on the market can handle the size of most intranet-focused directories, there are often

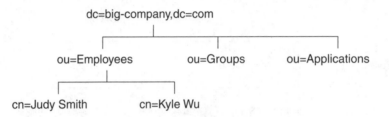

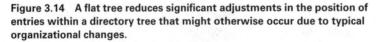

Figure 3.14 A flat tree reduces significant adjustments in the position of entries within a directory tree that might otherwise occur due to typical organizational changes.

political or other nontechnical motivations for splitting the data across multiple machines. Some products also allow for more granular access control when the tree is divided along more meaningful organizational boundaries.

Geographic trees

There are still a few places where division of the tree must happen for reasons that are technical in nature. One such reason is geography: links between continents, countries, or even relatively small distances may not always be desired.

In such situations, having a directory that is slow or inaccessible may limit your ability to deploy directory-enabled applications globally without decreasing that application's ability to function reliably. To get around this issue, the most common solution is to design a directory tree that is geographic, rather than organizational. The diagram in figure 3.15 shows a tree designed this way.

In this example, the regions are quite large and broad, but it would be entirely possible to split the tree into smaller regions. Typically, each region will have a master copy of the data in that region, with referrals or replicated copies of the data in other regions.

Because geographic and political boundaries do not always match, this type of directory tree may not solve any problems in the area of distributed management. In fact, it may contribute to management issues if political and geographic boundaries

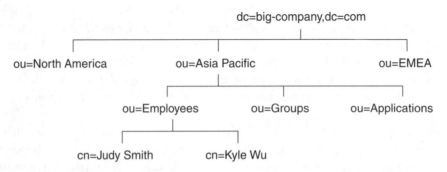

Figure 3.15 Geographic trees allow directories to be split in ways that make sense to ensure availability.

CHAPTER 3 EXPLORING THE LDAP NAMESPACE

overlap poorly. Considering that many company help desks and support organizations are regional in order to be available at the right time to local users, a high likelihood exists in many organizations that geographic distribution will work well with existing political boundaries.

In the organizational tree design, one issue is that employees may move between organizations. Although this is true to an extent with the geographic design, it is less of a problem because in many companies, transfers normally occur within a particular region. This benefit may not be realized if people move between regions frequently. Even if movement is rare, a process needs to be in place for coordinating it.

In the end, this design may be more complicated and difficult to maintain than the flat tree described earlier. You can avoid using this type of tree and use a flat tree by simply replicating the entire contents of a centralized directory containing a flat tree to other directories in the various regions. Directory servers that support multi-master replication can even allow for entries to be managed directly in multiple regions if bandwidth permits. Unfortunately, not all directory services support multi-master replication; so, if a user in another region needs to make a change to an entry, the possibility exists that the change will not be able to proceed if network or other issues are involved.

3.4.2 Internet directories

Internet directory designs tend to be much different than intranet designs, because they're outwardly focused and need to be specialized for containing customers or users rather than people in the internal organization. There are exceptions, but they usually more closely resemble either an intranet or extranet design.

The types of trees most commonly used for Internets are:

- Internal and external users
- External users with groups
- Application branches

Internal and external users

One way to organize an Internet directory is to split the tree into two sets of users. The first set contains the people on the organization's staff who might use such an application with special privileges. The other set contains those users who belong to a potentially much larger base of external users. The diagram in figure 3.16 shows how such a tree might look.

The advantage of separating these users is that there are usually significantly different processes and restrictions for the management of each group. External users, shown in figure 3.16 under the ou=Users branch of the directory tree, may be able to create themselves with as little information as an email address. However, internal users, under the ou=Staff branch, must be added by a privileged administrator based on the staff member's responsibilities in the organization.

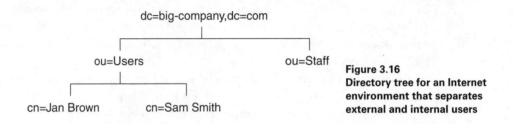

Figure 3.16
Directory tree for an Internet
environment that separates
external and internal users

There is no reason the `ou=Staff` portion of the tree cannot simply contain the information from an intranet-focused directory. In fact, it can be arranged in one of the intranet designs discussed in the previous section.

External users with groups

Do different classes of external users need different levels of privileges? Are there mailing lists that some customers belong to, but others do not? If the answer to either of these questions is yes, you should consider the early addition of a branch of the directory tree dedicated to the storage of group information that can be used in these situations. The diagram in figure 3.17 shows how such a tree might look.

Once again, the `ou=Staff` portion can contain either a small set of users with management rights within an application or some representation of the information in an intranet-focused directory service.

This approach has a disadvantage. Having a single Groups branch that is not subdivided does not allow different Internet applications to create their own groups easily without cluttering the Groups directory with groups from all applications. One way to resolve this situation is to add more hierarchy to the Groups branch; however, doing so tends to automatically isolate each application without taking into account that there should be some level of group sharing between applications.

Application branches

One potential solution to the issue just mentioned is not to create a top-level Groups branch at all. Rather, understand that groups are only one piece of information that will be used to make application-level decisions. For example, in addition

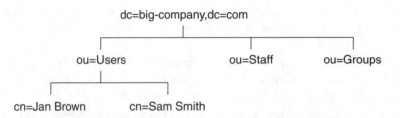

Figure 3.17   A directory tree with a group branch allows for easier segmentation of external users and the creation of groups that can facilitate access control and mailing lists.

CHAPTER 3   EXPLORING THE LDAP NAMESPACE

to groups, applications might want to store general configuration information in the directory. Additionally, certain groups, configurations, or other information may be used not so much for a single application as for a global setting that applies across the Internet environment.

Figure 3.18 shows a tree that fits this type of information. In this tree, a special Applications branch contains a separate branch for each application. Those applications in turn may have configurations, groups, and other branches that are useful to that application. In addition to having a branch for each application, this tree also designates a branch for global groups and configuration that allows certain information to apply across the Internet environment.

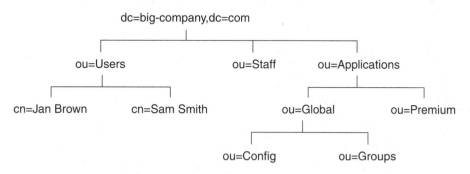

Figure 3.18 A branch containing information for applications is added to allow more extensive use of the directory in the Internet environment.

Such a tree gives you incredible flexibility when you're developing a directory that can be used by many Internet applications. However, it does make the directory's design more complex overall, and may not be easy to support with off-the-shelf provisioning and security applications.

3.4.3   Extranet directories

Extranets are becoming predominant, and the use of directories in extranets is getting to be a necessity. However, extranet directory design is extremely tricky, because much of it depends on multiple political entities. For this reason, much of the design for an extranet directory is highly dependent on the ability of the partners to agree on how people, groups, and other information will be managed.

The types of trees most commonly used for extranets include:

- Equal partners
- Internal and external with partner type segmentation
- Internal and external with partner segmentation

In addition to these three extranet-focused designs, an extranet directory may also use designs similar to those mentioned for the other directory types—particularly flat trees like those advocated for intranet design, and trees that only separate internal and external users, as shown in the Internet design section. Both of these alternate designs are particularly applicable if partners are generally small and do not have their own directory servers that might be used to seed or synchronize the most basic user information.

Equal partners design

The most basic extranet design simply acts as if each partner is completely equal and will be directly managing or otherwise providing its information. In figure 3.19, both big-company and componentco are equal within the directory tree. This design works well if big-company and componentco have their own directory environments and perceived value (single sign-on) to extranet users for people in both companies.

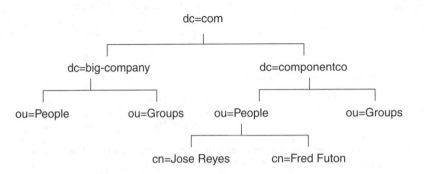

Figure 3.19   Equal partners design is one way to name information in an extranet directory such that multiple companies are represented within a single directory namespace.

This design doesn't make much sense if one company will be maintaining all of the directory information, or even if the second company will be managing its users through interfaces provided by the first company. This design also doesn't make sense in cases with smaller numbers of users, because segmentation between users can often be done just as easily with attributes. You should restrict the use of this design to instances where both companies have a significant exposure to directories and will potentially implement direct links between pieces of their directory environments.

Internal and external with partner type segmentation

When discussing directory trees for Internet directories, we showed a tree in which internal and external users are separated. Such a design also works well in a hub-and-spoke extranet environment where one company hosts the directory environment and everyone else uses it.

One way to extend this design within an extranet environment is to segment the "spoke" companies based on the their function (supplier, customer, and so forth). This

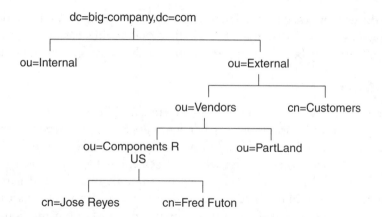

Figure 3.20 This directory tree segments partners by both name and function in order to allow for partial replication and better access control in some directories.

design is useful if certain applications are pointed at a directory that might be partially replicated to an application directory, which will be accessed only by a certain type of partner. Figure 3.20 shows this type of directory tree.

This tree is obviously quite a bit more complicated than the trees shown previously. As mentioned earlier, the more complicated the tree, the more difficult it may be to manage. One issue with managing this particular tree would be the use of off-the-shelf applications. Many may not be flexible enough to allow user management in the right parts of the directory.

Internal and external with partner segmentation

Rather than add an extra layer for partner type, you may simply want to flatten the tree a little such that the only segmentation under the external branch is by company. This design is a better choice if there is no perceived difference between how different types of partners will be managed or replicated. Figure 3.21 shows an example of this kind of tree.

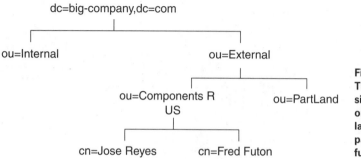

Figure 3.21 This directory tree is similar to the previous one, but it removes the layer that segments partners by type or function.

Like the previous design, this design's drawback is its complexity, but it does simplify situations where a partner might be both a vendor and a customer. Once again, the biggest issue may be in the support for off-the-shelf management applications.

3.5   SUMMARY

This chapter introduced the concept of the hierarchical LDAP namespace and entry naming. We discussed various potential design types and their respective advantages and disadvantages. In the end, the key thing to remember is that a flat tree is best, but you can add hierarchy where it helps with management and applications.

You also learned that entries are named by a unique distinguished name; these names must be unique and should be static whenever possible. We also discussed why distinguished names should almost never contain a personal or organizational name.

In chapter 4, we move from discussing directory concepts and design to understanding its most basic operation: searching.

C H A P T E R   4

Search criteria

This chapter delves into the world of LDAP searching. We will be answering the following questions:

- What makes up the LDAP search criteria? When are they used?

- What are the search base and scope? How do they affect the entries returned?

- How is the search filter constructed? What common pitfalls do you need to avoid with search filters?

- What search criteria offer the best performance? Worst?

- What similarities and differences exist between LDAP searches and SQL queries?

4.1 PERFORMING A SEARCH

When an LDAP client asks a directory server for information, it does so by passing a relatively simple set of search criteria that tells the server a number of things:

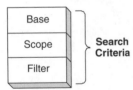

Figure 4.1 At minimum, the search criteria are made up of the base, scope, and filter, which determine the *where* and *what* of a search.

- What part of the directory tree will be searched.
- What qualities must returned entries contain or not contain.
- What information from matching entries should be returned.

The server will take these criteria, determine whether the connected client has the privileges necessary to perform a search using the given criteria, and return all the results the client is authorized to receive. Figure 4.1 shows some of the more important search criteria.

4.2 WHERE TO SEARCH: BASE AND SCOPE

The criteria used to determine the portion of the directory tree to which the search will be applied involve two factors. The first factor is the search *base*. The base is simply the distinguished name of an entry in the directory that will be the topmost entry associated with the search. The other factor is the search *scope*. The server uses the scope to determine how far below the search base it will look for entries that match the rest of the search criteria.

4.2.1 Search base

In chapter 3, we spent considerable time discussing the directory tree and LDAP namespace. Specifying a search base is simply a way for you to confine your search to branches of the tree. Note that searches never crawl up the tree from the search base—they occur only at or below the base.

Examples of search bases might be:

- dc=manning,dc=com
- ou=Authors,dc=manning,dc=com

These bases could also contain multivalued RDNs or other components allowed in the distinguished names of entries.

Some special search bases also exist. Servers supporting LDAPv3 support the Root Directory Server Entry (RootDSE) which is represented by an empty distinguished name (""). As you will see soon, this search base, combined with other search criteria, returns important information about the server's capabilities. Other special search bases exist for retrieving server schema and monitoring information.

4.2.2 Search scope

As mentioned previously, the search scope tells the server exactly which entries at or below the search base should be evaluated. The LDAP protocol defines three search scopes:

- Base
- One-level
- Subtree

In this section we will look at what entries can be returned with each of these search scopes.

Base scope

In figure 4.2, a search for Sam Smith's record will never return results, because that record is not evaluated as part of the search. However, a search for an entry with any `objectClass` value will return the `dc=manning,dc=com` entry.

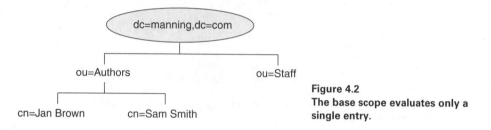

Figure 4.2
The base scope evaluates only a single entry.

The LDAP protocol does not offer an operation to read an entry from the directory by name. Instead, you can read an entry directly by specifying a search with a search base equal to the distinguished name to be read, and a base search scope.

One-level scope

The one-level scope allows you to search only those entries directly below the base you specified for the current search (see figure 4.3). This scope will not return the entry located at the search base. A search on the presence of the `objectClass` attribute will have the effect of listing all of the search base's immediate children.

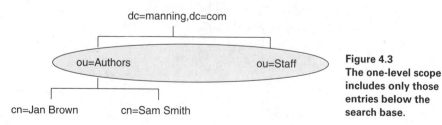

Figure 4.3
The one-level scope includes only those entries below the search base.

This is an important scope when you're creating graphical applications that need to open and close branches of the directory tree. If you expect that the application will need to traverse the entire directory tree below the base, one-level scope is the way to do it unless the number of entries in the directory is small enough that returning and caching the full tree will be more efficient.

Subtree scope

Rather than return only the immediate children of the search base, the subtree scope returns all descendants matching the given filter. Searching for the presence of `objectClass` will return all entries below the search base. Unlike the one-level search, the subtree search evaluates the base as well as entries below the base in the tree. Figure 4.4 shows the results of a subtree search from the top of the directory tree.

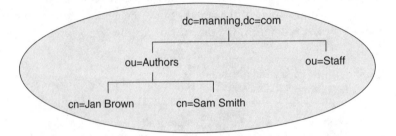

Figure 4.4   The subtree search returns all descendants of the base, including the base.

Most applications that do not have detailed directory tree requirements use subtree searching to find entries where the distinguished name of the entry is not already known.

4.3   WHAT TO EVALUATE: SEARCH FILTERS

If the search scope and base tell you where to look for matching entries, the search filter tells you under what conditions an entry in the specified location should be returned. LDAP filters can be as simple as requiring that returned entries have a particular attribute. More complex filters can contain many different tests that can be used to determine if an entry should be returned.

There are seven basic types of LDAP filters:

- Presence
- Equality
- Substring
- Greater-than or equal

- Less-than or equal
- Approximate
- Extensible

It is also possible to combine these filters using AND/OR filters and to negate filters or groups of filters using NOT filters.

The filter or set of filters supplied by the client is applied by the server against each entry in the location identified by the scope and base. If the filter is true for the entry, then that entry will be returned. If it's false, the entry is ignored and not returned as part of the search results.

4.3.1 Presence filters

A presence filter simply requires that an entry have any value for a particular attribute type. Figure 4.5 shows an example of a presence filter that returns any entry with the sn (surname) attribute.

Example: sn=*

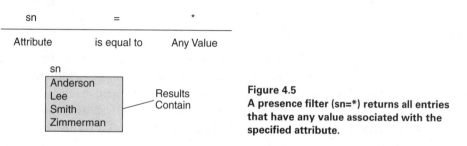

Figure 4.5
A presence filter (sn=*) returns all entries that have any value associated with the specified attribute.

Using the ldapsearch command and what you've already learned about filters, you can create a complete search using a presence filter:

```
> ldapsearch -b "dc=manning,dc=com" -s sub "(objectClass=*)"
```

Notice the parentheses around the filter. Although they are not necessary with most LDAP clients when using a single search filter, it is good practice to always surround each filter component with parentheses—this is the way standards documents state that filters should appear.

You will get results in LDIF that look something like this:

```
dn: cn=John Johnson,dc=manning,dc=com
cn: John Johnson
sn: Johnson
objectClass: person
objectClass: top

(more entries...)
```

This entry is returned because it is at or below the `dc=manning,dc=com` branch of the directory tree, as specified by the base and scope arguments, and contains an `objectClass` attribute as required by the search filter.

Had the filter been (`uid=*`), this entry would not have been returned, because it does not contain that attribute. Nor would the entry have been returned had the scope been `base` rather than subtree (`sub`).

A presence filter of (`objectClass=*`) with a scope of base and a search base equal to a particular distinguished name is a common way to read in an entry where the distinguished name is already known. This filter works because every entry is required to have one or more associated `objectClass`es. The ability to read an entry this way is important, because the distinguished name itself is not an attribute and is not typically evaluated as part of matching the search filter.

For example, suppose you do the following search:

```
> ldapsearch -b "dc=manning,dc=com" -s sub "(dc=*)"
```

The John Johnson entry will not be retrieved, because of the nonevaluation of the distinguished name. Using (`cn=*`) would return the entry because the entry contains the `cn` attribute, not because the distinguished name contains that attribute.

4.3.2 Exact equality filters

An equality matching filter limits the entries returned as part of the search results to those that contain a specified attribute and value. This is different from presence matching, which only asks that an entry contain a given attribute. Figure 4.6 expands a simple equality filter that looks for entries with `Smith` in the `sn` attribute.

The following example using the `ldapsearch` command also shows an equality search:

```
> ldapsearch -b "dc=manning,dc=com" -s sub "(sn=Johnson)"
```

The John Johnson entry will be returned by this search, because it contains the `sn` attribute with an associated value of `Johnson`. Because the `sn` attribute is defined as case insensitive, doing an exact search for (`sn=johnson`) or (`sn=joHnSoN`) will also return the John Johnson entry. Appendix A offers a reference to a large number of standardized attribute types, including their syntax.

Example: sn=Smith

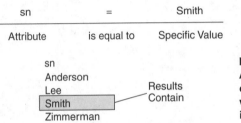

Figure 4.6
An equality filter (`sn=Smith`) returns any entry that contains the given attribute with a value equal to the value specified in the filter.

Most directory servers offer their best performance for equality searches. This is the case partly because of easier indexing, but also because exact equality searches are the most commonly used search filters in applications that make programmatic use of directories.

To understand why, consider an application that uses the directory as a repository for identity information. When given an ID, the application wants passwords and other information associated with that identity. When the application performs such a lookup to find this information, it does so in the most exact way possible. After all, if you log in as jjohnson, it is important that there is no ambiguity about whether jjohnson is John Johnson or Jeff Johnson. Therefore, the application might query on a unique attribute called uid that contains unique user identities, such as jjohnson. This process ensures that the application can locate an exact entry. Mail-relaying software typically performs similar exact matching, because it is imperative that email for a single email address be delivered only to the appropriate mail servers and mailboxes.

These common uses do not mean that exact equality matching is not used to perform searches that might return multiple results—far from it. White pages applications, unlike security applications, need to find as many matches as possible for potentially ambiguous user input. After all, users are unlikely to know that they should look up John Johnson as jjohnson. In fact, a user may be unaware that John's name is actually Jonathan. In this type of situation, an exact match on a nonunique field is both possible and useful. A search for a last name of Johnson offers a good choice of matches from which to select.

Similarly, an administration interface that assigns users to groups or roles might need to do this type of matching in order to give administrators the ability to locate appropriate users. Once added, the service that uses these groups and roles would use exact equality matching to locate the exact entry identified as part of a given group.

4.3.3 Substring matching

As we just mentioned, white pages applications have different requirements than many other types of applications. The basic need is for the ability to match the partial information a user might know with a list of results that have a good chance of being what that user needs. LDAP offers additional types of matching to meet these higher requirements.

The most commonly used search filter, other than exact equality and presence, is the substring filter. The substring filter looks simple, but is in fact much different than it first appears.

Figure 4.7 shows both a valid and an invalid substring search filter. The valid filter shows a search for the characters *Don* anywhere in the cn attribute. The invalid filter

Right: cn = *Don*

Wrong: cn = *D*nl*

Figure 4.7
An example of a substring filter that correctly queries for entries containing *Don* anywhere in the value, along with an illegal search filter that attempts to use multiple middle substring components

doesn't work because LDAP substring filters do not use true wildcards the way file system listings or regular expressions do.

A substring search can be performed by the an `ldapsearch` command like the following:

```
> ldapsearch -b "dc=manning,dc=com" -s sub "(sn=Johns*)"
```

This command will return all entries with `sn` attribute values beginning with the characters *Johns*. Such a search is called an *initial substring* search, because it looks for the specified characters at the start of attribute values.

Substring searching can also be performed to match the middle and end of attribute values, as the following two examples show:

```
> ldapsearch -b "dc=manning,dc=com" -s sub "(sn=*ohns*)"
```

```
> ldapsearch -b "dc=manning,dc=com" -s sub "(sn=*son)"
```

Finally, you can use a combination of these types of substring searches. The following examples match first at the beginning and middle of the entry, then the beginning and end, and finally the middle and end:

```
> ldapsearch -b "dc=manning,dc=com" -s sub "(sn=J*ns*)"
```

```
> ldapsearch -b "dc=manning,dc=com" -s sub "(sn=Jo*son)"
```

```
> ldapsearch -b "dc=manning,dc=com" -s sub "(sn=*oh*son)"
```

Figure 4.8 shows two examples. One is valid and shows a substring search that looks for *Do* anywhere within the `cn` attribute and *ley* at the end; the other is invalid because it contains multiple substrings in the middle.

Right: cn=*Do*ley **Figure 4.8**

Wrong: cn=*D*nl*y **An example that uses only contains (*Do*) and final (*ley) substring matching along with another example of a bad filter that inserts too many criteria**

As we stated earlier in this section, many people first exposed to LDAP look at the asterisks (*) and assume that LDAP supports full wildcard matching like that available in most command shells and file-searching applications. Others incorrectly assume that the asterisks imply support for regular expressions. Neither of these assumptions is valid. LDAP's support for substring searching is limited to the exact types of filters documented in this section.

Substring searches are closer to creating and combining multiple search filters. For example, the first filter in figure 4.8 is equivalent to a combination filter like `(&(cn=*Do*)(cn=*ley))` that uses ANDing of filters, as shown in the next section.

Figure 4.9 brings the initial, contains, and final substring components together for a single search filter, and also shows that adding any other components to the filter makes it invalid.

Right: cn = Cla*Do*ley

Wrong: cn = Cla*ton*Do*ley

Figure 4.9
An example of a substring filter using initial (`Cla*`), contains (`*Do*`), and final (`*ley`) substring matching, along with a bad filter that attempts to use too many wildcards

One final note about substring matching is related to performance. Substring filters are universally slower than exact and presence filters. However, substring searches that include only initial or final substrings will typically perform better than substring matches in the middle of a string.

4.3.4 Ordered matching (greater than/less than)

Greater- and less-than searches operate in much the same fashion as equality searches. These searches are called *ordering matches* because they require the server to know the order of the attribute value of the search filter relative to values for that attribute in all entries in the directory.

Figure 4.10 expands a greater-than-or-equal-to search to show its components. Notice that because the filter includes both equality and entries larger than the specified value, it returns the entry whose sn attribute is equal to Smith in addition to entries with greater values.

Example: sn>=Smith

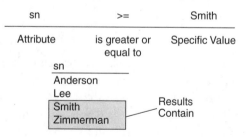

Figure 4.10   Greater-than-or-equal-to filters return entries that contain attribute values greater than or equal to the value specified in the filter.

The greater-than-or-equal-to search is designated by the >= identifier. All entries with a particular attribute value that is greater than or equal to the one in the filter are returned. Here is an example of using the ldapsearch command-line tool to perform such a search:

```
> ldapsearch -b "dc=manning,dc=com" -s sub "sn>=Johnson"
```

A value is determined to be greater than or equal to a particular value according to the attribute's syntax and matching rules. Chapter 2 goes over matching rules and syntax in detail, and appendix A lists information about these characteristics for most standard attributes.

The reverse of a greater-than-or-equal-to filter is the less-than-or-equal-to filter. This filter uses the <= operator and returns all entries with an attribute value that is less than or equal to the value in the filter.

Example: sn<=Smith

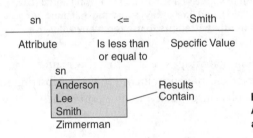

Figure 4.11 gives an example of using the less-than-or-equal-to filter to find entries whose sn attribute is less than or equal to Smith.

Generally speaking, ordered searching is not used as frequently as some of the other types of filters. This is the case because most LDAP-enabled applications use directories for either security (which primarily requires exact searches) or white pages (which generally require both exact and substring searches).

4.3.5 Approximate filters

LDAP supports a type of filter for doing approximate matching. Approximate matching is generally useful in white pages applications when a human attempts to search for a name but is unsure of the exact spelling.

An example of an approximate search is

```
> ldapsearch -b "dc=manning,dc=com" -s sub "(sn~=Donnelley)"
```

This search tells the directory server to return entries that have an sn value that is similar to Donnelley. The actual algorithm that the server uses to determine whether a particular value is a match is entirely up to the server. Many servers support an algorithm like Soundex, but it is difficult for a developer to know in advance what the server will return; so, you should generally restrict such searches to instances where user input is being used to offer a user a list of potential matches to choose from.

You can find more information about Soundex at http://www.bluepoof.com/ Soundex/info.html. Directory server documentation will generally describe the actual algorithm used.

4.3.6 Multiple filters: AND and OR operators

You can easily combine multiple filters in LDAP to make more complex filters that provide more precise results. One way filters can be combined is by using the AND (&) operator, which returns an entry only if all the specified filters are true. Figure 4.12 shows an example of two filters being tied together by this operator, and the entries the resulting combined filter will match.

Example: (&(sn=Smith)(title=President))

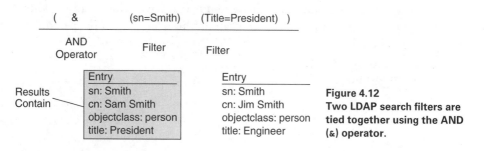

Figure 4.12
Two LDAP search filters are tied together using the AND (&) operator.

The number of filters that can be tied together by the AND operator is not limited to two. In fact, many filters can be included to make the search more precise. For example:

```
(&(sn=Smith)(title=President)(cn=Jim*))
```

Note that you simply add additional filters within the set of parentheses that include the AND operator.

In addition to the AND operator, LDAP can return entries under the condition that any of the filters are true by using an OR (|) operator. Figure 4.13 shows an example of two filters brought together by the OR operator and the results of a search using that filter.

Example: (|(sn=Smith)(title=President))

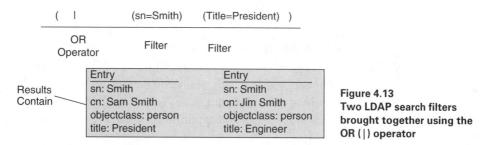

Figure 4.13
Two LDAP search filters brought together using the OR (|) operator

These complex filters can themselves be only a single part of an even more complex search filter. Consider this example:

```
(&(|(objectClass=person)(objectClass=inetOrgPerson))(sn=Smith))
```

When the server reads this filter, it will return entries that contain either the `person` or `inetOrgPerson` `objectClass`, but that also contain `Smith` in the `sn` attribute.

4.3.7 Negative filters: the NOT operator

Sometimes you want to eliminate results that have values that you know will make a particular entry undesirable. You can do this using NOT (!) operator to create a negative filter. Figure 4.14 shows the NOT operator in action.

Example: (!(sn=Smith))

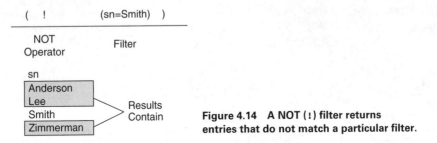

Figure 4.14   A NOT (!) filter returns entries that do not match a particular filter.

Keep in mind that a negative filter is not the same as the != operation you may be familiar with from various programming languages. Rather, the NOT operator indicates that any entry that does not match a particular filter will be returned.

Thus if you are negating the sn=Smith filter as in figure 4.14, even entries that do not contain the sn attribute will be included in the results. If you wanted to require that the sn attribute also exist, you would create a complex filter using the AND operator discussed previously:

```
(&(sn=*)(!(sn=Smith)))
```

4.3.8 Extensible searching and matching rules

In chapter 2, we discussed the concept of matching rules. With extensible searching, matching rules can be associated with a particular search operation.

Extensible searching using matching rules is one of LDAP's more esoteric features and is rarely used by most clients and applications. However, when used correctly, this feature offers considerable power.

To understand how extensible searching works, it is first important to remember what we discussed in section 2.3.3 related to matching rules. An extensible search filter simply adds an explicit matching rule to the search filter, such as the following example:

```
(sn:1.2.3.4.5=Hartman)
```

This filter says to use the 1.2.3.4.5 matching rule to return entries where the sn attribute equals Hartman. If the server defines the 1.2.3.4.5 matching rule to be case sensitive, the entry with sn=Hartman will match, but sn=hartman will not.

4.4 WHAT TO RETURN:
THE ATTRIBUTE RETURN LIST

The final part of a full set of LDAP search criteria is a list of attributes to return. If the list is empty, all nonoperational attributes of the entry will be returned. *Operational* attributes are typically those used by the server that should rarely be displayed to an end user unfamiliar with their use. Such attributes can vary by directory vendor, but they tend to include attributes involved in storing a server's access control lists, change time stamps, and other information. Attribute types in the return list that do not exist, either in the server's schema or as part of a returning entry, will be ignored with no error messages or other exceptional behavior.

The distinguished name is always returned. If only the distinguished name is to be returned, the LDAP client should pass an attribute that will not be returned in an entry. One good attribute to use is dn, because there is no such attribute in any entry. Many people make the mistake of thinking that because some LDAP clients return the distinguished name in a way that looks like a value for an attribute called dn, this is in fact an attribute. Not so.

What about removing the dn from search results? It isn't possible to do so using the attribute return list. Because, as we just mentioned, the distinguished name is not an attribute, it will not be affected in any way by the attribute return list.

You might wonder why you'd want to remove any or all attribute values from a returned entry in the first place. In a white pages context, there are few reasons to remove all attributes.

However, many other applications use only a limited subset of an entry. For example, an application using a directory for authentication may need only two attributes: uid and userPassword. If the entry also contains a photo or other information, it will be inefficient to simply have the server return an entire entry.

Similarly, an authorization application may already have the distinguished name of an authenticated user and want to find the distinguished names of groups to which the user belongs without necessarily returning the groups' entire member lists. In this case, you can pass a pseudo-attribute like dn to remove all attributes.

4.5 LDAP SEARCH CRITERIA VS. SQL QUERIES

Most developers who are familiar with databases have used SQL to create database queries. Many similarities exist between the functionality of LDAP criteria and SQL queries. For the benefit of readers who are familiar with SQL but not as familiar with LDAP, this section looks at some of the similarities and differences.

4.5.1 Similarities between SQL SELECT and LDAP search criteria

First, let's look at the similarities, beginning with a simple SQL SELECT statement:

```
SELECT firstname,lastname FROM table WHERE lastname='Johnson'
```

In this statement, `firstname` and `lastname` are the fields to be returned by the query. The list of fields to return is similar to the use of an attribute return list in LDAP, as mentioned in the previous section. Additionally, the `WHERE` clause includes an expression that is similar to an LDAP exact equality search.

Ignoring pieces of the `SELECT` statement (such as `table`) that apply only in a database environment, you can easily reconstruct this query as an LDAP search filter:

```
> ldapsearch -b "dc=manning,dc=com" "(sn=Johnson)" givenname sn
```

Note that you simply add a search base and use the LDAP-equivalent of `lastname` in your search filter. You do a similar substitution in the list of attributes to be returned.

4.5.2 Differences between SQL SELECT and LDAP search criteria

Getting beyond these basic, easy mappings, it is increasingly difficult to show similarities, or even convert, between the type of search filter used in LDAP and an SQL SELECT statement. As its simplest, expressions in the `WHERE` clause are very different from LDAP search filters and are usually not one-to-one mappings. At a more fundamental, architectural level, the relational and LDAP information models do not map easily to each other.

Fundamental differences include things such as a lack of RDBMS concepts such as joins or even tables in LDAP, or the concept of LDAP hierarchy and object classes in an RDBMS. For example, an SQL JOIN involves bringing information from multiple tables into a single result. LDAP has no such concept, because LDAP information is always pulled from an entry, and all clients have the same view of the data with exceptions for access control.

4.6 INCREASING SEARCH PERFORMANCE

Although it is beyond the scope of this book to describe exact techniques for increasing performance in specific directory products, you can consider a number of general areas when shooting for better search performance. The most common issue people have when querying LDAP servers is that some search filters return results extremely quickly, whereas other search filters take forever, time out, or hit resource limits on the same server. These are almost always indexing issues. Virtually all LDAP servers have settings that specify which attributes are indexed or hashed. Adding indices increases disk usage and update time, but will likely be the only way that searches can be completed in a timely manner on larger directories.

Just because a server responds well to one type of search does not mean it will respond similarly to other types of searches. Proper indexing will almost always give better performance. For example, most directory servers allow an attribute to be indexed separately for exact and substring searches. If only exact indexes are created, a substring search will be unacceptably slow. Simply performing several searches on an unindexed attribute may be enough to cause denial of service—intentionally or not. Application developers absolutely must know what kind of searching the server is set up to support.

You should minimize the number of times you open and close connections. Opening and binding connections can be rather heavy, so opening a new connection for each search is extremely inefficient.

One of the simplest way to improve performance is to request only those attributes needed in the results. Doing so will reduce I/O and network traffic, especially on larger result sets.

It is also a good idea to limit the scope of a search if possible. Doing so may have little effect in normal operation but reduces the possibility that your client will need to chase referrals or dereference aliases in parts of the directory tree that would not normally be pertinent to the query at hand.

A few directory servers index entries based on their location in the directory tree. Such an indexing strategy may result in slower search performance during subtree searches on deep directory trees. Most directory server products will suffer little or no search performance degradation with deeper trees or wider search scopes.

4.7 SUMMARY

In this chapter, you learned that the base, scope, and filter are the primary criteria used in an LDAP search. We went over the three possible LDAP scopes (base, one-level, and subtree) and discussed how each of them affects the returned results. The numerous examples of search filters we presented will be important throughout the rest of the book as we begin using LDAP. Finally, we discussed important considerations for getting optimal performance when you're searching a directory.

In the next chapter, we will discuss how the information received from an LDAP server can be represented and shared outside the directory using common formats such as LDIF and DSML.

C H A P T E R   5

Exchanging directory information

It is often necessary to share or use directory information outside the directory server. You can do so by writing that directory information to text files written to well-known specifications. With LDAP-enabled directories, the specifications that tend to be used are the following:

- LDIF
- DSML

This chapter introduces each of these interchange formats and answers the following questions:

- How does data look when it's formatted to each specification?
- What are the advantages and disadvantages of each? When should they be used?
- What kinds of data can be represented in each specification? What limitations exist?
- How does DSMLv2 go beyond the interchange specification defined by DSMLv1?

5.1 REPRESENTING DIRECTORY INFORMATION OUTSIDE THE DIRECTORY

When retrieving information from a data repository, it is often desirable to store the results of the retrieval for later use. In a relational database environment, this data might be stored as an extract in a format like CSV, where each returned field is separated by a comma or similar separator.

Directories that support LDAP have an information model that doesn't lend itself to rows and comma-separated fields. Instead, you use other extract formats that relate better to the LDAP information model.

The first and most widely used of these formats is LDIF. Until this point in the book, we have used this format without introducing it. We could do so because the format is quite simple and intuitive on the surface, particularly with simple entries that contain only textual information. The following is an example of an entry in LDIF format:

```
dn: cn=Sam Smith,dc=manning,dc=com
cn: Sam Smith
sn: Smith
objectClass: person
objectClass: organizationalPerson
```

The other format is the DSML, which is used to represent directory information in XML. Although this format tends to look more complex at first glance, the fact that it is based on XML means that more and better application program interfaces are available to read and write these files. Additionally, DSML leverages XML, so it's considerably more extensible. In version 1 of the specification, entries and schema could be represented. Version 2 extends the specification to represent actual directory protocol operations. The following is the same entry that expressed previous in LDIF, this time written in DSML:

```
<dsml:dsml xmlns:dsml="http://www.dsml.org/DSML">
  <dsml:directory-entries>
    <dsml:entry dn="cn=Sam Smith,dc=xyz,dc=com">
      <dsml:objectclass>
        <dsml:oc-value>person</dsml:oc-value>
        <dsml:oc-value>organizationalPerson</dsml:oc-value>
      </dsml:objectclass>
      <dsml:attr name="cn">
        <dsml:value>Sam Smith</dsml:value>
      </dsml:attr>
      <dsml:attr name="sn">
        <dsml:value>Smith</dsml:value>
      </dsml:attr>
    </dsml:entry>
  </dsml:directory-entries>
</dsml:dsml>
```

The DSML listing is longer and looks more complex, but the general flow of elements and data should be familiar to most people who have used XML.

Throughout the rest of this chapter, we will explore these interchange formats in more detail, as well as the advantages and disadvantages of each.

5.2   *LDAP DATA INTERCHANGE FORMAT*

As you just saw, LDIF can be a simple way of representing directory information as text. Nearly all directory servers support it for import and export, and most LDAP APIs will read or write it as necessary. After several years as a de facto standard, LDIF is now properly documented as RFC 2849 from the IETF.

In addition to representing full entries, LDIF can also be used to exchange entry changes and even schemas, when combined with the textual representation of schemas that we discussed in chapter 2.

LDIF is restricted to printable text. This means binary values must be encoded using the Base64 standard. (Base64 is a standard that is commonly used in a wide variety of situations and is not specific to directory services.)

5.2.1   Expressing entries in basic LDIF

We walked through an LDIF sample earlier in the chapter. Let's look at that entry again and use it to better understand the LDIF format:

```
dn: cn=Sam Smith,dc=manning,dc=com
```

The first thing you'll notice is that this first line, like all the others, can be broken in two by a colon (:). In this line, the left side is dn and the right side is cn=Sam Smith,dc=manning,dc=com.

In LDIF, the left side is usually an attribute type name. When you're creating full entries, lines like the previous one are the only exception, because they designate the fully qualified distinguished name of the entry. This name is constructed per our previous discussions in chapter 3.

Once the entry has been named, you specify all of its attributes in much the same way you specify its distinguished name. The left side of the colon is the attribute name, and the right side contains a single value of that attribute:

```
cn: Sam Smith
sn: Smith
```

Multivalued attributes are expressed in multiple lines, with a single line representing each value. The example entry contains a multivalued objectclass attribute, which is represented in LDIF as

```
objectClass: person
objectClass: organizationalPerson
```

The five lines we've shown are enough to construct a full LDAP entry in LDIF that could be added using a typical import utility, or even the command-line tool `ldap-modify` that comes with most directory servers. The command line with `ldap-modify` would be

```
> ldapmodify -D cn=admin -w manager -a
dn: cn=Sam Smith, dc=manning,dc=com
cn: Sam Smith
sn: Smith
objectclass: person
objectclass: organizationalperson
```

The entry could also be specified in a file rather than being fed as input to the program.

Wrapping long values

If the value is extremely long and will wrap to multiple lines, you simply insert a line-feed and continue the value on another line. The following `description` attribute demonstrates this technique:

```
description: This is a very long description that will
 take up multiple lines to display.
```

The `description` is the equivalent of a single attribute value in LDAP that does not have the linefeed at the end of the first line.

Handling binary and other special attribute values

Binary values, such as photographs, digital certificates, and values that contain characters outside printable ASCII, must be encoded using Base64 when used in LDIF. A few other special cases exist that can also require attribute values to be encoded in Base64 to prevent confusion.

Base64 is a popular, well-documented standard that is also used for, among other things, encoding email attachments. In general, it uses 4 bytes for every 3 bytes of binary information, which means the size of the encoded data will be larger than the original data.

The `postalAddress` attribute in the next example shows a Base64-encoded value:

```
postalAddress:: RWRnZWhhbSBIb2xsb3cNCldpbmNoZXN0ZXIgV2F5
```

Notice the two colons after the attribute name. The double colon is a special designation used to indicate that the value that follows is Base64 encoded.

In addition to characters that fall outside printable ASCII, values should be encoded in Base64 if they begin with a space, colon, or less-than sign (<). Also be aware that it is possible to mix plain text and Base64-encoded values in the same entry, or even for a particular multivalued attribute.

5.2.2 Writing LDAP changes as LDIF

As mentioned earlier in the chapter, LDIF can represent changes to LDAP entries in addition to the entries themselves. This is done by using the `changetype` designator and providing information relevant to the type of change being performed. Because adding an entry is considered a change, the simplest change that can be performed is the `add` change type. The following example shows the previous LDIF entry as an `add` change:

```
dn: cn=Sam Smith, dc=manning,dc=com
changetype: add
cn: Sam Smith
sn: Smith
objectclass: person
objectclass: organizationalperson
```

This entry can now be added using the `ldapmodify` command, assuming you place the contents of the previous LDIF into a file called change.ldif:

```
> ldapmodify -D cn=admin -w manager <change.ldif
```

Notice that you do not use the `-a` option to indicate that you are adding entries. Thus you can intermix `add` changes with other types of changes. One other type of change you might use is the `modify` change. The next example shows how to add a `description` attribute to the existing entry:

```
dn: cn=Sam Smith,dc=manning,dc=com
changetype: modify
add: description
description: This is a description
```

Once again, the first line indicates the distinguished name of the entry, and the second line tells which type of change you are performing. The third line says you're adding a value to the `description` attribute. If a value already exists for the `description` attribute, it will not be discarded when you add the new one, whose value is on the final line.

To make multiple changes to the same entry, separate those change lines with a line containing a single dash (-). The following shows a slightly more complex `modify` change type example:

```
dn: cn=Sam Smith,dc=manning,dc=com
changetype: modify
delete: description
-
replace: postalAddress
postalAddress: 101 N. Maple St.
postalAddress: P.O. Box 141
-
add: l
l: Herscher
```

The first modification to the entry deletes the existing `description` values. You then replace any existing `postalAddress` attribute values with the two specified values. Finally, you add the `l` attribute with a value of `Herscher`.

If any one of these changes is invalid when decoded from LDIF and transmitted to an LDAP server, the server will reject all the changes in that sequence of modifications. An example of an invalid change might be if `postalAddress` is not allowed by the server's schema, or if access controls do not permit one of the changes.

5.2.3   **Representing schemas in LDIF**

As we stated at the beginning of this chapter, it is possible to represent LDAP schemas in LDIF. Although this is true, it is not as common as representing entries themselves and is usually done only in the context of writing schema changes to a directory server.

In fact, no new operators are necessary in LDIF to add schema presentation capabilities. Instead, you simply use a set of defined attribute types and the syntax defined in IETF RFC 2252 (discussed in detail in chapter 2). What follows is an example of a single object class as defined using this standard:

```
objectclasses: ( 2.5.6.6 NAME 'person' SUP top
 MUST ( sn $ cn ) MAY ( userPassword $ telephoneNumber
 $ seeAlso $ description ) )
```

This example indicates that an object class called `person` is a subclass of the `top` object class and must contain the `sn` and `cn` attributes, but may also contain `userPassword`, `telephoneNumber`, `seeAlso`, and `description` attributes.

Notice that the attribute name is `objectclasses`, not `objectClass`. This `objectclasses` attribute can be part of entries of the `subschemaSubentry` object class. In addition to holding information about object class definitions, the `subschemaSubentry` object class can hold other schema information, including attribute types, syntaxes, and matching rules. The following lines show an attribute type definition in LDIF:

```
attributetypes: ( 2.5.4.35 NAME 'userPassword' EQUALITY
 octetStringMatch SYNTAX 1.3.6.1.4.1.1466.115.121.1.40
 USAGE userApplications )
```

This example defines the `userPassword` attribute as being of a particular `syntax` and using the `octetStringMatch` matching rule.

If you were going to add a new attribute to a directory's schema by running `ldap-modify` or a similar command on a created LDIF file, the file might look like this:

```
dn: cn=schema
changetype: modify
add: attributetypes
attributetypes: ( 1.2.3.4 NAME 'myAttribute'
 DESC 'My Little Attribute' )
```

This example indicates that you are adding an attribute with the specified characteristics to the schema.

Holding schemas in LDIF is very useful when you're creating and distributing applications with custom schemas. It allows the new schema to be added to most directory servers in a relatively painless way without messing with the server's configuration.

5.2.4 Advantages and disadvantages of LDIF

The clearest advantage of LDIF is that it is so simple to use and read. It also maps closely to the information model used by LDAP. With its almost nonexistent learning curve and built-in support with most directory servers and directory-aware products, LDIF will likely remain popular for some time.

LDIF's biggest disadvantage is that it is so closely tied to LDAP. In addition, nothing that isn't directory-aware will know how to use it. Thus most text editors will not be able to do simple syntax checking, and most applications will have no existing framework for using or validating these types of files.

We will now look more closely at DSML, which in many ways serves a similar purpose to LDIF. As you will see, DSML serves this purpose in an entirely different way that is more complicated, but more extensible and easier to use in environments not geared toward directory services.

5.3 DIRECTORY SERVICES MARKUP LANGUAGE

DSML is an XML vocabulary for representing directory information. Directory information stored or transformed into DSML can be shared with other applications that support DSML. You will create such applications in chapters 10 and 12.

5.3.1 Why use DSML?

Because it is based on XML, you can use DSML as a generic import/export format for directory data. After all, directory information sometimes needs to flow beyond the bounds of a network or outside a company. DSML can store both schemas and data, making it much easier for these exported entries to be used outside their original context.

Another reason to use DSML is that many new applications and application servers are XML enabled. Thus they can use technologies such as XSL stylesheets to generate dynamic content based on data published in XML without creating application logic at the presentation layer. DSML also enables XML-based web services using standards like SOAP to easily share directory information. Figure 5.1 shows how DSML can be used as a format to encode information that comes from a directory prior to being presented to a DSML-enabled client.

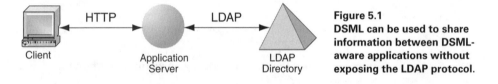

Figure 5.1
DSML can be used to share information between DSML-aware applications without exposing the LDAP protocol.

CHAPTER 5 EXCHANGING DIRECTORY INFORMATION

It is possible to create a DSML service that completely abstracts the use of LDAP and data access from both the business logic and presentation layers in a typical e-business application. Standards such as XSL Transformations (XSLT) provide the ability for basic DSML documents to be transformed and injected into the flow of useful web-based applications with minimal effort, as shown in figure 5.2.

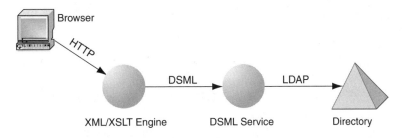

Figure 5.2   XSLT and DSML together may be used to build simple directory-centric applications with very little actual programming.

As we mentioned earlier, one of LDIF's big weaknesses is that few general-purpose applications know how to deal with it. For example, figure 5.3 shows a Java development tool with XML capabilities that is able to take advantage of the fact that DSML is defined in XML and uses XML markup.

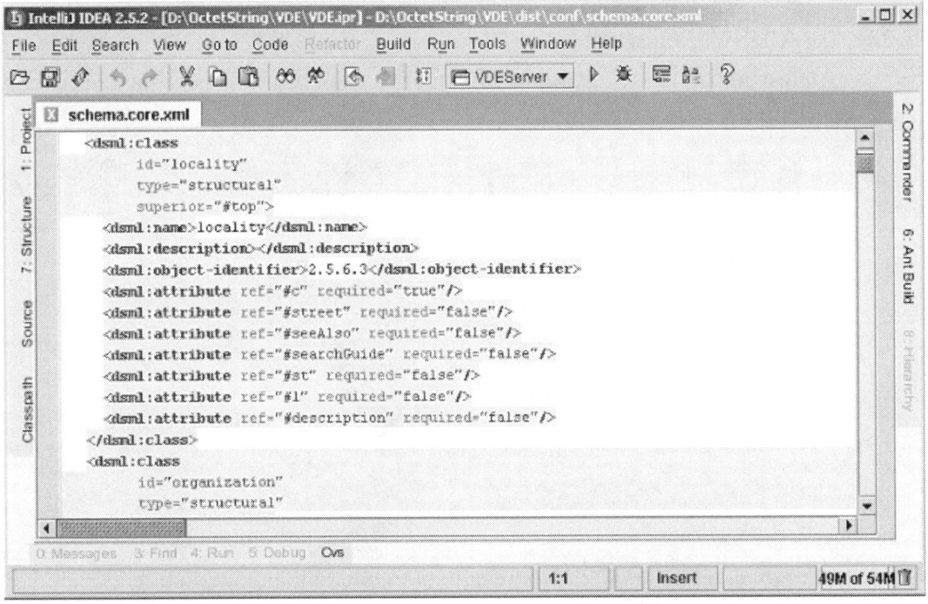

Figure 5.3   Many programs, such as this Java IDE, support XML editing and syntax checking and can simplify the creation and management of DSML documents.

This is one way in which DSML wins out over LDIF in generic directory information interchange, in cases where the data may be used outside a directory context. With full APIs for XML parsing and manipulation in nearly every modern programming language, the handling of DSML documents will only become easier.

5.3.2 Getting started with DSML

Many LDAP-enabled directory servers do not support DSML out of the box. Thus it is often necessary to use middleware to enable DSML access to LDAP information. Additionally, services that support DSML typically support only DSMLv1, which does not support the encoding of directory operations in XML, but which does offer the ability to encode entries and schema information in XML.

DSMLv2, the next generation of DSML, has extended DSMLv1 to act as an interchange format not just for entries and schemas, but also for full directory operations. The DSMLv2 standards are managed and published by the Organization for the Advancement of Structured Information Standards (OASIS). The full draft of the DSML standard, as well as information about adoption, can be found on the OASIS DSML site: http://www.oasis-open.org/committees/dsml/.

This is not an introductory book on XML, but if you're familiar with HTML, you should be able to understand the general flow of a DSML document: it consists of opening and closing elements and data in between. Elements may have XML attributes associated with them that are included within the opening brackets. Let's walk through an example to help you understand the elements that make up a DSML document.

5.3.3 A DSML example

Listing 5.1 is an example of a DSML structured document containing a directory entry for Janet Smith.

Listing 5.1 janet.xml

```
<dsml:dsml xmlns:dsml="http://www.dsml.org/DSML">
  <dsml:directory-entries>
    <dsml:entry dn="cn=Janet Smith,dc=xyz,dc=com">
      <dsml:objectclass>
        <dsml:oc-value>top</dsml:oc-value>
        <dsml:oc-value>person</dsml:oc-value>
      </dsml:objectclass>
      <dsml:attr name="cn">
        <dsml:value>Janet Smith</dsml:value>
      </dsml:attr>
      <dsml:attr name="sn">
        <dsml:value>Smith</dsml:value>
      </dsml:attr>
    </dsml:entry>
  </dsml:directory-entries>
</dsml:dsml>
```

In XML, everything starting in angle brackets (< and >) is called an *element*. Thus `<dsml:entry>` and `<dsml:directory-entries>` are both elements.

Some elements have attributes. Do not confuse XML attributes with LDAP attributes—XML attributes simply supply information about a particular element. In the previous example, one element is `<dsml:attr>`, which is used to start an LDAP attribute. One of the XML attributes of this element is called `name` and contains the name of the LDAP attribute you will be representing.

Elements are usually ended by prefixing the element name with a slash. For example, the tag `</dsml:entry>` indicates the end of the `<dsml:entry>` element that began earlier in the file.

Elements are nested within other elements. Elements that come between the start and end tags of an element are that element's *children*. However, the following is illegal:

```
<dsml:dsml ...>
   <dsml:directory-entries>
       <dsml:entry ...>
           ... entry definition ...
       </dsml:entry>
   </dsml:dsml>
</dsml:directory-entries>  ◁—— Incorrect!
```

In this broken example, the `dsml:directory-entries` element is a child of the `dsml:dsml` element. Children must be closed before their parents.

The `<dsml:directory-entries>` element indicates that you will be listing directory entries between that element tag and the `</dsml:directory-entries>` tag. Each individual entry begins with the `<dsml:entry>` element tag, which has an XML attribute specifying the distinguished name of the entry being defined.

Once inside the entry, things diverge a bit from LDIF. The entry's object classes are treated differently from its other attributes and isolated in the `<dsml:object-class>` element and its child element `<dsml:oc-value>`. The earlier Janet Smith example assigns the entry to the `top` and `person` object classes.

Finally, the attributes of each entry are listed in the `<dsml:attr>` element tag. Each value of that attribute is listed between its `<dsml:value>` child element tags. The Janet Smith example has only two non-`objectClass` attributes: `cn` and `sn`.

You can list multiple entries in the DSML file by creating more `<dsml:entry>` structures under the `<dsml:directory-entries>` tag.

5.3.4   Handling binary values in DSML entries

Like LDIF, DSML is meant to contain only printable characters and is ill-suited for direct display of binary blobs, such as images. When you're storing such information, you need to use Base64 encoding, just as you do in LDIF.

Unlike in LDIF, where you simply use double colons to indicate that the following value is encoded, in DSML you set the encoding XML attribute in `<dsml:value>` to indicate the type of encoding you have used for the specified value:

```
<dsml:attr name="cacertificate">
  <dsml:value encoding="base64">
    MIICJjCCAY+...
  </dsml:value>
</dsml:attr>
```

This example indicates that Base64 encoding was used on the specified value.

5.3.5   Entry changes and DSML

In LDIF, you store entry changes rather than full entries by specifying a change type and associated information. DSMLv1 has no such capability and is restricted to storing full entries.

To an extent, DSMLv2 resolves this problem by allowing the representation of entire directory operations, such as add, modify, and delete. In fact, DSMLv2 even supports representing searches and controls. However, this functionality is not roughly equivalent to LDIF in its simplicity or even its purpose. DSMLv2 is geared toward web services in which DSML-encoded operations are transmitted between a DSMLv2 client and a web service supporting DSMLv2; such web services either directly provide information or act against an LDAP directory to provide information. Therefore, they are not truly used as an interchange format for managing directory information outside the directory.

We discuss DSMLv2 in this context in more detail in chapter 12.

5.4   DEFINING DIRECTORY SCHEMAS WITH DSML

As we already mentioned, DSML not only represents entries, but also has elements for defining directory schemas. This functionality is useful in that it allows a single document to contain both directory entries and the schemas those entries use, making it possible to recreate any unavailable schemas as desired. DSML can be used to store schema information that includes object classes and attribute types.

5.4.1   DSML object classes

Here is an example of a DSML document containing the schema definition for the `person` object class:

```
<dsml:dsml xmlns:dsml="http://www.dsml.org/DSML">
  <dsml:directory-schema>
    <dsml:class id="person" superior="#top" type="structural">
      <dsml:name>person</dsml:name>
      <dsml:description>Person as defined in RFC2256
      </dsml:description>
      <dsml:object-identifier>2.5.6.6</dsml:object-identifier>
      <dsml:attribute ref="#sn" required="true"/>
```

```
        <dsml:attribute ref="#cn" required="true"/>
        <dsml:attribute ref="#userPassword" required="false"/>
        <dsml:attribute ref="#telephoneNumber" required="false"/>
        <dsml:attribute ref="#seeAlso" required="false"/>
        <dsml:attribute ref="#description" required="false"/>
      </dsml:class>
      ... additional object class and attribute type definitions ...
    </dsml:directory-schema>
  </dsml:dsml>
```

This is equivalent to the following definition in RFC 2256.

```
( 2.5.6.6 NAME 'person' SUP top STRUCTURAL
MUST ( sn $ cn ) MAY ( userPassword $ telephoneNumber
$ seeAlso $ description ) )
```

Notice how the DSML definition uses references to indicate where the definition for a particular attribute type can be found. This is similar to the way HTML references information within the same document.

Most of the tags are self explanatory, if you understand the components that make up an object class (discussed in detail in chapter 2). The required flag separates the attributes that must be part of the entries of that object class from the attributes that are optional.

5.4.2   DSML attribute types

The definition of an attribute type being referenced might look like the following one for telephoneNumber:

```
<dsml:attribute-type id="telephoneNumber">
  <dsml:name>telephoneNumber</dsml:name>
  <dsml:description>Telephone Number from RFC 2256
  </dsml:description>
  <dsml:object-identifier>2.5.4.20</dsml:object-identifier>
  <dsml:syntax bound="32">1.3.6.1.4.1.1466.115.121.1.50
  </dsml:syntax>
  <dsml:equality>telephoneNumberMatch</dsml:equality>
  <dsml:substring>telephoneNumberSubstringsMatch</dsml:substring>
</dsml:attribute-type>
```

This DSML attribute type definition would appear between the <dsml:direc­tory-schema> start element and the </dsml:directory-schema> end element. The telephoneNumber attribute type defined here is identical to that defined using the form in RFC 2256:

```
( 2.5.4.20 NAME 'telephoneNumber' EQUALITY telephoneNumberMatch
 SUBSTR telephoneNumberSubstringsMatch
 SYNTAX 1.3.6.1.4.1.1466.115.121.1.50{32} )
```

Once again, all the elements map almost directly to the various attribute type components we discussed in chapter 2.

5.5   *XSLT and DSML*

XSL is a stylesheet language for XML. XSLT vocabulary is used by XSL to transform one XML document into another.

Because DSML is simply an XML document type, XSLT can be used to transform DSML documents into other formats that are more useful to a particular application (see figure 5.4).

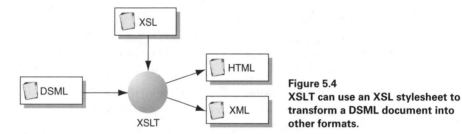

Figure 5.4
XSLT can use an XSL stylesheet to transform a DSML document into other formats.

One example would be a simple white pages application that consisted entirely of a stylesheet that translated search results into HTML. Other examples would be translation from DSML into specialized XML document styles that have been devised for different vertical industry segments.

5.5.1   Converting DSML to HTML using XSLT

One such format into which you can translate a DSML document is HTML, which is natively viewable by any web browser. A stylesheet that creates HTML output from DSML is shown in listing 5.2. Even if you aren't familiar with XSLT, you can scan the stylesheet and see that it basically lists HTML tags around DSML elements. The DSML entry is transformed into a heading, and the attribute types and values are placed into an HTML table.

> **Listing 5.2   simple.xsl**

```
<xsl:stylesheet version="1.0"
    xmlns:xsl="http://www.w3.org/1999/XSL/Transform">
  <xsl:template match="/">
    <html>
      <head>
        <title>Results</title>
      </head>
      <body>
        <h1>Results</h1>
        <xsl:for-each select=
            "dsml:dsml/dsml:directory-entries/dsml:entry">
          <h4>
            <xsl:value-of select="@dn"/>
          </h4>
```

```
            <table border="1">
              <xsl:for-each select="dsml:attr">
                <tr>
                  <th>
                    <xsl:value-of select="@name"/>
                  </th>
                  <xsl:for-each select="dsml:value">
                    <td>
                      <xsl:value-of select="."/>
                    </td>
                  </xsl:for-each>
                </tr>
              </xsl:for-each>
            </table>
          </xsl:for-each>
        </body>
      </html>
    </xsl:template>
</xsl:stylesheet>
```

This stylesheet could be used to transform the janet.xml file (listing 5.1) into the HTML file shown in listing 5.3. Examples of doing this in both Perl and Java can be found in chapters 10 and 12.

Listing 5.3   janet.html

```
<html>
  <head>
    <title>Results</title>
  </head>
  <body>
    <h1>Results</h1>
    <h4>cn=Janet Smith,dc=xyz,dc=com</h4>
    <table border="1">
      <tr>
        <th>cn</th>
        <td>Janet Smith</td>
      </tr>
      <tr>
        <th>sn</th>
        <td>Smith</td>
      </tr>
    </table>
  </body>
</html>
```

XSLT is not limited to generating HTML. You could easily write a different stylesheet that transforms the janet.xml file into another type of document. Doing so would not require you to change the janet.xml file in any way. In fact, this separation between data and presentation is part of what makes XML so attractive when sharing information of this nature.

5.6   SUMMARY

DSML is an important new standard that can be used to represent directory information from an LDAP-enabled directory in XML in such a way that it can be exchanged and transformed without disrupting the data involved. DSML compares favorably to LDIF in its ability to store schema as well as entry information. Additionally, with the growing popularity of XML APIs such as SAX (Simple API for XML) and DOM (Document Object Model), DSML offers the ability to access directory information to programmers and applications that are not as well versed in directory technology.

In the next chapter, we move from discussing LDAP and directory concepts to learning about one of the APIs that enables you to begin putting theory into practice in Perl.

LDAP management

Information that exists in directories must be managed, as must the server itself. This part of the book examines techniques that you can use to manage directories effectively with LDAP.

The examples in this part of the book use Perl and the Net::LDAP module. Chapter 6 walks through using the module to communicate effectively with an LDAP-enabled directory service.

Chapter 7 explores ways to manage the information in an LDAP-enabled directory. Examples are included in Perl for managing users, groups, and other types of entries.

In many cases, the information in an LDAP-enabled directory originates in another data store, or must be provided to another data store. Chapter 8 introduces synchronization and migration techniques, with examples in Perl.

Chapter 9 looks at how you can use LDAP to access monitoring and configuration information in many directory services. Doing so will let you better manage service availability.

Finally, chapter 10 builds on your knowledge of DSML from chapter 5 to include using the standard as a data interchange format that can simplify interactions between a directory service and other services with which it must interact.

C H A P T E R 6

Accessing LDAP directories with Perl

This chapter introduces the Net::LDAP module for Perl, which we will use throughout the book in our programming examples. We selected Perl as the primary language for examples in this part for two reasons. First, a huge number of people are familiar with Perl—especially the type of people who manage and implement directories. And second, Perl is highly regarded as a glue language that can be used easily to bring together different types of information. The flow of Perl code is relatively human readable and similar in syntax to many other popular programming languages, thus allowing a wide variety of readers to understand this book without necessarily being coders.

By the end of this chapter, we will have answered the following questions:

• What modules exist for accessing LDAP from Perl? How are they different?

• How can Net::LDAP be used to connect and authenticate to an LDAP-enabled directory server?

- How can Net::LDAP be used to search, compare, and manipulate directory entries?
- How can LDAP errors and exceptional conditions be handled with the Net::LDAP module?

6.1 LDAP ACCESS FROM PERL

When this book was first drafted, it used something called PerLDAP to allow Perl to access LDAP. PerLDAP was initially released in August 1998 as part of Netscape's Mozilla open source effort. It was developed by Leif Hedstrom from Netscape and this book's author as a consolidation of two earlier Perl modules for accessing LDAP.

PerLDAP is divided into two parts:

- An object-oriented programming interface written completely in Perl
- A back-end interface to a standard API written for C language developers (Perl XS)

Figure 6.1 shows PerLDAP's general architecture.

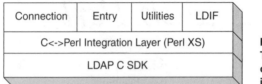

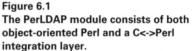

Figure 6.1
The PerLDAP module consists of both object-oriented Perl and a C<->Perl integration layer.

We will not, however, be using PerLDAP in this chapter. Instead, we will use a different module called Net::LDAP that was developed by a prolific Perl developer named Graham Barr.

Unlike PerLDAP, the Net::LDAP module does not require the module to be compiled using a C compiler on different servers, making it much easier to install on systems without freely available bundled compilers, such as Windows. Mr. Barr has implemented an entire ASN.1 module that is used to encode and decode the appropriate LDAP messages as necessary directly in Perl. Doing this has also simplified the use of controls and other LDAPv3 features that were not easily available from the PerLDAP module.

Why did we look at the architecture of the PerLDAP module if we will not be using it? Simply because it is available for download in many places, and it is important to understand the advantages and disadvantages of using it versus the Net::LDAP module. Because PerLDAP is quite popular and many existing scripts and tools use it, appendix B shows several of the examples from part 2 of this book rewritten using PerLDAP.

6.2 GETTING STARTED WITH NET::LDAP

Now that we have discussed the Net::LDAP module and how it differs from PerLDAP, let's begin exploring how you can use Net::LDAP to access LDAP-enabled directory services. We'll start by setting up the environment and connection.

6.2.1 Using the module

To utilize the functionality provided by Net::LDAP—or any Perl module, for that matter—you must first list the modules you will be using. You do so with the use command:

```
use Net::LDAP;
```

This line is all that's necessary to begin accessing LDAP directories from Perl. If this line does not work when run independently, the Net::LDAP module is most likely not installed. (The "Getting Started" section at the beginning of this book describes how to obtain the module.)

6.2.2 Opening a connection

Perl scripts cannot communicate with an LDAP server until a connection is opened. You open a connection to the LDAP server by creating a new Perl object of the Net::LDAP class. Here is an example that opens a connection to the LDAP server on the local machine:

```
my $conn = new Net::LDAP("localhost");
```

This example attempts to access the directory server running on port 389 on the local host. If the connection is unsuccessful, the $conn variable will be undefined. You can detect this situation easily with the next few lines:

```
if (!$conn)
{
    print "Error Opening Connection!";
}
```

In addition to the host name, you can specify a port. Doing so is important if the LDAP server you are using does not listen to the default port (389):

```
my $conn = new Net::LDAP("localhost",port=>10389);
```

You may remember that LDAP is an asynchronous protocol, but the Net::LDAP class supports only synchronous operations. In Perl this normally isn't an issue, particularly for the types of scripts you will be putting together in this part of the book. Writing an application where blocking on a search or modify operation would be a problem (such as an interactive program with a GUI) makes support for asynchronous operations more important.

6.2.3   Binding to the directory

LDAP allows a connection to be bound as an entry within the directory; operations are then performed as this entry. For example, if an entry named `uid=admin,dc=man-ning,dc=com` exists with a password, binding as that entry with a correct password allows you to use that entry's identity when performing the operations that follow. Binding is useful because it allows the server to know who is doing a search or modify operation, which in turn offers the potential for granular authorization.

By default, Net::LDAP either does not bind to the directory or binds anonymously, depending on the version of the LDAP protocol being used. Either way, the server regards the initial state of the connection as being bound anonymously. You can authenticate to the server by passing a login and password to the `bind()` method on your returned `Net::LDAP` object. For example:

```
$conn->bind(dn => "cn=Admin", password => "abc123");
```

The result is interesting when you bind with an entry name without specifying a password:

```
$conn->bind(dn => "cn=Admin", password => "");
```

It gives you a connection without requiring a password. This invalidates the use of LDAP as a secure data store, right?

Not exactly. This result is called a *reference bind*, and the connection is still bound anonymously. Using reference binds, an application that uses the directory anonymously can give the server an idea of who is accessing it.

To see where this approach might be useful, let's say you have a monitor program that checks an entry in the server every minute. You might bind as `cn=monitor` without a password so that the server can log the fact that the monitor program is accessing it.

However, in most cases, a reference bind is useless. It is usually only important to remember that it exists when you're using LDAP to validate passwords in an application, in which case you should discard attempts to bind without passwords.

Some applications need to switch credentials on an existing connection. This requirement is common in cases where a login needs to be performed as a userid rather than as a distinguished name. The bind operation can be used multiple times in a single LDAP session. Binds that occur after the initial bind will make the server forget the connection's previous credentials.

The bind operation always takes the distinguished name. So, because users tend to use and remember a username like `janderson` much more easily than a distinguished name like `uid=janderson, ou=Authors, dc=manning,dc=com`, you need to go through extra steps to let a user bind using the information they know.

You can use a code segment like that in listing 6.1 to let users log in using a given username and password, rather than directly with a distinguished name.

Listing 6.1   username_bind.pl

```
use Net::LDAP;

$username = "janderson";
$password = "password";

$conn = new Net::LDAP("localhost",port=>389);
$mesg = $conn->search(base=>"dc=domain,dc=com",scope=>"sub",
                      filter=>"(uid=" + $username + ")");
$entry = $mesg->entry(0);

if ($entry) {
    if ($conn->bind(dn=>$entry->getDN(),password=>$password)) {
        print "Authentication Successful!\n";
    } else {
        print "Authentication Failed!\n";
    }
}
```

Listing 6.1 first opens an anonymous connection to the LDAP server—in this case, one running on the current machine. It then performs a search for entries with a uid attribute that matches the $username variable, which in this listing is hard-coded to janderson. The first entry returned is placed in the $entry variable if it exists.

If the $entry value does not contain a value, you do not do anything further. However, if an entry is returned, you extract the distinguished name from it and use that along with the password listed in the $password variable to rebind to the server with the credentials of that returned entry.

6.3   SEARCHING WITH NET::LDAP

Now that you've opened your connection and perhaps even authenticated yourself to the LDAP server, the next logical step is to do something. Searching is the most common LDAP operation. It is also the most complex, so it is a good one for us to get out of the way early with some examples. Chapter 4 discusses much of the complexity associated with searching; you can refer to it to better understand elements such as search filters that you will use in this section's examples.

6.3.1   Performing a search

Assuming you already have a connection to the directory, you simply use the search() method on your previously established connection object:

```
$mesg = $conn->search(base=>"dc=domain,dc=com", scope=>"sub",
                      filter=>"(objectClass=*)");
```

This code makes a request to the server to return all the entries under the dc=domain,dc=com portion of the directory tree. The part of the tree you are searching (the search base) is the first argument to the `search()` method, followed by the scope and a standard LDAP search filter string.

The search returns an object that contains the LDAP message returned by the server. Once the search completes, you can print each returned entry in LDIF format quite easily with the following code:

```
$ldif = new Net::LDAP::LDIF("-","w");

for ($i = 0; $i < $mesg->count; $i++) {
  my $entry = $mesg->entry($i);
  $ldif->write_entry($entry);
}
```

The code creates a new `Net::LDAP::LDIF` object that will be used to write entries in LDIF format. You then cycle through each of the returned entries and write them out. Although you could access each entry object manually and print the contents, the `Net::LDAP::LDIF` object does more than just print basic attributes: it handles the encoding of binary attributes into printable characters using the Base64 standard.

Listing 6.2 shows the complete `simple_search` program.

Listing 6.2 simple_search.pl

```
use Net::LDAP;
use Net::LDAP::LDIF;

my $conn = new Net::LDAP("localhost");

$mesg = $conn->search(base=>"dc=domain,dc=com", scope=>"sub",
                      filter=>"(objectClass=*)");

$ldif = new Net::LDAP::LDIF("-","w");

for ($i = 0; $i < $mesg->count; $i++) {
  my $entry = $mesg->entry($i);
  $ldif->write_entry($entry);
}

$ldif->done;

$conn->unbind;
```

When run, the `simple_search` program gives you output that looks something like the following:

```
dn: uid=ssmith,dc=domain,dc=com
objectClass: inetOrgPerson
cn: Sam Smith
sn: Smith
uid: ssmith
```

To change this program so it returns only the attributes in which you are interested, you can add an argument to the `search()` method. This argument is an array reference containing a list of attributes to be returned:

```
$entry = $conn->search(base=>"dc=domain,dc=com", base=> "sub",
                       filter=>"objectClass=*", attrs=>["cn"]);
```

Changing the `simple_search` program to use this search results in the program returning the `cn` attribute but not other attributes, such as `sn`:

```
dn: uid=ssmith,dc=domain,dc=com
cn: Sam Smith
```

Notice that the distinguished name is still returned; the distinguished name is not an attribute and is always returned as part of a matching search result.

6.3.2 Understanding search scopes

We discussed search scopes in chapter 4. Here we will look at how these scopes can be applied to search operations in the Net::LDAP module.

As in LDAP, three search scopes are available for use with Net::LDAP:

- Base
- One-level
- Subtree

Base scope

Using the base scope tells the server to apply the rest of your search criteria only against the entry given as the base for the search. As shown in figure 6.2, you can return only a single entry with such a search.

In figure 6.2, a search for Sam Smith's record will never return results, because that record is not evaluated as part of the search. However, a search for an entry with any `objectClass` value will return the `dc=domain,dc=com` entry.

In Net::LDAP, you can use a base scope by passing the string `"base"` as the second argument to a `search()` request:

```
$mesg = $conn->search(base=>"dc=domain,dc=com",scope=>"base",
                      filter=>"objectClass=*");
```

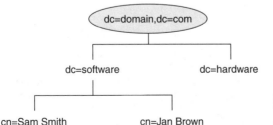

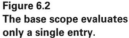

Figure 6.2
The base scope evaluates only a single entry.

One-level scope

The one-level scope allows you to search only those entries directly below the base you specified for the current search. It will not return the entry located at the search base. A search on the presence of the objectClass attribute will list all of the search base's immediate children.

Figure 6.3 shows the entries that are evaluated by a one-level search where the search base is dc=domain,dc=com.

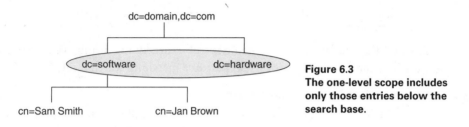

Figure 6.3
The one-level scope includes only those entries below the search base.

You can tell Net::LDAP to request a one-level scope by using "one" as the second argument to the search() method:

```
$entry = $conn->search(base=>"dc=domain,dc=com",
                  scope=>"one", filter=>"objectClass=*");
```

Subtree scope

Rather than return only the immediate children of the search base, the subtree scope returns all descendants matching the given filter. Searching for the presence of objectClass returns all entries below the search base.

Figure 6.4 shows the entries that are evaluated by a subtree search from the top of the directory tree.

A subtree scope in Net::LDAP is designated by the string "sub" in the second argument to the search() method:

```
$mesg = $conn->search(base=>"dc=domain,dc=com",
                  scope=>"sub", filter=>"objectClass=*");
```

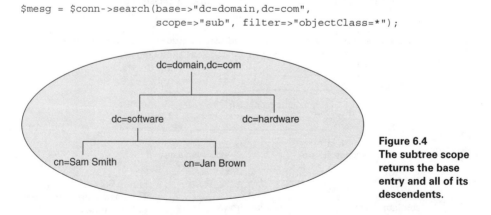

Figure 6.4
The subtree scope returns the base entry and all of its descendents.

6.3.3 LDAP search filters

We touched on search filters in our previous examples, primarily by testing for the presence of the objectClass attribute. By doing so, you instruct the server to return all entries covered by the scope of the search.

Although many of the search filters in this book's examples are relatively straightforward, search filters can be complex. Detailed information about how to read and construct LDAP search filters can be found in chapter 4.

6.3.4 Using search results

The simple_search example shown earlier isn't much more useful than the ldapsearch tool that comes with most LDAP server distributions. You begin to see real value when you use Perl to act on the results of an LDAP query.

You do so by acting on Perl objects of the Net::LDAP::Entry type that you can extract from the search results. Acting directly on those objects, you can do something simple to retrieve a particular attribute's values:

```
@cn_values = $entry->get_value("cn");
```

This line puts the values of the cn attribute into the @cn_values array. Because LDAP attributes can contain multiple values, @cn_value can contain multiple values.

You can extract individual values from this array by using Perl array operators:

```
$onevalue = $cn_values[0];
```

You can also read only the first value by placing the results of get_value into a scalar instead of an array, as shown here:

```
$onevalue = $entry->get_value("cn");
```

6.3.5 Limiting attribute retrieval

Entries can contain any number of attributes. However, simply because the attribute exists doesn't mean you want to retrieve it.

For example, there is little use in retrieving a telephone number if you are building an application to programmatically route email. In this instance, you can expand your search command with a few additional arguments:

```
$mesg = $conn->search(base=>"dc=domain,dc=com", scope=>"sub",
                      filter=>"objectClass=person",attrs=>["mail"]);
```

The attrs argument to the search() method limits the returned attributes to those specified in the array reference following it. Using this new argument, the previous search will return only the mail attribute.

The entry object returned by the following search will contain only mail, cn, and sn attributes, in addition to the entry's distinguished name:

```
$mesg = $conn->search(base=>"dc=domain,dc=com", scope=>"sub",
                      filter=>"objectClass=person",
                      attrs=>["mail","cn","sn"]);
```

As shown in both examples, there is no need to return attributes used in the search filter.

In some cases, the value of the attribute isn't important. In those situations, you can prevent attribute values from being returned by the server. When set to `true`, the argument `typesonly` notifies the server that it should return only the names of attributes and not their values:

```
$mesg = $conn-search(base=>"dc=domain,dc=com",scope=>"sub",
                    filter=>"objectClass=person",typesonly=>true);
```

The entry object returned from this search will produce LDIF output in the same vein as the following:

```
dn: uid=sjones, dc=domain, dc=com
cn:
sn:
```

6.3.6 Handling referrals

A server that doesn't contain part of the tree referenced by the search request may refer the client to a server that does contain the information needed. It is up to the client to handle these referrals and redirect its query to the right server.

Net::LDAP greatly simplifies this process. Unfortunately, it offers no way to retrieve the value of these referrals without following them. In normal use, this is not an issue; but in some types of monitoring applications, this limitation opens the potential for your request to be sent a server other than the one to which you had originally connected.

6.4 MANIPULATING ENTRIES

We've focused up to now on retrieving information from the directory. Let's begin to look at the process for manipulating directory entries. Note that prior to making changes to the directory, you will virtually always need to bind as a directory user with adequate power.

6.4.1 Updating an entry

Updating an entry in Net::LDAP is extremely easy, because the `Net::LDAP::Entry` class is designed to record change activity. Before updating, you need to retrieve the entry that you plan to change. You do so with a simple search operation:

```
$mesg = $conn->search(base=>"dc=domain,dc=com",scope=>"sub",
                    filter=>"(uid=cdonley)");
$entry = $mesg->entry(0);
```

You can now perform an add, replace, or delete for any attribute type. Here are a few examples:

```
$entry->add("telephonenumber","+1-847-555-1212");
$entry->add("facsimileTelephoneNumber",["+1-815-555-1212",
        "+1-847-555-1213"]);
```

```
$entry->replace("pager","+1-212-555-1212");
$entry->delete("manager");
```

The first line adds a single value to the `telephonenumber` attribute. The next line adds the `facsimileTelephoneNumber` attribute with the values within the brackets. The third line replaces the value of the `pager` attribute with the one specified. The final line removes all the values for the `manager` attribute.

Once you have finished making changes to the entry, you simply tell the entry to update using a particular open connection that is authenticated appropriately:

```
$entry->update($conn);
```

6.4.2 Adding new entries

Adding a new entry is similar to updating an existing entry, with the exception that new entries must first be created and assigned a distinguished name before they can be persisted:

```
$entry = new Net::LDAP::Entry();
$entry->dn("uid=jsmith, dc=domain, dc=com");
```

Now you can use the same four ways of manipulating the entry object that you used earlier when updating existing entries.

When you finish setting all the necessary attributes in your new entry, you simply pass it to the `add()` method:

```
$conn->add($entry);
```

6.4.3 Deleting an entry

Deleting an entry is probably the simplest operation you can perform with Net::LDAP. Here is an example of how incredibly easy it is:

```
$conn->delete("uid=edonley,dc=domain,dc=com");
```

That's it. No confirmation or other protections—so be certain you really want to perform this operation before you do it.

You can't change more than one entry at a time using a single delete operation. Thus you cannot do something like the following if child entries exist:

```
$conn->delete("dc=domain,dc=com");
```

You need to delete the entries below the `dc=domain,dc=com` entry before you can delete it.

6.4.4 Renaming an entry

The rename operation is a relatively recent addition to the LDAP protocol. Virtually all LDAPv3-compatible servers support renaming entries that have no children. Many servers do not support renaming of entire subtrees.

You might wonder why renaming is so difficult with LDAP. Consider for a moment what needs to happen if you rename an organization or other type of entry that typically has descendants. All of those descendants need to be renamed to reflect the new name of their parent. What if that organization has 100,000 entries?

Even when you're changing a single entry's RDN, it is important to remember that changing the distinguished name this way may require you to update any groups or other types of entries that have references to this entry.

Some directory servers include relational integrity plug-ins that you can use to automatically update groups and other objects in the directory when a referenced entry is deleted or renamed. The LDAP protocol makes no guarantees about relational integrity; thus if an application needs to work across multiple directory platforms, you can't rely on this functionality.

Net::LDAP supports modification of distinguished names through the moddn() method on the Net::LDAP class. The following line allows you to change a userid from ljensen to lsmith in the RDN:

```
$conn->moddn("cn=ljensen,dc=domain,dc=com",
           newrdn=>"uid=lsmith");
```

As mentioned in chapter 3, designing namespaces with unique identifiers rather than more change-prone attributes will reduce the need for this type of functionality.

6.5   COMPARING ENTRIES

It is possible to compare a specific directory entry with given criteria using the Net::LDAP module. This functionality is made possible by the compare() method on the connection class:

```
if ($conn->compare("uid=lfranklin,dc=domain,dc=com",
                   attr=>"sn", value=>"Franklin"))
{
    print "The last name of this entry is Franklin!\n";
}
```

This example isn't terribly practical. However, the compare operation in general isn't terribly practical, because you often need to do a search for an entry just to find the distinguished name—few people know the distinguished name of the entry they want to compare.

Distinguished names are often meaningless in relation to the human-readable identity of an entry. Although we have been using the common name and a human-readable userid in the distinguished name for many of the examples in this chapter, you probably would not do so in a real directory. Thus the only reliable way to find the distinguished name of an entry is to search for it using a known identifier, such as a userid or name. Because you would have already performed a search, you would likely have simply returned the sn attribute as part of the result set and done a comparison using programming logic rather than perform another LDAP operation.

The compare operation is useful when permission is not given to read a particular attribute from an entry but the entity accessing the directory is allowed to compare that attribute. For example, this technique was often used in ancient times with the `userPassword` attribute. The attribute was usually restricted, but certain users were often given access to compare a string to the password stored in an entry in the directory. A successful comparison indicated a correct password. This practice is now relatively defunct, because passwords are rarely, if ever, stored in plain text on the directory server unless the intent is to further protect the password over the wire through advanced authentication mechanisms. We'll explore alternative ways to do this when we discuss security in chapter 13.

6.6 HANDLING ERRORS

Exceptional conditions happen for various reasons when working with Net::LDAP. Perhaps you tried to bind as a nonexistent user or supplied the wrong password. In a search, the search base may not have existed. When making a change, the connection may not have been bound as an appropriate user.

When any of these types of situations happen, the operation you performed will fail. You can test for such a failure by checking to see whether the `code` variable is defined on the returned LDAP message object:

```
if ($mesg->code())
{
    print "An Error Occurred: Error #" . $mesg->code . "\n";
}
```

In real life, you'll probably want to print a meaningful error message rather than a cryptic error number. You can do so by retrieving the `error` variable from the returned LDAP message:

```
$errorString = $mesg->error();
print "Error: " . $errorString . "\n";
```

6.7 SUPPORT FOR ENCRYPTED/SSL CONNECTIONS

Although most LDAP servers encrypt user passwords on disk, servers and APIs have only recently begun to support encrypted transmission of passwords. Without network encryption, the directory is only as secure as the network link between client and server. For a small switched intranet, this level of security might be sufficient. Unfortunately, this is not the case when you're sending sensitive passwords and other data over the Internet. To get around this issue, some servers allow for the encryption of the entire session, rather than just the password, using the Secure Sockets Layer (SSL); but SSL has never been part of the LDAP standard.

With LDAPv3, the SASL has been added to the standard. This standard was originally devised by the developers of the IMAP as a way of allowing the client and server to negotiate the way passwords and data are transmitted. It serves the same purpose in LDAP.

If you have used VeriSign or another CA to generate a client certificate for your web browser, it is possible to export that certificate in such a format that it can be used by Net::LDAP to open an encrypted connection to an LDAP server supporting SSL.

6.8 SUMMARY

In this chapter, we discussed the performance of every major LDAP operation using the popular Net::LDAP module. We reviewed in detail the way that the search criteria discussed in chapter 4 directly impact the search results obtained using this module. We covered important limitations when renaming and deleting entries, and provided more information about best practices for naming directory entries.

The next chapter explores using the technology we discussed in this chapter to effectively manage the content of a directory server with Perl.

C H A P T E R   7

Managing directory entries, groups, and accounts

It is common for a directory to be deployed without much consideration for ongoing management. Such oversight tends to lead to isolated directories that are difficult to manage over time and not properly integrated into related business processes.

In this chapter, we will explore a few models for managing directory entries and create some new tools that simplify this process. By the end of this chapter, we will have answered the following questions:

- What are the most common models for managing information in directories?

- How do you build a simple web-based tool for adding users to a directory? What if that tool needs to work with data from existing sources?

- How can groups be managed in the directory? What about account information?

- What issues are involved when you're managing directory entries that refer to objects other than people and groups?

7.1 COMMON TYPES OF MANAGED ENTRIES

Before we go deeper into managing information in an LDAP server, let's take another look at what you are actually managing. We've discussed the concept of entries throughout the book and noted how they are made up of attributes. It's important to realize that an entry can be *anything*. Prior to this chapter, we didn't need to distinguish between various types of data being stored in the directory. However, as you manage this information, you must look at the characteristics of different types of information that are typically managed in a directory.

The most common type of information stored in a directory pertains to people and accounts. As in real life, people are unique entities; therefore each person typically has a single entry within a directory that describes various characteristics about them.

Accounts are different: a single person may have multiple accounts, and a single account may be associated with multiple people. This difference is key when you're managing accounts, because you must manage not only accounts but also the association between those accounts and an account owner. For example, in a perfect world, it would be nice to disable all the accounts associated with a terminated employee.

Groups and roles tend to be associated with other entries (often people or accounts) to allow applications to treat the associated entries in a similar manner. For example, you might want a group entry that contains a list of all the people who should get a certain type of email or have access to a particular application.

Other types of entries exist as well, and you can make new types by creating custom object classes and attributes. The key thing to remember when reading this chapter is that many entry management techniques apply to all types of entries. However, when we discuss managing specific types of information, such as user accounts, the techniques used may not be as applicable to other types of information.

7.2 ENTRY MANAGEMENT MODELS

There are three primary models for entry management:

- Centralized administration
- Distributed administration
- User self-administration

In general, there is no right or wrong model to use. However, the model you choose should reflect the type of entries being managed, the ratio of administrators to entries, and the nature of the applications using the directory information.

7.2.1 Centralized administration

Centralized administration is the easiest to develop and deploy quickly, especially in organizations with minimal directory management needs. In this model, a central group receives and processes add, modify, and remove requests each time an entry must be changed. Whether the group performing management is an IT organization

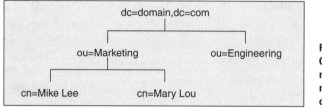

Figure 7.1
Centralized administration means that all entries are managed by a single organization.

or a project group is not relevant, as long as the administrators have nearly identical management responsibilities to the same group of users. Figure 7.1 shows that in this scenario, all the entries in the directory tree are managed by a single organization.

Centralized administration requires only minimal administration infrastructure. In addition, its central nature reduces the potential for the duplication of effort that can sometimes occur in other models.

Such an administrative environment can result in long lead times for entry provisioning, because the central group can become a bottleneck when information needs to be created or changed. However, this is the only viable solution in many computing environments.

Some people make the mistake of assuming that centralized control is the most secure solution. In fact, centralized control often has the undesired result of putting too much trust in a central body that has little experience with the entities needing management. For example, consider an extranet environment consisting of a hub company and many spoke companies. Figure 7.2 shows this type of environment.

Central administration is not as secure in this example because Company A, B, or C may hire and fire people at will and may not have an adequate process for notifying the central administrators about these changes.

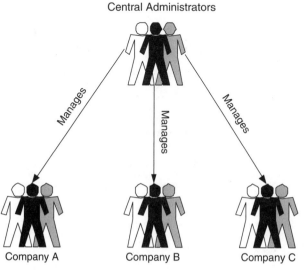

Figure 7.2
Central administrators in an extranet environment are responsible for managing everyone in that environment.

7.2.2   Distributed administration

The extranet scenario just described is perfect for the distributed administration model. This model was born of the need to reduce reliance on a centralized body. As the name implies, a centralized body may coordinate or manage key pieces, but most administration is delegated to other groups.

Figure 7.3 shows how this model might work given the previous example. You now have delegated administrators for each of the companies. These delegated administrators are responsible for the users in the extranet environment belonging to their company.

This arrangement does two good things: it makes administration highly scalable, and it reduces administrative bottlenecks. Such an environment scales because each company can grow rapidly without having to increase the number of central administrators substantially. Administrative bottlenecks are removed because there is no longer a need to wait for approval from a group of central administrators. Companies requiring higher levels of service can simply appoint additional delegated administrators.

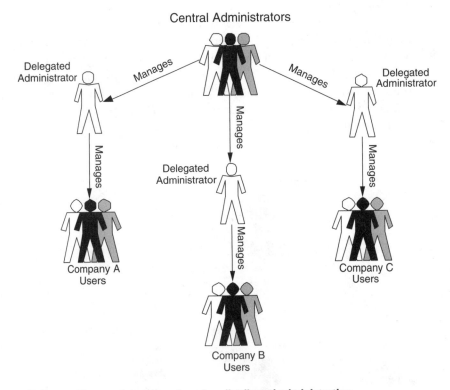

Figure 7.3   The previous example, using distributed administration

The delegated administration environment is not new, and it is not limited to people. One of the best examples of a distributed administration model is the Internet DNS. Although a centralized body manages the very highest level of Internet domain names (.com, .edu, and .org), everything else is delegated hierarchically. Thus if you control domain.com, you can add the entries ldap.domain.com and admin.domain.com; you can even delegate the administration of everything under users.domain.com to yet another group.

In LDAP, this model of administration is common for intranets where a company already has existing administrative domains that are normally responsible for managing their respective areas. Many off-the-shelf software packages exist to meet the need to handle this kind of distributed administration. These tools are generally referred to as *provisioning tools*; they manage directories as well as other user data stores, such as those used by many operating systems.

The namespace used by a particular directory can play an important role in the viability of the distributed administration model. This is the case because flat namespaces can be difficult to distribute. Conversely, as seen with the DNS, administration of hierarchical namespaces can be easily distributed. Figure 7.4 shows a namespace that is divided along administrative boundaries, assuming that each organization maintains its own entries.

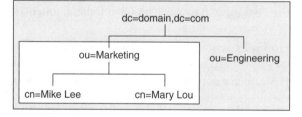

Figure 7.4
In distributed administration, a central administrative authority delegates administration of entries in certain parts of the directory tree to other bodies.

Because it is also possible to distribute management based on information contained within an entry rather than just its name, a flat or nearly flat namespace does not prevent distributed administration. Chapter 3 describes the advantages and disadvantages of many types of LDAP namespaces in terms of both management and use.

7.2.3 User self-administration/self-service

In Internet environments where users expect dynamic access to resources, user self-management is the norm. Consider what would happen if Amazon.com required you to wait until someone created an account before you could buy a book. Reverting to centralized or even distributed administration in such an environment is a sure-fire way to lose business, because people don't have the instant access they need to make spontaneous transactions.

Self-administration usually involves the use of forms that allow end users to change their own entries in the directory. This creation process may be done from scratch, as when a new user subscribes to a site like Amazon.com.

In one variation on the self-administration model, web applications have the ability to create and update information about users in certain parts of the directory. Other parts of the directory—perhaps for employees with more privileges—may have more restricted self-management. Figure 7.5 shows a directory tree in which Internet users might be separated from other users to allow for a different level of self-management.

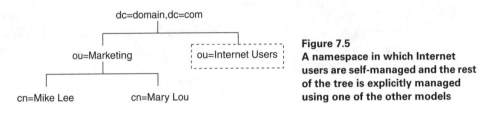

Figure 7.5
A namespace in which Internet users are self-managed and the rest of the tree is explicitly managed using one of the other models

The practice of populating much of the directory entry based on preexisting data is common in environments with existing users. Typically, the user supplies a key that joins new information with existing information in another data repository. For example, an online airline reservation application might autocreate an Internet account for you and then assign a password based on the frequent flier number you submit.

Security can be employed by sending only initial password information or other confidential data to a location that has been previously verified as belonging to the account owner. For example, such information may be sent to a postal or email address.

Many Internet sites that offer self-administration are more concerned with preventing users from abusing the system than with verifying users' identities. For example, some online email systems allow users to create a new account without human intervention but then send an initial password to an existing email address. This process allows the sites to limit users to a single account and helps track down the senders of abusive email.

7.3   CREATING PEOPLE ENTRIES

Because information about people is commonly stored in a directory server, this is a good time to examine how you can get that information into the directory. Our first example will show how to add an entry from scratch; the other demonstrates how to assemble an entry based on new input combined with existing information. We'll use simple web-based examples, although you can just as easily do any of these examples as command-line tools by removing the web-related code.

7.3.1 People entries via a web form

Figure 7.6 This output from adduser.pl shows a new user being successfully created.

Now that we have looked at a few of the models for entry administration, let's walk through a simple example of how to add a user entry. In this example, you will create a user entry based on input to a web form. Such a tool could be used either by central or distributed administrators in addition to self-provisioning environments.

In addition to the Net::LDAP module discussed in chapter 6, you will use a module called CGI written by Lincoln Stein. The Net::LDAP module will be used to access and manipulate the directory, and the CGI module will simplify the handling of web forms.

Figure 7.6 shows how the example adduser.pl code might look in a web browser when called as a CGI script. Listing 7.1 shows the complete code for the adduser.pl script.

Listing 7.1   adduser.pl

```perl
use CGI qw/:standard/;
use Net::LDAP;

my $server = "localhost";
my $port = 389;
my $user = "cn=Administrator";
my $pass = "password";
my $org = "dc=domain,dc=com";

print header,
    start_html('Add User'),
    h1('Add User'),
    start_form,
    "First Name:",textfield('givenname'),p,
    "Last Name:",textfield('sn'),p,
    "UserID:",textfield('uid'),p,
    "Mail:",textfield('mail'),p,
    submit("Add"),end_form,hr;
```

```
if (param()) {
    my $ld = new Net::LDAP($server,port=>$port);
    $ld->bind(dn=>$user,password=>$pass);
    my $givenname = param('givenname');
    my $sn = param('sn');
    my $uid = param('uid');
    my $mail = param('mail');
    my $cn = "$givenname $sn";
    my $dn = "uid=$uid,$org";
    my $objectclass = "inetOrgPerson";

    print "Adding User: ",$dn,p;

    my $entry = new Net::LDAP::Entry();

    $entry->dn($dn);
    $entry->add("objectclass",$objectclass);
    $entry->add("givenname",$givenname);
    $entry->add("sn",$sn);
    $entry->add("uid",$uid);
    $entry->add("mail",$mail);
    $entry->add("cn",$cn);

    my $mesg = $ld->add($entry)
    if ($mesg->code) {
        print "Failed: ",$mesg->error;
        exit;
    }
    print "Okay!",p;
}
```

Understanding the code

You begin with the standard use lines that load the modules needed by this program. Notice that the code uses the CGI module. The qw/:standard/ option simply tells the module which functions you would like to use:

```
use CGI qw/:standard/;
use Net::LDAP;
```

The next few lines initialize some variables related to the LDAP server with which you want to communicate. You will need to change these to reflect values that work in your environment:

```
my $server = "localhost";
my $port = 389;
my $user = "cn=Administrator";
my $pass = "password";
my $org = "dc=domain,dc=com";
```

You print the top part of the form using basic functions made available by the CGI module. In this example, you collect only very basic information. In a full version, you would obviously expand this part of the code to include anything you needed that could not be derived:

```
print header,
    start_html('Add User'),
    h1('Add User'),
    start_form,
    "First Name:",textfield('givenname'),p,
    "Last Name:",textfield('sn'),p,
    "UserID:",textfield('uid'),p,
    "Mail:",textfield('mail'),p,
    submit("Add"),end_form,hr;
```

Now you check to see if any form data has already been posted. This step is necessary because the same script is being called to both draw and parse the form. You can do this using the `param()` function provided by the CGI module. If it is defined, data has been passed and this `if` statement will return `true`:

```
if (param()) {
```

If form data has been passed, you create a new LDAP connection object using the connection information specified previously and collect the data passed by the web browser. Note that you also derive the common name (cn) and distinguished name (dn) from some of the other available values. If no form data has yet been posted, nothing is left for the script to do, because the form was already drawn:

```
my $ld = new Net::LDAP($server,port=>$port);
$ld->bind(dn=>$user,password=>$pass);
my $givenname = param('givenname');
my $sn = param('sn');
my $uid = param('uid');
my $mail = param('mail');
my $cn = "$givenname $sn";
my $dn = "uid=$uid,$org";
my $objectclass = "inetOrgPerson";

print "Adding User: ",$dn,p;
```

The next step is to create a new LDAP entry and populate it with the information you collected previously:

```
my $entry = new Net::LDAP::Entry();

$entry->dn($dn);
$entry->add("objectclass",$objectclass);
$entry->add("givenname",$givenname);
$entry->add("sn",$sn);
$entry->add("uid",$uid);
$entry->add("mail",$mail);
$entry->add("cn",$cn);
```

The add() method in the connection class can now be called to create the new entry in the directory. As mentioned in chapter 6, adding the values only changes the entry in memory. Changes are not committed to the directory until the add() method is called:

```
my $mesg = $ld->add($entry);
if ($mesg->code) {
    print "Failed: ",$mesg->error;
    exit;
}
print "Okay!",p;
}
```

That's it. Now you simply plug the script into the appropriate place on your web server and try it out.

NOTE   If you click the Add button a second time with the same UserID value, you will get the following message:

```
Adding User: uid=juser,o=test
Failed: Already exists
```

Doing a query using the simple_search.pl example from chapter 6, you can see this entry in LDIF:

```
dn: uid=juser,dc=domain,dc=com
cn: Joe User
sn: User
uid: juser
givenname: Joe
mail: juser@domain.com
objectclass: top
objectclass: person
objectclass: inetOrgPerson
objectclass: organizationalPerson
```

Once again, notice how the objectclass attribute contains both the object class you assigned to the entry and the object classes from which you are inheriting. Otherwise the entry contains exactly what was submitted.

7.3.2   People entries based on existing data

As we already mentioned, in some cases you may have existing data that will be used to instantiate new things. Let's look at an example that allows you to create a user entry that uses existing information as a base. This technique is useful in reducing the amount of data that must be entered when some information already exists about the entity being created. In this example, you will pull in information from an existing user repository, but it is perfectly reasonable for this information to come from databases or even other directories.

The output of the example addimportuser.pl script looks something like figure 7.7. Listing 7.2 shows the complete code for the addimportuser.pl script.

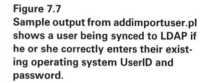

Figure 7.7
Sample output from addimportuser.pl shows a user being synced to LDAP if he or she correctly enters their existing operating system UserID and password.

Listing 7.2   addimportuser.pl

```
use CGI qw/:standard/;
use Net::LDAP;

my $server = "localhost";
my $port = 389;
my $user = "cn=Admin";
my $pass = "manager_password";
my $org = "dc=domain,dc=com";
my $maildomain = "domain.com";

print header,
    start_html('Sync User'),
    h1('Sync User'),
    start_form,
    "UserID: ",textfield('uid'),p,
    "Password: ",password_field('password'),p,
    submit("Sync"),end_form,hr;

if (param()) {
    my $ld = new Net::LDAP($server,port=>$port);
    $ld=>bind(dn=>$user,password=>$pass);
    my $uid = param('uid');
    my $password = param('password');

    my ($login,$pass,$userid,$groupid,$quota,
        $comment,$gecos,$home,$shell,$expire) = getpwnam($uid);

    if (!$login || crypt($password,$pass) ne $pass) {
        print "Invalid Username or Password.",p;
```

```
        print "Crypt: $pass",p;
        exit;
    }
    $gecos =~ /(\w+)$/;
    my $sn = $1;
    my $dn = "uid=$uid,$org";
    my $entry = new Net::LDAP::Entry();
    $entry->dn($dn);
    $entry->add("objectclass",[ "top", "person", "inetOrgPerson" ]);
    $entry->add("cn",$gecos);
    $entry->add("sn",$sn);
    $entry->add("userPassword","{crypt}$pass");
    $entry->add("uid",$uid);
    $entry->add("mail","$uid\@$maildomain");

    print "Adding $dn.",p;
    my $mesg = $ld->add($entry);
    if ($mesg->code) {
        print "Failed: ",$mesg->error;
        exit;
    }
    print "Okay!";
    exit;
}
```

Understanding the code

Again, you begin with the standard use lines that load the modules needed by this program:

```
use CGI qw/:standard/;
use Net::LDAP;
```

Be sure to change the variables to reflect your environment:

```
my $server = "localhost";
my $port = 389;
my $user = "cn=Admin";
my $pass = "manager_password";
my $org = "dc=domain,dc=com";
my $maildomain = "domain.com";
```

Next, you print a basic HTML form and check to see if any form data has already been passed to your script. As in the last example, you use the same script to display and parse the form, so you must check to see if form data has already been posted in order to change the script's behavior depending on how it is run:

```
print header,
    start_html('Sync User'),
    h1('Sync User'),
    start_form,
    "UserID: ",textfield('uid'),p,
```

```
    "Password: ",password_field('password'),p,
    submit("Sync"),end_form,hr;

if (param()) {
```

You now create an authenticated connection object and gather the form data entered by the user:

```
my $ld = new Net::LDAP($server,port=>$port);
$ld->bind(dn=>$user,password=>$pass);
my $uid = param('uid');
my $password = param('password');
```

The next few lines do the fancy work necessary to find the existing information that will be used to instantiate information within your new entry. This particular example should work fine if you are using a Unix /etc/passwd file that uses crypt-style passwords. This style is the default on most traditional Unix platforms and is usually an option on newer Unix-based operating systems. Some recent Linux and BSD distributions use MD5 passwords by default, and many systems use shadow files. You will need to change these lines in either of these cases. Under Windows NT, you can use one of the special modules (Win32::NetAdmin) for accessing the NT account information:

```
my ($login,$pass,$userid,$groupid,$quota,
    $comment,$gecos,$home,$shell,$expire) = getpwnam($uid);

if (!$login || crypt($password,$pass) ne $pass) {
    print "Invalid Username or Password.",p;
    print "Crypt: $pass",p;
    exit;
}
```

Here you parse out the last name from a field that you expect to contain the user's full name. You also generate a distinguished name for this entry:

```
$gecos =~ /(\w+)$/;
my $sn = $1;
my $dn = "uid=$uid,$org";
```

Now you create a new Net::LDAP::Entry object and populate it with the information you were able to collect and derive earlier. Notice how you are able to derive the mail attribute from the uid attribute, a static mail domain, and a defined creation pattern (uid plus @ plus mail domain). This is a common way to reduce the amount of data entry needed to create a directory entry:

```
my $entry = new Net::LDAP::Entry();
$entry->dn($dn);
$entry->add("objectclass",[ "top", "person", "inetOrgPerson" ]);
$entry->add("cn",$gecos);
$entry->add("sn",$sn);
$entry->add("userPassword","{crypt}$pass");
$entry->add("uid",$uid);
$entry->add("mail","$uid\@$maildomain");
```

Finally, you call the add() method to communicate your desired change to the LDAP server:

```
print "Adding $dn.",p;
$mesg = $ld->add($entry);
if ($mesg->code) {
    print "Failed: ",$mesg->error;
    exit;
}
print "Okay!";
exit;
}
```

7.3.3 Summary of creating entries

You now have two methods of creating new entries in the directory. The difference between these methods is the way in which most of the initial user data is input. In the first example, the person accessing the web page enters most of the data by hand, whereas in the second example, you use a minimal amount of information from the person accessing the web page to locate more extensive existing information that can be used to populate the directory.

Generally speaking, if good information already exists, there is no reason not to use it. In chapter 8, which discusses synchronization and migration, we talk about automating some types of directory population. The previous example also works well to give administrators and end-users the ability to link accounts when no common key currently exists to link that information.

Neither of these examples spends much time dealing with error conditions, such as those that occur when an entry already exists within the directory or bad data is entered. Such error checking is shown extensively in chapter 6 and is left as an exercise for you.

Another likely improvement for any production use of these examples would be to add an input to accept a login and password for an administrative user. The existing examples do not require authentication by the web user and perform activities on the directory as a superuser. This approach is insecure and is easily remedied by requiring authentication on the web form or server.

7.4 CREATING AND MAINTAINING GROUPS

Group entries in LDAP lump together other entries such that applications can treat those other entries in a similar manner. Entries often share commonalities with other entries. For example, several people may belong to the same department, and many printers may be situated on the same floor.

When you're managing entries, it is often important to put them into groups based on these commonalities—the whole idea of LDAP is to allow sharing of information across multiple applications. Grouping people or accounts inside an application does not promote this type of information cross-functionality. On the other hand, specifying groups within the directory allows these groups to be reused. For example, a group that contains a list of managers can be used both for security and as an email list.

In LDAP, groups can be managed two ways: explicitly and dynamically. Not all directory servers support dynamic groups, although support for them is becoming more common.

7.4.1 Explicit groups

Explicit groups' members are listed explicitly. The standard object class for group entries is `groupOfUniqueNames`, so named because each member is the distinguished name of an entry that belongs to this group.

Explicit groups work wonderfully in situations where members are relatively static or people are allowed to add themselves as members. An example of the latter would be an email mailing list to which anyone can subscribe.

Here is an LDAP group shown in standard LDIF format:

```
dn: cn=My Explicit Group,dc=manning,dc=com
objectclass: groupOfUniqueNames
cn: Explicit Group
uniquemember: uid=hall,dc=manning,dc=com
uniquemember: uid=csmith1,dc=manning,dc=com
```

This example group has two members; each member is specified by a distinguished name in the directory. Most directory servers will not check to be sure the distinguished names listed actually exist in the directory. In addition, the LDAP protocol has no expectation that if the distinguished name for a user changes, the value of `uniquemember` will change automatically. This lack of dependable relational integrity has been cited throughout the book as a consideration for namespace design.

> **NOTE** Sun One and other directory servers offer the ability to use plug-ins and other mechanisms to maintain relational integrity. Although these tools are generally reliable, they are also proprietary; it is unwise to depend on this functionality.

When allowing for automatic group management, it can be useful to populate the `owner` attribute with the distinguished name of the group's owner. For example:

```
dn: cn=My Explicit Group,dc=manning,dc=com
objectclass: groupOfUniqueNames
cn: Explicit Group
owner: uid=wu1,dc=manning,dc=com
uniquemember: uid=hall,dc=manning,dc=com
uniquemember: uid=csmith1,dc=manning,dc=com
```

One gotcha with the `owner` attribute is that many applications do not include the distinguished name listed in that attribute as an actual member of the group. So, if the owner is also a member, they should be specified twice.

7.4.2 Dynamic groups and LDAP URLs

A weakness with explicit groups is that many groups' membership changes frequently. An obvious example is a group based on a division or department. In such situations, it may be better to simply say that the group contains all the entities that match a given criteria.

For example, a particular department-based group may contain all the entries whose attribute department is set to AAAA. Therefore, if a person's entry is changed to reflect a departmental change, any groups built by referencing this attribute will automatically reflect this change.

Dynamic groups use LDAP Universal Resource Locators (URLs). The format for LDAP URLs is defined by the IETF in RFC 2255 and can be used to represent LDAP search criteria as a single string. Here's an example URL:

```
ldap://localhost:389/dc=manning,dc=com?cn,sn?sub?(objectclass=person)
```

In this example, the first part (ldap://localhost:389) specifies that the URL refers to an LDAP connection to the server running on port 389 of localhost. The next part of the URL (dc=manning,dc=com) specifies the search base, and the comma-separated list after the first question mark includes the list of attributes to return. If you leave the return list empty, all attributes will be returned. Finally, the last major component in this example is the LDAP filter.

If you wanted to use this filter to create a dynamic group, you would add the filter to an entry with the groupOfURLs objectclass:

```
Dn: cn=My Dynamic Group, dc=manning, dc=com
Objectclass: groupOfURLs
Memberurl: ldap:///dc=manning,dc=com??sub?(objectclass=person)
```

This group would include all entries on the current server under the dc=manning,dc=com branch with an objectclass of person as members of the dynamic group. You could use a more complex search filter to narrow the types of people to include in the group.

Dynamic groups are not a well-documented standard, but they are becoming increasingly well supported by major directory vendors. When you need to create groups larger than a moderate size, dynamic groups can ease overall group management.

7.5 REPRESENTING AND MANAGING ACCOUNT INFORMATION

Accounts and people are often two different things. Whereas accounts may be specific to applications or systems, people are unique entities. In this section, we'll look at managing user accounts, rather than information about unique individuals or groups.

For many organizations, a worthy goal would be to represent and manage account information in an LDAP-enabled directory service. Doing so would allow user accounts for groups of machines to be managed centrally, reducing security risks from stale accounts and allowing linkage to people entries (as discussed later in this chapter). Unfortunately, because different systems are designed to require different account information, no single object class could possibly cover everything from IBM RACF to Microsoft Windows. For example, a Unix account entry needs to be associated with a login shell that makes a difference in the user's environment when using a system. The choice of shell may even differ among Unix systems, let alone the fact that there is no such concept on a system running Windows 2000.

7.5.1 Unix user accounts

Most Unix-based operating systems, including Linux, come out-of-the-box using simple structured flat files to store user and group account information. Sun's NIS is available on most Unix platforms as a means of sharing information about accounts and groups, and other data that may be needed across multiple systems. NIS is, in many ways, a simple operating system–specific directory service.

With its flat namespace and limited extensibility, NIS is a directory service with limited scalability. However, schema definitions exist for representing NIS data in an LDAP directory. Combined with plug-ins for specific operating systems, it is often possible to use LDAP to store information that would normally be found in NIS, with the result of completely replacing NIS.

The RFC 2307 specification from the IETF defines a number of object classes, as shown in table 7.1.

Table 7.1   Object classes defined by RFC 2307

Object class	Description
posixAccount	Attributes corresponding to fields in a common passwd file
shadowAccount	Password and password expiration information
posixGroup	Group and group membership information
ipService	Port and protocol used by various IP services
ipProtocol	Internet Protocol to protocol number mappings
oncRpc	RPC mappings
ipHost	Host to IP address mappings
ipNetwork	Network name to network address mappings
nisNetgroup	Grouping of hosts and/or users
nisMap	Description of an NIS map
nisObject	Entry in an NIS map
Ieee802Device	Auxiliary object class for any device with a MAC address
bootableDevice	Auxiliary object class for any device with boot parameters

Although all the object classes defined by RFC 2307 are useful in directory-enabling the management of Unix servers, we will focus for now on account and group information. This information is stored in the `posixAccount`, `shadowAccount`, and `posixGroup` object classes.

The attribute types allowed and required by `posixAccount` are virtually identical to the fields found in a standard passwd file: `uid`, `userPassword`, `uidNumber`, `gidNumber`, `gecos`, `homeDirectory`, and `loginShell`. The only additions not normally found in the Unix passwd file are `cn` and `description`.

Adding users with Net::LDAP

You can construct a simple text-based interface for adding new users with Net::LDAP; see listing 7.3. This technique is similar to what you did with people entries using web forms earlier in the chapter.

Listing 7.3   account_add.pl

```perl
use Net::LDAP;

$conn = new Net::LDAP("localhost");
$conn->bind(dn=>"cn=Admin",password=>"password");

print "Username: ";
$username = <>;

print "Password: ";
$password = <>;

print "UID#: ";
$uid = <>;

print "GID#: ";
$gid = <>;

print "Full Name: ";
$gecos = <>;

print "Home Directory: ";
$home = <>;

print "Shell: ";
$shell = <>;

$entry = new Net::LDAP::Entry();
$entry->add("uid",$username);
$entry->add("uidNumber",$uid);
$entry->add("gidNumber",$gid);
$entry->add("gecos",$gecos);
$entry->add("homeDirectory",$home);
$entry->add("loginShell",$shell);
$entry->add("userPassword",$password);
$entry->add("cn",$username);
```

```
$dn = "cn=" . $username . ", ou=Division A, ou=Accounts," .
     " dc=domain, dc=com";
$entry->dn($dn);

$mesg = $conn->add($entry);
if ($mesg->code) {
   print "An error occurred adding the account to the directory.\n";
   die $mesg->error;
}
print "Account added successfully!\n";
```

You begin by using the connection class to open an authenticated connection:

```
use Net::LDAP;

$conn = new Net::LDAP("localhost");
$conn->bind(dn=>"cn=Admin",password=>"password");
```

With your connection open, you can begin gathering the information you need to create a user account:

```
print "Username: ";
$username = <>;

print "Password: ";
$password = <>;

print "UID#: ";
$uid = <>;

print "GID#: ";
$gid = <>;

print "Full Name: ";
$gecos = <>;

print "Home Directory: ";
$home = <>;

print "Shell: ";
$shell = <>;
```

Now that you have all the necessary information, you can construct your entry object. Notice that the code uses the posixAccount object class defined by RFC 2307:

```
$entry = new Net::LDAP::Entry();
$entry->add("uid",$username);
$entry->add("uidNumber",$uid);
$entry->add("gidNumber",$gid);
$entry->add("gecos",$gecos);
$entry->add("homeDirectory",$home);
$entry->add("loginShell",$shell);
$entry->add("userPassword",$password);
```

Although you've populated the entry with all the information you collected, two constructed elements are still missing:

- Distinguished name
- Required cn attribute

Much of how you construct the distinguished name or assign the common name depends on how you have structured your namespace. Remember that whichever attribute you use as your naming component needs to be unique at a particular level in the directory tree.

Perhaps the best way to represent accounts in the directory tree is to distinguish them by the fact that they are accounts and by the administrative domain to which they belong. For example, let's use the directory tree in figure 7.8.

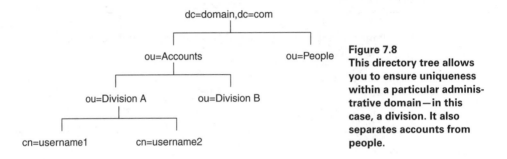

Figure 7.8
This directory tree allows you to ensure uniqueness within a particular administrative domain—in this case, a division. It also separates accounts from people.

You can assign the value of the uid attribute to the common name and construct the distinguished name using the common name as the naming component:

```
$entry->add("cn",$username);

$dn = "cn=" . $username . ", ou=Division A, ou=Accounts," .
    " dc=domain, dc=com";
$entry->dn($dn);
```

You can now simply add the entry to the directory:

```
$mesg = $conn->add($entry);
if ($mesg->code) {
    print "An error occurred adding the account to the directory.\n";
    die $mesg->error;
}
print "Account added successfully!\n";
```

Running this new code gives you output that looks something like the following:

```
Username: hjones
Password: abc123
UID#: 100
GID#: 100
```

```
Full Name: Harry Jones
Home Directory: /home/hjones
Shell: /bin/ksh
Account added successfully!
```

There is obviously room for improvement; you could add such features as auto-incrementing UID counters, more intelligent defaults for home directories and shells, and perhaps automatic generation of usernames based on full name or some local account naming standards. If you were ambitious, you might also decide to create a web-based front-end that would present a better user interface, as in the example earlier in this chapter.

You should also strengthen security by removing the hard-coded password and requiring that the person running the script enter his own credentials upon execution. Turning off or masking the password as it is typed would also be a worthwhile enhancement, as would encrypting the password prior to storage in the directory.

7.5.2   Linking Unix accounts to people

Storing accounts in a more generalized directory service, rather than in a specialized directory that exists solely for account information, simplifies linking accounts to the people that own them. Doing so is important in hire-fire scenarios where changes to data in human resources information systems automatically cause the creation, modification, or deletion of accounts in other systems. Such seamless account management is virtually impossible without strong mappings between accounts and people.

You can create this linkage either by putting an identifier for the person within the account, or by putting an identifier for the account within a person entry. Because a person may have more than one account, such an identifier within a person entry will be multivalued.

Adding the following bold code to the previous example will ask the administrator for the `employeeNumber` to be associated with the new account and add it to the account. Of course, the object class being used must allow that attribute:

```
print "Shell: ";
$shell = <>;

print "Employee#: ";
$employeeno = <>;

$entry = new Net::LDAP::Entry();
$entry->add("uid",$username);
$entry->add("employeeNumber",$employeeno);
```

You can easily search the directory for the distinguished name of the entry containing the specified employee number. Doing so offers input validation and allows you to store the information in an attribute with a distinguished name syntax that can be easily used in most directories to allow employees to change certain account information, such as their shell.

7.6 MANAGING OTHER INFORMATION

So far, we've focused on managing people, accounts, and groups. Although this type of information is important in most directories, LDAP's flexibility offers you the ability to easily represent other types of entities—everything from organizations to network devices.

Managing these other types of information in the directory makes sense only when there is some agreement on a common schema, because directories are most useful in their ability to share information that can be used by multiple applications. If nobody agrees on a schema, there is little advantage in using a directory over a database.

It would be out of our scope to try to present specific management tools for each type of information being managed; most would be similar to those presented earlier in this chapter. However, we will explore some of the issues associated with managing different types of information—particularly information for which there is some consensus on a common schema.

7.6.1 Security services information

The most common current application for directories besides white pages and user management is storing information for security services. Such information often includes authorization policies and credentials used for authentication.

We have already discussed managing account passwords. Storing password information in other locations is beneficial in another case: single sign-on. Certificates, required for strong public key authentication, may be stored with an entry just as passwords are, but there is less necessity to do so. The unique management issues associated with single sign-on and certificate storage are discussed in more detail in chapter 12.

Managing policy information is different, because it involves more than management of a single data element: it depends on the representation of rules that have been externalized from application logic. Most applications and services storing this type of information currently use proprietary schemas and namespaces structured in a way that allows the representation of more complex relationships. If you're interested in managing policy information, you'll need to get the vendor's policy schema and namespace.

7.6.2 DNS information

The inventors of LDAP explicitly state that it is not designed to be a replacement for DNS: DNS is a naming service, whereas LDAP is a directory service. However, this difference does not mean that LDAP cannot or should not be the source of information used by a local DNS service. In fact, the latest versions of Bind include the ability to source DNS records in an LDAP directory. This functionality is interesting, but without a proper management tool, it would be much more difficult to manage DNS information in the directory than it would be to manage it in existing file-based stores. People with experience managing DNS servers know that the most common problems occur when someone makes a typographical error in a configuration file and thereby invalidates a large number of records.

A simple administration interface would make it possible to create distributed DNS management tools with better audit trails and access control than a typical file-based solution. Such an interface would also be less error-prone than the approach just mentioned.

7.6.3 Directory Enabled Networking information

The DEN initiative was introduced in chapter 1. As mentioned there, it is primarily focused on object modeling. More directories are beginning to support schemas derived from these models.

On the LDAP side, there is little difference between managing a person and managing a router. The big question is, "Where does information come from?" In the case of a router, you can poll information from it dynamically using SNMP or possibly from a database used by applications like HP OpenView, Tivoli, and others of this nature.

Although the DEN schema is becoming well defined, the limitations on DEN's acceptance stem primarily from a lack of native support for related standards within the products that need to be managed. For example, you can manipulate information about a router in the directory and even write a separate application to read that configuration from the directory periodically and write it to the particular router—but it is much more desirable for the router to be able to read the directory itself to "self-configure" as necessary. This approach would allow smarter, more dynamic network configuration.

7.6.4 Card catalog information

One of the pilot schemas included with the University of Michigan LDAP server can be used to create a card catalog for documents. Entries using this schema do not store the documents themselves, but rather store the metadata about these documents. The only disadvantage is that most existing applications don't understand this schema out-of-the-box; in addition, better systems undoubtedly exist for providing this functionality using the web and databases.

7.7 SUMMARY

There are three common models for managing directories: centralized, distributed, and self-administration. Most environments use some mix of these three models to develop a good, balanced management system.

In this chapter, we walked through the creation of several web-based tools for adding users, both from scratch and with existing information. We also looked at managing groups and accounts, with several examples that show how a typical Unix or Linux account can be managed in a directory. Finally, we discussed some of the issues involved in storing information that is not related to people or groups in the directory.

In the next chapter, we move from manual entry management to automated mechanisms for getting information into the directory server.

CHAPTER 8

Synchronizing LDAP information

No directory exists in a vacuum. New tools and products are making directory co-existence and migration much easier tasks than they used to be. Unfortunately, no tool is smart enough to understand the idiosyncrasies of every environment.

In this chapter, we look at the process of moving information to and from an LDAP directory. We will answer these questions:

- What are the three basic approaches to managing data flow?
- What aspects of the data stores must be understood prior to successful migration or synchronization?
- What is LDIF, and how can it be used for data interchange?
- How can data be migrated to an LDAP directory? What issues exist when joining with existing data?
- What is the best way to synchronize from an LDAP directory?
- What are the issues with bidirectional synchronization?

8.1 APPROACHES TO DATA FLOW MANAGEMENT

There are three basic approaches to managing data flow between various data repositories:

- Replication
- File export/import
- Scripting

Each approach has benefits and drawbacks that make it a good choice for some situations and a horrifying nightmare in others.

In addition to these basic approaches, a whole segment of the directory market is devoted to tools designed to ease directory integration issues. These tools are divided into synchronization products called *metadirectories* and real-time transformation products called *virtual directories*. Metadirectories try to take out some of the legwork of the data access, time-stamping, and basic transformation that we show throughout this chapter. Virtual directories, on the other hand, take the approach that the information was just fine where it was before, and the solution is to change the presentation of information rather than the location of information. Both types of tools are discussed in more detail at the end of chapter 1.

8.1.1 Replication

Replication is the process of exactly duplicating data between directories (see figure 8.1). Replication is a way of creating copies of information for purposes such as geographic distribution of data, performance, scalability, and redundancy.

Although many servers support replication to other servers from the same vendor, there is currently no standard for LDAP replication. However, the IETF is in the process of developing a standard called LDUP.

Even if standard replication existed, it is not always necessary or desirable for all information to be duplicated between two directories. Additionally, not all data sources can be queried or replicated using the LDAP standards.

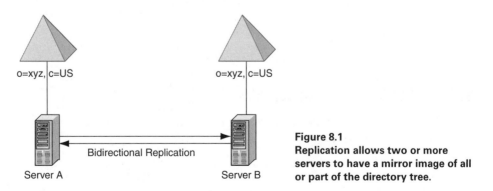

Figure 8.1
Replication allows two or more servers to have a mirror image of all or part of the directory tree.

8.1.2   File export/import

Exporting a data file from one directory server and then importing that same data to a different server does not require special protocol support by either server. Figure 8.2 shows how data can be exported from one server and imported into another. Between the import and export process, the data can easily be manipulated as necessary to meet the needs of applications using the second directory.

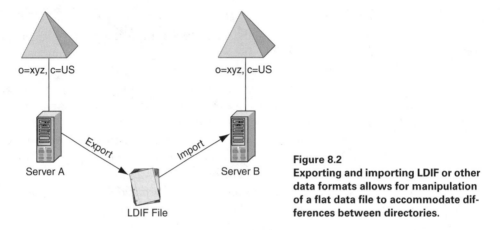

Figure 8.2
Exporting and importing LDIF or other data formats allows for manipulation of a flat data file to accommodate differences between directories.

Adding to the benefits of this approach is the fact that two well-defined formats, LDIF and DSML, exist for data files containing LDAP entries. The drawback of this approach is that delays usually associated with periodic exports and imports can potentially let data get out of sync.

8.1.3   Scripting

The process we'll focus on throughout this chapter is scripting. *Scripting* is the process of using languages such as Perl to access, transform, and update information in a way that allows it to flow effectively from one data store to another. Although scripting isn't as tightly coupled with the server as replication, scripted synchronization and migration allow you to perform data transformation, schema mapping, and namespace translation as you read entries from one directory and place them in another directory. It also allows you to easily select and synchronize only the subset of data that should be shared between servers.

8.2   DATA FLOW ANALYSIS

Prior to jumping into synchronization and migration, it is important for you to understand the type of up-front analysis that must be done to make this process successful.

8.2.1 Schema mapping

Schema mapping is required when the two data stores use different attribute types or data fields to store the same information. For instance, consider a situation in which an LDAP-enabled directory has a custom attribute called `buildingLocation-Code`. If a peer in another part of the organization creates another attribute in her directory called `locationCode`, it will be necessary to create an entry in a mapping table indicating that the two attributes are the same (figure 8.3).

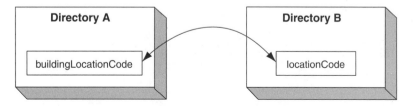

Figure 8.3 The attribute `buildingLocationCode` in one directory is the same as `locationCode` in another.

8.2.2 Determining the authoritative source

The most important thing to remember when moving data is that some data is better than other data. If you are simply migrating from one data store to another (for example, from a spreadsheet to LDAP), the source data is obviously more interesting than the empty destination data store. In situations where multiple data sources are being migrated, or where synchronization is being performed, finding the authoritative source for each attribute is absolutely critical.

The authoritative source can only be determined by careful analysis of each of the data repositories being connected. Generally speaking, the authoritative source will contain the freshest and most accurate version of the information stored in a particular attribute. For example, you might see that a facilities database is constantly updated with location codes, whereas an enterprise LDAP server rarely gets direct updates. In that situation, the facilities database is probably the authoritative source. As shown in figure 8.4, it is completely possible for different parts of the whole to be authoritative in different repositories.

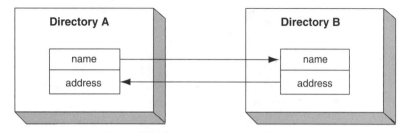

Figure 8.4 The `name` attribute is authoritative in directory A, whereas `address` is authoritative in directory B.

Let's envision a thriving company that has, over time, deployed various data stores. Among these data stores are the company's HR system, email directory, and facilities database. After some analysis, you might determine that the email directory is the authoritative source for email information; HR is authoritative for department, job title, and related information; and the facilities database is an excellent source for telephone and location information (see figure 8.5).

Figure 8.5 Each data store has a set of attributes for which it should be authoritative. Here, the authoritative attributes in each data store are bold.

Be sure to consider the information from chapter 7 about entry management. The directory most often used as a destination for data in other repositories may itself be authoritative for certain fields, depending on the model used to manage directory entries.

8.2.3 Data transformation

Data transformation is necessary because not all systems represent the same information in an identical fashion. For example, figure 8.6 illustrates a circumstance in which one data store maintains a user's department as an account code and another system uses text that describes the department. To synchronize information from the first data store to the second, you must first transform the data in the first system such that it matches the format of the data in the second.

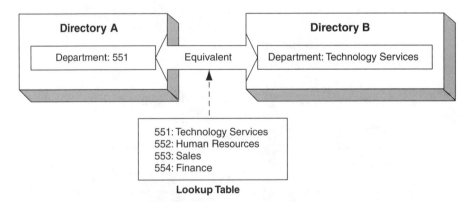

Figure 8.6 Department 551 is equal to Technology Services. Directory A uses a numeric representation, whereas directory B uses a string description.

8.2.4 Namespace translation

The namespaces on two servers may not be the same. In fact, even when you're synchronizing LDAP servers within the same company, the namespace often varies in depth and RDN usage. Figure 8.7 shows a company with two directories in which everything is the same except the top-level naming components.

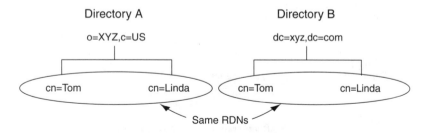

Figure 8.7 Directories using the same RDNs, but under different trees, cannot be synchronized using true replication. However, they are not as difficult to synchronize programmatically.

In the simplest cases, solving synchronization and migration issues related to namespace differences may be as easy as changing the root naming context (such as o=xyz,c=us to dc=xyz,dc=com). Many situations, such as the one shown in figure 8.8, require that such translation be more intelligent. This is usually the case when depth and RDN attributes vary between servers.

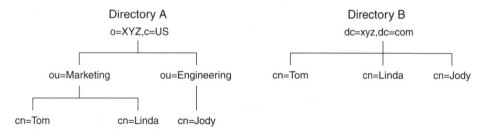

Figure 8.8 Directory A has a deeper namespace than directory B. Any synchronization between the two directories will require smarter namespace translation.

Many data stores do not support LDAP-style distinguished names, thus making this more a process of namespace generation than translation. For example, the database in figure 8.9 does not offer any real hierarchy that relates to the hierarchy shown in the directory server.

In such cases, you will need to derive the hierarchy based on other information. For example, if you always use dc=xyz,dc=com as the suffix and the namespace is flat below that, you can put all the database information into entries beneath that level.

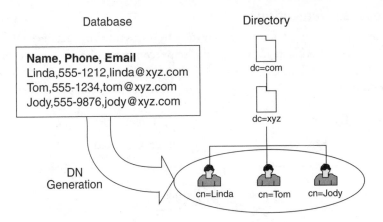

Database

Directory

Name, Phone, Email
Linda,555-1212,linda@xyz.com
Tom,555-1234,tom@xyz.com
Jody,555-9876,jody@xyz.com

dc=com

dc=xyz

DN
Generation

cn=Linda   cn=Tom   cn=Jody

**Figure 8.9   A database without a hierarchical namespace requires you
to generate distinguished names for new entries.**

If you're dividing the directory tree organizationally or geographically, other information in the database will help you determine the namespace to use within the directory.

8.3   INTERCHANGE FORMATS

Two formats exist for representing LDAP information outside the directory server. The first, LDIF, is a convention supported by a wide variety of existing directory vendors. The other, DSML, is the emerging standard and is based on XML. Both of these standards were covered in great detail in chapter 5, but here is a simplified review.

8.3.1   LDAP Data Interchange Format

The LDIF file format is not a core LDAP standard, but it is a widely followed convention that is supported by many LDAP servers and applications. We'll use LDIF in many examples throughout this chapter. These examples will take advantage of Net::LDAP's support for LDIF.

At its most basic, LDIF is written as follows:

```
dn: <entry distinguished name>
objectclass: <objectclass-1>
objectclass: <objectclass-n>
<type-1>: <value-1>
<type-1>: <value-2>
<type-2>: <value-3>
```

The first line always indicates the distinguished name of the entry to follow. The next few lines indicate the object classes that the entry uses. The remaining lines simply associate a value with a particular attribute type.

Here is an example of a real entry represented as LDIF:

```
dn: cn=Joe Schmoe, dc=xyz, dc=com
objectclass: top
objectclass: person
cn: Joe Schmoe
sn: Schmoe
telephoneNumber: +1-847-555-1212
```

In cases where the text is not printable, such as with an audio clip or a JPEG photo, the value of the entry is Base64 encoded. The Base64-encoded value is then separated from the attribute type by two colons rather than one:

```
jpegPhoto:: <Base64 encoded jpeg photo>
```

In addition to binary values, the following types of values also must be Base64 encoded when written in LDIF format:

- Values that begin with a semicolon (;) or space
- Values that contain characters outside printed ASCII

If the line is longer than can normally be displayed without wrapping (such as a long Base64-encoded value), you can continue the line by beginning a new line with a single space. The following two attributes are exactly the same:

```
cn: Joe Sch
<1 space>moe
```

```
cn: Joe Schmoe
```

8.3.2 Directory Services Markup Language

As introduced in chapter 5, DSML is a relatively new standard that has been developed by Bowstreet with participation from IBM, Microsoft, Sun, Novell, and Oracle. Here is an example of what an LDAP entry might look like if encoded using DSML:

```
<dsml:entry dn="cn=Joe Schmoe,dc=xyz,dc=com">
    <dsml:objectclass>
        <dsml:oc-value>top</dsml:oc-value>
        <dsml:oc-value>person</dsml:oc-value>
    </dsml:objectclass>
    <dsml:attr name="cn"><dsml:value>Joe Schmoe
      </dsml:value></dsml:attr>
    <dsml:attr name="sn"><dsml:value>Schmoe
      </dsml:value></dsml:attr>
    <dsml:attr name="telephoneNumber">
      <dsml:value>+1-847-555-1212<dsml:value>
    </dsml:attr>
</dsml:entry>
```

This code may not be quite as easy to read as LDIF, but it has the advantage of being readable by any application or editor that supports XML and is aware of the DSML document type definitions.

Not only does DSML define a way for directory entries to be represented in XML, it also does the same for directory schemas. We'll look at DSML in greater detail in chapters 10 and 12. Included there are examples of how to use a Perl XML parser to read entries written to the DSML specification. We will also explain how to read the DSML schema for an object class. Both of these techniques make it possible to use DSML easily as an import/export format in a directory integration process.

8.4   MIGRATION TO LDAP

In this book, we consider migration to be a one-time movement of data from one data source to another (see figure 8.10). Sometimes this process is performed more than once, but the basic idea is that the old data source goes away and is replaced by a new one after a defined cut-off time.

Figure 8.10
Directory migration is typically a one-way, one-time movement from a legacy data store to a directory service supporting open standards, like LDAP.

8.4.1   Migrating a simple table

A wide variety of data sources can be represented as tables, including databases and spreadsheets. For this reason, we'll begin by looking at how to migrate a table containing information you would like to put into your directory.

For the sake of example, we will concentrate on migrating a few simple data elements:

```
Smith,Bob,847-555-1212,bsmith@xyz.com
Johnson,Joe,815-555-1212,jjohnson@xz.com
```

The comma-separated lines represent two people. The first two columns make up the person's name, and the latter two make up the telephone number and email address.

NOTE   Picking an appropriate field separator is important. Although this example uses commas for simplicity, commas appear often in data. It may be wise to instead use a separator that needs less special treatment. One commonly used separator that fits the bill is the pipe (|) character.

Before you can do anything with this data, you need to look at the namespace and schema you plan to use. For the sake of example, let's assume all your entries exist below a naming context of dc=xyz,dc=com and your RDNs are made up of the uid attribute and the value to the left of the at sign (@) in an email address.

Here is a bit of Perl code to read the previous lines from standard input and create their distinguished names:

```
while ($line = <>)
{
    chop $line; # remove the trailing linefeed
    ($last,$first,$telephone,$email) = split(/,/,$line);
    ($username,$domain) = split(/@/,$email);
    $dn = "uid=" . $username . ",dc=xyz,dc=com";
    #... do something ...
}
```

This code begins by reading an entire line, and then splits it into the various components based on what you declared each of the four fields to represent. The code then parses the email address into the username and domain components and uses the username as part of the distinguished name.

Consider for a moment what you need to do in the "do something" block. If you wanted to write an import file, you could simply write out the entry to LDIF. Otherwise, you might decide to use Net::LDAP to write directly to the directory server.

Actually, Net::LDAP makes it easy to do things either way. Let's replace the "do something" comment with the following lines:

```
$entry = new Net::LDAP::Entry();
$entry->dn($dn);
$entry->add("sn",$last);
$entry->add("cn","$first $last");
$entry->add("givenName",$first);
$entry->add("uid",$username);
$entry->add("mail",$email);
$entry->add("telephoneNumber",$telephone);
$entry->add("objectclass",[ "top","person" ]);
$ldif = new Net::LDAP::LDIF("-","w");
$ldif->write_entry($entry);
$ldif->done;
```

These lines insert the parsed values you read from the comma-separated file into an entry object. You then use the write_entry() method available on the Net::LDAP::LDIF class to print the entire entry in LDIF format. This LDIF output can now easily be imported into a number of LDAP servers.

If you want to create an entry in an LDAP server directly from your script, it is just as easy to add the following line instead of the previous LDIF-related code:

```
$conn->add($entry);
```

This line requires that the $conn variable be a reference to an open LDAP connection that is authenticated as a user with permission to add entries to the server.

The complete code appears in listing 8.1.

Listing 8.1   migrate_table.pl

```perl
use Net::LDAP;
use Net::LDAP::Entry;

$conn = new Net::LDAP("localhost");
$conn->bind(dn=>"cn=Admin",password=>"password");

while ($line = <>)
{
    chop $line; # remove the trailing linefeed
    ($last,$first,$telephone,$email) = split(/,/,$line);
    ($username,$domain) = split(/@/,$email);
    $dn = "uid=" . $username . ",dc=xyz,dc=com";
    $entry = new Net::LDAP::Entry();
    $entry->dn($dn);
    $entry->add("sn",$last);
    $entry->add("cn","$first $last");
    $entry->add("givenName",$first);
    $entry->add("uid",$username);
    $entry->add("mail",$email);
    $entry->add("telephoneNumber",$telephone);
    $entry->add("objectclass",[ "top","inetOrgPerson" ]);
    $conn->add($entry);
}
```

8.4.2   Migrating from multiple sources

Imagine that you have a second table you would like to migrate with the table from the previous section. For the sake of example, let's use the following table. The first field is the username, the second is a password, and the third is a full name:

```
bsmith,jump4joy,Robert Smith
jjohnson,hit1back,Joe Johnson
```

Here is the original table. We'll call it the email table:

```
Smith,Bob,847-555-1212,bsmith@xyz.com
Johnson,Joe,815-555-1212,jjohnson@xyz.com
```

When presented with such a situation, it is often useful to begin by glancing at a few records from each data source to find similarities. Doing so is helpful because you need to be able to join the entries from both data sources into a single LDAP entry. Looking at the example, it is apparent that the username is the same in both tables. Note that although a full name is also present in both tables, it will not offer an exact match in all cases—for example, Bob Smith is known as Robert Smith in the password database.

It is important to know that you have the same general information (full name) available in both tables. Thus you need to make a decision about the authoritative data source. Picking the authoritative data source usually means picking the data that most accurately reflects what needs to be stored in the LDAP entry.

Let's say that after careful consideration, you determine that the email table most accurately reflects the appropriate value for your common name attribute in LDAP. (It may still be useful to store alternative names in another attribute that it can be searched on.) Listing 8.2 shows the code to migrate these two tables.

Listing 8.2 migrate_two.pl

```perl
use Net::LDAP;
use Net::LDAP::Entry;

$conn = new Net::LDAP::Conn("localhost");
$conn->bind(dn=>"cn=Admin",password=>"password");

open(EMAILDB,"email.txt");
while ($line = <EMAILDB>)
{
    chop $line; # remove the trailing linefeed
    ($last,$first,$telephone,$email) = split(/,/,$line);
    ($username,$domain) = split(/@/,$email);
    $dn = "uid=" . $username . ",dc=xyz,dc=com";
    $entry = new Net::LDAP::Entry();
    $entry->dn($dn);
    $entry->add("sn",$last);
    $entry->add("cn","$first $last");
    $entry->add("givenName",$first);
    $entry->add("uid",$username);
    $entry->add("mail",$email);
    $entry->add("telephoneNumber",$telephone);
    $entry->add("objectclass", [ "top","inetOrgPerson" ]);
    $entries{$username} = $entry;
}
close (EMAILDB);

open(PASSDB,"password.txt");
while ($line = <PASSDB>) {
    chop $line;
    ($uid,$password,$name) = split(/,/,$line);
    $entry = $entries{$uid};
    $entry->add("userPassword",$password);
    $conn->add($entry);
}
close(PASSDB);
```

Understanding the code

As with all scripts using an LDAP server, you first connect to the server using appropriate credentials:

```
$conn = new Net::LDAP("myserver");
$conn->bind(dn=>"cn=Admin",password=>"password");
```

Next you open the first data file for reading. In this case, you begin with the email database. After opening the file, you loop through each record:

```
open(EMAILDB,"email.txt");
while ($line = <EMAILDB>)
{
```

You parse the various fields from the line and derive the uid attribute from the email address. Here you are also using the uid value as the entry's RDN:

```
chop $line; # remove the trailing linefeed
($last,$first,$telephone,$email) = split(/,/,$line);
($username,$domain) = split(/@/,$email);
$dn = "uid=" . $username . ",dc=xyz,dc=com";
```

With all the fields parsed, you can now instantiate a new entry to hold all the information:

```
$entry = new Net::LDAP::Entry();
$entry->dn($dn);
$entry->add("sn",$last);
$entry->add("cn","$first $last");
$entry->add("givenName",$first);
$entry->add("uid",$username);
$entry->add("mail",$email);
$entry->add("telephoneNumber",$telephone);
$entry->add("objectclass",[ "top","inetOrgPerson" ]);
```

Rather than store the entry directly, you instead put it into a hash using the username as the key. Doing so allows you to add content from your second data store before writing to the directory:

```
$entries{$username} = $entry;
}
```

Now that processing is completed on the first data file, you close it and open the second file:

```
close (EMAILDB);

open(PASSDB,"password.txt");
while ($line = <PASSDB>) {
```

Parsing this file is much easier, because you only care about the uid and password fields. You also do not need to create a new distinguished name, because the base entry has already been created:

```
chop $line;
($uid,$password,$name) = split(/,/,$line);
```

You use the `uid` from the record to find an entry with a corresponding `uid` in the hash. Once retrieved, you add only the `userPassword` attribute:

```
$entry = $entries{$uid};
$entry->add("userPassword",$password);
```

Because this is the last data store used to construct this record, you now add the entry. If you had additional data stores, you would simply readd it to the hash:

```
    $conn->add($entry);
}
close(PASSDB);
```

You could have added the nicknames from the second data store to the user's directory entry. Some organizations store multiple names for a user in the `cn` attribute, but because value ordering cannot be guaranteed, doing so may cause the server to return the alternative name to applications expecting a single name.

NOTE   Active Directory defines an attribute called `anl`, or Alternative Name Lookup. This attribute can be used to store alternative names, but it is not supported by most LDAP vendors.

8.4.3   Adding new information to existing entries

Often, the purpose of migration is not to seed a new directory, but to add information to existing entries. An example is a situation in which you would like to initialize the passwords in the directory with information in another data source. In such cases, you want to look at existing entries and update a subset of attributes that may or may not already exist.

As when migrating from multiple sources, you first need to decide which attribute you can use to link data in the two sources. This process is similar to the one that you followed when combining rows from multiple tables in the last example.

Let's change the previous example to read in the new information from a file. Then you'll read in the existing entry and change only those attributes for which the information you've read can be considered authoritative.

Here is the table you will read. The first field is the userid, the second contains the full name, the third contains a company affiliation, and the fourth contains the user's password:

```
johns,John Smith,XYZCorp,johnpassword
marthaj,Martha Jones,XYZCorp,marthapassword
```

Listing 8.3 shows how you can add new password information to existing entries on the directory server.

Listing 8.3   update_password.pl

```perl
use Net::LDAP;

$conn = new Net::LDAP("localhost");
$conn->bind(dn=>"cn=Admin",password=>"password");

open (MYFILE,"inputfile");
while ($line = <MYFILE>)
{
    chop $line; # remove tailing linefeed
    ($userid,$name,$company,$password) = split(/,/,$line);
    $mesg = $conn->search(base=>"dc=xyz,dc=com",
                          scope=>"sub",
                          filter=>"(uid=$userid)");
    $entry = $mesg->entry(0);
    if (!$entry)
    {
        print "Warning: Entry '$userid' was not found.\n";
    } else {
        $entry->replace("userPassword",$password);
        $entry->update($conn);
        print "Updated Password for Entry '$userid'.\n";
    }
}
close (MYFILE);
```

Understanding the code

In this example, you make the (not always good) assumption that the userid in the file is the same as an existing userid in the LDAP server. You don't really care about anything except the password:

```perl
use Net::LDAP;

$conn = new Net::LDAP("localhost");
$conn->bind(dn=>"cn=Admin",password=>"password");

open (MYFILE,"inputfile");
while ($line = <MYFILE>)
{
    chop $line; # remove tailing linefeed
```

Next, you parse out each of the components in the input line:

```perl
    ($userid,$name,$company,$password) = split(/,/,$line);
```

You perform a standard LDAP search to find the entry with a userid that matches the one read from your input file:

```perl
    $mesg = $conn->search(base=>"dc=xyz,dc=com",
                          scope=>"sub",
                          filter=>"(uid=$userid)");
    $entry = $mesg->entry(0);
```

If no entry matches, you print a warning and skip it. In some environments, this lack of a match may be a more serious error that indicates the source data and the directory server are out of sync. In other environments, not all users in one data store exist in another:

```
if (!$entry)
{
    print "Warning: Entry '$userid' was not found.\n";
```

If the entry is found, you replace the userPassword attribute with the password from the file:

```
} else {
    $entry->replace("userPassword",$password);
```

Once again, the entry is not updated on the server until the update() method is called:

```
    $entry->update($conn);
    print "Updated Password for Entry '$userid'.\n";
    }
}
close (MYFILE);
```

Notice how you simply replace the value in the LDAP entry with the authoritative values from your input file. No other attributes are affected.

8.5   JOINING RELATED INFORMATION

A common concept when integrating information between data repositories, such as directories, is that of joining related information. The idea is that in the beginning, parts of the whole exist in different repositories. In the simplest cases, the different repositories share a common key that can be used to join those parts into the whole. For example, if Linda Richards has accounts on both the mainframe and Unix with a common login name of lrichards, it should be possible to join information from each of those accounts by simply querying each repository and combining the results.

8.5.1   Multikey matches

In the perfect world, a common key would always exist in disparate data sources that would allow you to easily join the related information contained in them. Unfortunately, the situation is not always so ideal.

When a single key cannot be used to make an entry unique, you can sometimes use two or more fields that by themselves would not offer a unique identity but that together allow data from two or more sources to be joined. A common example in everyday computing is the way an email address combines a local account name that could never be unique across a billion Internet users with a fully qualified host name that is registered and guaranteed to be globally unique. The example using fuzzy matching in the next section shows the combining of name and department information in an attempt to use multiple criteria to join information in one repository with another when the repositories don't share a common key.

8.5.2 Fuzzy matching

Fuzzy matching means trying to join records based on the fact that they look like a close match, although there may not be enough common information to make an obvious match. Joining data this way has been the subject of much research, especially in the realm of data warehousing. Some companies sell products to do this sort of thing with database tables. You will obviously not be able to match such sophistication, but we'll demonstrate a basic technique that directory managers have used for some time.

By looking at multiple fields, you can come up with a general probability that two records refer to the same subject. For example, given a person's name and department number and the fact that a department in this example company has about 25 people, you can say with relative certainty that if these two fields match, they have a high probability of being the same.

Here is an example of a data file that contains nonunique names. Because this situation is always a possibility, you need to use other fields to help match these records to information in the LDAP-enabled directory:

```
Smith,Bob,847-555-1212,Sales
Johnson,Joe,815-555-1212,Development
Smith,Bob,815-555-9999,Development
```

Listing 8.4 shows how you can use fuzzy matching to join information in this table with existing entries in the directory.

Listing 8.4 fuzzy_update.pl

```perl
use Net::LDAP;
use Net::LDAP::Entry;

$conn = new Net::LDAP("localhost");
$conn->bind(dn=>"cn=Admin",password=>"password");

while($line = <>)
{
    chop $line;
    ($last,$first,$phone,$department) = split(/,/,$line);
    $mesg = $conn->search(base=>"dc=xyz,dc=com",scope=>"sub",
            filter=>"(&(department=$department)(cn=$first $last))");
    $entry = $mesg->entry(0);

    if (!$entry) {
        $entry = new Net::LDAP::Entry();
        $entry->dn("cn=$first $last,dc=xyz,dc=com");
        $entry->add("objectClass","organizationalPerson");
        $entry->add("cn","$first $last");
        $entry->add("sn",$last);
```

```
    $entry->add("telephoneNumber",$phone);
    $entry->add("department",$department);
    $conn->add($entry);
} else {
    $entry->replace("telephoneNumber",$phone);
    $entry->update($conn);
    }
}
```

■

Understanding the code

As usual, you begin by opening a connection to the server. In this case, you bind as an administrator or other user with the privileges necessary to make changes:

```
$conn = new Net::LDAP("localhost");
$conn->bind(dn=>"cn=Admin",password=>"password");

while($line = <>)
{
    chop $line;
    ($last,$first,$phone,$department) = split(/,/,$line);
```

You attempt to match the name and department of an entry that already exists in LDAP. By using both searches in your filter, you are more likely to avoid matching entries that you shouldn't:

```
    $mesg = $conn->search(base=>"dc=xyz,dc=com",scope=>"sub",
            filter=>"(&(department=$department)(cn=$first $last))");
    $entry = $mesg->entry(0);
```

If no entry is returned, the next `if` statement is true. You proceed to create a new entry using the information in the file:

```
    if (!$entry) {
        $entry = new Net::LDAP::Entry();
        $entry->dn("cn=$first $last,dc=xyz,dc=com");
        $entry->add("objectClass","organizationalPerson");
        $entry->add("cn","$first $last");
        $entry->add("sn",$last);
        $entry->add("telephoneNumber",$phone);
        $entry->add("department",$department);
        $conn->add($entry);
    } else {
```

If an entry is returned, the name and department matched. The only other attribute that is not guaranteed to be in sync is the telephone number, which you replace here:

```
        $entry->replace("telephoneNumber",$phone);
        $entry->update($conn);
    }
```

There are two potential problems. First, if the department has changed, you might not get a match when you want one. Second, if your department has two people with the same name, you may match the wrong person.

Although this script works well if departments are relatively small and names are the same between data sources, in a department with 1,000 employees and different name representations, the probability of matching records that refer to different subjects increases dramatically. Smarter processes will check the first name for potential nicknames and other factors that will ensure a higher ratio of good matches.

8.6   SYNCHRONIZATION

The concept of synchronization is closely related to migration. Many of the techniques for matching entries for migration also apply to synchronization. Unlike migration, which generally happens only once, synchronization is a periodic process of finding new changes and propagating them as necessary.

8.6.1   Synchronization to LDAP

When synchronizing, it is important to decide how best to determine whether entries in your source data store have changed. If you look at the data source from the previous section, you see that this is not as simple as it may look at first:

```
Smith,Bob,847-555-1212,bsmith@xyz.com
Johnson,Joe,815-555-1212,jjohnson@xyz.com
```

Although you could easily delete old entries and rewrite them with the same process used to migrate them in the first place, this approach is highly inefficient and has its own problems. If you overwrite the information in the target directory with the data in the previous table, you'll have difficulty determining which entries in the table have been deleted since the previous synchronization.

You can get around this issue by keeping a copy of the previous table and comparing the contents with the current table to find those entries that have been deleted since the last synchronization. In cases where synchronization is being done from data sources (such as structured files) where this type of comparison is easy, this approach can also be a simple way to determine which entries have changed, thus reducing the number of directory operations needed to perform synchronization.

Another way to solve this problem is to keep a change log. Many directory servers use this technique to keep track of entries that need to be replicated to other servers. You can do this by trapping updates to the data store (using database triggers, for example), or by logging changes with the tools used to make changes to the data.

Another approach to determine which entries to synchronize involves tagging each row of data with a last-modified time:

```
Smith,Bob,847-555-1212,bsmith@xyz.com,199908231145
Johnson,Joe,815-555-1212,jjohnson@xyz.com,199908041830
```

By tagging the rows, you can easily check to see if the entry has changed since the last time the information was synchronized.

8.6.2 Synchronization from LDAP

Synchronizing data from LDAP to another data source is similar to doing the reverse. Synchronizing from LDAP to other repositories is important when an LDAP-enabled directory will be an authoritative source of information but that information is also needed in other legacy applications that do not natively support LDAP. However, the way you locate changes and match rows with entries is somewhat different.

Many LDAP servers support an operational attribute called `modifyTimestamp` that automatically reflects the last time an entry was changed. With such functionality available, you can search on this attribute to find entries that have changed. Listing 8.5 shows how you can use this operational attribute to your advantage.

Listing 8.5 sync_from_ldap.pl

```perl
use Net::LDAP;

$conn = new Net::LDAP("localhost");
$conn->bind(dn=>"cn=Admin",password=>"password");

open (TIMEFILE,"lastrun.timestamp");
$lastrun = <TIMEFILE>;
chop $lastrun;
close TIMEFILE;

print "Last Run was " . $lastrun . ".\n";

$mesg = $conn->search(base=>"dc=xyz,dc=com",scope=>"sub",
        filter=>"(modifyTimestamp>=$lastrun)");
$count = $mesg->count;

for ($i = 0; $i < $count; $i++)
{
    $entry = $mesg->entry($i);
    $cn = $entry->get_value("cn");
    ($first,$last) = split(/ /,$cn);
    $phone = $entry->get_value("telephoneNumber");
    $email = $entry->get_value("mail");
    $row{$email} = "$last,$first,$phone,$email";
}

while ($line = <>)
{
    chop $line;
    ($last,$first,$phone,$email) = split(/,/,$line);
    if ($row{$email})
    {
        print $row{$email} . "\n";
    } else {
        print $line . "\n";
    }
```

```
}
($sec, $min, $hour, $day, $month, $year, @extra) = gmtime();
$month++;
if ($month < 10) {
      $month = "0" . $month;
}
if ($day < 10) {
      $day = "0" . $day;
}
if ($min < 10) {
      $min = "0" . $min;
}
if ($hour < 10) {
      $hour = "0" . $hour;
}
if ($sec < 10) {
      $sec = "0" + $sec;
}
$year = $year + 1900;

open (TIMEFILE,">lastrun.timestamp");
print TIMEFILE $year . $month . $day . $hour
           . $min . $sec . "Z\n";
close TIMEFILE;
```

Understanding the code

Again, you begin by using the proper module and opening a connection. You need only authenticate as an entry with enough access to read the entries you want to synchronize:

```
use Net::LDAP;

$conn = new Net::LDAP("localhost");
$conn->bind(dn=>"cn=Admin",password=>"password");
```

Now you set the last time the script was run. You'll read this information from a file that is generated at the end of each run. The time stamp is in the form yyyymmddh-hmmssZ, where yyyy is the year, mm is the month, dd is the date, and hhmm is the hour and minutes. The trailing Z indicates that the time and date is in Universal Time Coordinate (UTC), which is the same as Greenwich Mean Time (GMT):

```
open (TIMEFILE,"lastrun.timestamp");
$lastrun = <TIMEFILE>;
chop $lastrun;
close TIMEFILE;

print "Last Run was " . $lastrun . ".\n";
```

Next you perform a search for all time stamps larger than the one recorded at the end of the last run:

```
$mesg = $conn->search(base=>"dc=xyz,dc=com",scope=>"sub",
        filter=>"(modifyTimestamp>=$lastrun)");
$count = $mesg->count;
```

You loop through each of the matching entries:

```
For ($i = 0; $i < $count; $i++) {
{
```

In this example, you retrieve the common name from the entry and split it in half to get the first and last name. In most environments this step is not adequate, because people often have middle names or generation qualifiers attached to their names that also must be included:

```
$entry = $mesg->entry($i);
$cn = $entry->get_value("cn");
($first,$last) = split(/ /,$cn);
```

You retrieve the rest of the information you would like to synchronize using the standard getValue() method:

```
$phone = $entry->get_value("telephoneNumber");
$email = $entry->get_value("mail");
```

Because you have not yet read in your data file, you store this information in a hash in memory, with the email address acting as the key. The value associated with the key is a record in the format of the data file:

```
$row{$email} = "$last,$first,$phone,$email";
```

Now that you've finished processing this entry, you advance to the next:

```
}
```

Once you have recorded your changes in the %row hash, you can read the input file and substitute your changes:

```
while ($line = <>)
{
    chop $line;
    ($last,$first,$phone,$email) = split(/,/,$line);
```

After reading and parsing one line of input from the data file, you check to see if you read any changed entries from LDAP with the same email address. If so, you print the row from your %row hash:

```
if ($row{$email})
{
    print $row{$email} . "\n";
```

If the email address does not exist in the hash, no changes occurred, and you print the original line from the data file:

```
    } else {
        print $line . "\n";
    }
}
```

Finally, before you exit, you need to print out a current time stamp:

```
($sec, $min, $hour, $day, $month, $year, @extra) = gmtime();
$month++;
if ($month < 10) {
        $month = "0" . $month;
}
if ($day < 10) {
        $day = "0" . $day;
}
if ($min < 10) {
        $min = "0" . $min;
}
if ($hour < 10) {
        $hour = "0" . $hour;
}
if ($sec < 10) {
        $sec = "0" + $sec;
}
$year = $year + 1900;

open (TIMEFILE,">lastrun.timestamp");
print TIMEFILE $year . $month . $day . $hour
            . $min . $sec . "Z\n";
close TIMEFILE;
```

Note that if the synchronization process takes a while, entries may be changed between the time you perform your query and the time you write out the time stamp. You can alleviate this situation by getting the time before the search, but doing so will give you additional unwanted entries that were already returned. The real solution may be to do an occasional full synchronization.

This script doesn't give you the entries that have been deleted. Because deleted entries are removed from the LDAP-enabled directory's namespace, the situation becomes more complicated. However, there are workable alternatives. The most common way to get around this issue is to avoid using the delete operation and instead use a status attribute, such as employeeType. You change this attribute to deactivate the entry. You can then perform a search on this attribute to find entries that have been tagged for deletion. If you want to remove the entry, the synchronization script can perform the deletion from both sources.

8.6.3   Bidirectional synchronization

Bidirectional synchronization requires more consideration than any other type. It must deal with many issues in addition to the usual problems associated with trying to match a row of data with a particular entry, or entries with different names.

Bidirectional synchronization is generally most important when multiple active data repositories are being used and each is authoritative for part of the data. Synchronization is done to bring authoritative information to each of the nonauthoritative data repositories. In instances where multiple repositories are authoritative for the same attribute, bidirectional synchronization must determine which changes to propagate.

Needless to say, one of the most important issues that must be resolved is how to handle data mastering. In unidirectional replication, data is always mastered in one location and copied to another. With bidirectional data flow, you must be conscious of which location masters each piece of data.

An even more complicated situation exists when data must be mastered in multiple locations, because special types of conflicts may occur. The most important of these conflicts arises when two different data stores get updates to the same entry at about the same time. Depending on the process used for synchronization, one or both sources may end up containing improper information. Directories that support multimaster replication avoid this issue by using change sequence numbers that contain time and other information that lets you determine the order in which changes were applied.

However, in an environment where the data sources being synchronized are not of the same type, it is unlikely that a similar type of technique will be as effective. In such environments, it is best to either avoid multimastering of data completely, or set one of the sources to be more authoritative than the others for any information that would be adversely impacted in these types of situations.

8.7 SUMMARY

In this chapter, you learned about the three basic approaches to managing data flow across multiple data stores. You need to understand issues such as the authoritative sources and existing schemas before you can be successful at keeping your directory information up to date. Unlike chapter 7, which focused on manual data management, this chapter examined scripted approaches to automate as much of the directory information management process as possible.

Additionally, we presented several examples of tactical solutions to common synchronization and migration issues. These examples showed how to move information between databases and directories, as well as how to generate and search using directory time stamps.

In chapter 9, we move from discussing directory information management to looking at management and monitoring of operational information within the directory.

C H A P T E R   9

Accessing operational information in LDAP

Until now, this part of the book has focused on managing the information that resides in an LDAP-enabled directory. At this point, we will shift our focus to managing the server itself.

Not all of the techniques described in this chapter will work in all directories. Information given with each example specifies its requirements.

By the end of this chapter, we will have discussed topics that give you answers to the following questions:

- How do you get server information, such as schemas and available naming contexts, in a programmatic way?

- What is the best way to monitor the server?

- How should the server's replication with other servers best be monitored?

9.1 GETTING SERVER INFORMATION

If you want to write an application that accesses only a single LDAP server within a predefined environment, you can make assumptions about the server's schema and namespace. However, in many real-world situations, you can't make these assumptions. Instead, you ask the server to tell you about its environment and use its response as a guide for accessing it. In this section, we will look at how to use Net::LDAP (introduced in chapter 6) to get this information from the server.

9.1.1 Retrieving available root naming contexts

Before you can use an LDAP server, you need to know the available root naming contexts. Based on information in chapter 3, you know that the root naming context is the top level of the directory. Knowing this helps you determine automatically what you might set a default search base to within your applications. What better way to get started than by looking at a program that can query the server for this information?

The information is contained in an entry at the root of the directory tree. You can get it just as you get any other information from the server—by performing a search. Listing 9.1 shows this particular search. You use the search base of an empty string, a base scope, and a presence filter for the objectclass attribute.

Listing 9.1   get_root.pl

```perl
use Net::LDAP;

$conn = new Net::LDAP("localhost");

$mesg = $conn->search(base=>"", scope=>"base",
                      filter=>"(objectclass=*)");
$entry = $mesg->entry(0);

if ($entry)
{
    $ldif = new Net::LDAP::LDIF("-","w");
    $ldif->write_entry($entry);
    $ldif->done;
}
$conn->unbind;
```

Understanding the code

As usual, you begin by including the Net::LDAP module:

```perl
use Net::LDAP;
```

Next, you open the connection to the server. Be sure to change the parameters if you do not want to aim your requests at an LDAP server running on your local machine:

```perl
$conn = new Net::LDAP("localhost");
```

Now you perform a search on the directory's root entry (" "):

```
$mesg = $conn->search(base=>"", scope=>"base",
                        filter=>"(objectclass=*)");
$entry = $mesg->entry(0);
```

As discussed in chapters 4 and 6, only one entry can be returned on a base scope search. You print the entry's contents now and close the connection:

```
if ($entry)
{
    $ldif = new Net::LDAP::LDIF("-","w");
    $ldif->write_entry($entry);
    $ldif->done;
}
$conn->unbind;
```

The output of listing 9.1 actually gives you more information than you need. If you scan through the output, you'll notice an attribute type called namingContext. The value or values associated with this attribute type should give you a good picture of the top-level namespace provided by the server you queried.

9.1.2 Extracting object class information

Getting schema information is a little more complex than simply retrieving naming context information, because schema information is stored in the directory in a structured format that must be parsed. Recall from chapter 2 that schema information consists of syntax, object class definitions, and attribute type definitions.

Listing 9.2 demonstrates how to extract information about object classes from the server.

Listing 9.2   print_oclass_def.pl

```
use Net::LDAP;

my $conn = new Net::LDAP("localhost");
$conn->bind(dn=>"cn=Admin",password=>"manager");

my $mesg = $conn->search(base=>"cn=schema",scope=>"base",
                        filter=>"(objectclass=*)");
my $entry = $mesg->entry(0);

if (!$entry)
{
    print "Sorry, this server doesn't support schema discovery.\n";
    exit;
}

my @objectclasses = $entry->get_value{"objectclasses"}};

foreach my $oc (@objectclasses)
{
    my ($name, $desc, $sup, $must, $may, @must, @may, $match);
```

```
    if ($oc =~ /NAME '(.+)' DESC '(.*)'/)
    {
        $name = $1;
        if ($2 =~ /\w+/)
        {
            $desc = $2;
        }
    }
    if (grep (/^$name$/i,@ARGV))
    {
        $match = 1;
        if ($oc =~ /SUP (\w+)/)
        {
            $sup = $1;
        }
        if ($oc =~ /MUST [\(']+([$ \w]+)[\)']+/ ||
            $oc =~ /MUST (\w+)/)
        {
            $must = $1;
            $must =~ s/ //g;
            @must = split(/\$/,$must);
        }
        if ($oc =~ /MAY [\(']+([$ \w]+)[\)']+/ ||
            $oc =~ /MAY (\w+)/)
        {
            $may = $1;
            $may =~ s/ //g;
            @may = split(/\$/,$may);
        }
    }
    print "Name:\t$name\n" if ($match || $#ARGV < 0);
    print "Desc:\t$desc\n" if $desc;
    print "Sup:\t$sup\n" if $sup;
    print "Must:\t" . join("\n\t",@must) . "\n" if @must;
    print "May:\t" . join("\n\t",@may) . "\n" if @may;
    print "\n" if ($match);
}

$conn->close;
```

Understanding the code

First you open a connection to the LDAP server:

```
use Net::LDAP;

my $conn = new Net::LDAP("localhost");
$conn->bind(dn=>"cn=Admin",password=>"manager");
```

Now you read the entry at `cn=schema`. If no entry is returned, the server probably doesn't support schema discovery:

```
my $mesg = $conn->search(base=>"cn=schema",scope=>"base",
                         filter=>"(objectclass=*)");

my $entry = $mesg->entry(0);

if (!$entry)
{
    print "Sorry, this server doesn't support schema discovery.\n";
    exit;
}
```

The `objectclasses` attribute that is returned should be multivalued. Each value defines a single object class in the standard format detailed in chapter 1. You put these values into an array called `@objectclasses`. The `foreach` loop then cycles through each value so you can parse them out into a format that you can read without going blind from all the parentheses. You also declare a few of the variables you'll need as you parse a single object class definition:

```
my @objectclasses = $entry->get_value{"objectclasses"}};

foreach my $oc (@objectclasses)
{
    my ($name, $desc, $sup, $must, $may, @must, @may, $match);
```

In this program, you don't really care about the OID associated with the object class. You therefore begin by snatching the object class's name and description. You do this with a few Perl regular expressions:

```
    if ($oc =~ /NAME '(.+)' DESC '(.*)'/)
    {
      $name = $1;
        if ($2 =~ /\w+/)
            {
            $desc = $2;
        }
    }
```

You make this program a little fancy by allowing the person executing it to specify a list of object classes to be returned. Thus if you only want to see the definition for `organization`, you simply specify that when you execute the script. The `grep` expression tries to find the current object class in the list of arguments that you passed to the script:

```
    if (grep (/^$name$/i,@ARGV))
    {
        $match = 1;
```

If the current object class is one for which you want details, you parse out the superior class and the required and permitted attributes in the definition. Once again, this is done with Perl regular expressions. This first segment finds any object class superior to this one:

```
if ($oc =~ /SUP (\w+)/)
{
    $sup = $1;
}
```

Required attributes are specified by the MUST keyword. You parse these out and add them to a list. When parsing MUST and MAY, you need to take into account that each may be single or multivalued:

```
if ($oc =~ /MUST [\(']+([$ \w]+)[\)']+/ ||
    $oc =~ /MUST (\w+)/)
{
    $must = $1;
    $must =~ s/ //g;
    @must = split(/\$/,$must);
}
```

The next segment of code parses out the optional attributes from the definition by looking for the MAY keyword:

```
if ($oc =~ /MAY [\(']+([$ \w]+)[\)']+/ ||
    $oc =~ /MAY (\w+)/)
{
    $may = $1;
    $may =~ s/ //g;
    @may = split(/\$/,$may);
}
}
```

Now that you've completely parsed the line, you can do something useful, like print it in a human-readable format:

```
print "Name:\t$name\n" if ($match || $#ARGV < 0);
print "Desc:\t$desc\n" if $desc;
print "Sup:\t$sup\n" if $sup;
print "Must:\t" . join("\n\t",@must) . "\n" if @must;
print "May:\t" . join("\n\t",@may) . "\n" if @may;
print "\n" if ($match);
}

$conn->close;
```

Using this code, you can take cryptic definitions from an LDAP server and generate human-readable output. You could also use this same code as the basis for generating other types of output, such as XML/DSML or HTML.

9.1.3 Getting attribute type details

Being able to dynamically determine which object classes a server supports is pretty cool. It's almost as cool as knowing the syntax and other details of the attribute types of those object classes. You'll find that information in this section.

Listing 9.3 shows the code for getting attribute type definitions.

Listing 9.3   print_atype_def.pl

```perl
use Net::LDAP;

my $conn = new Net::LDAP("localhost");

my $mesg = $conn->search(base=>"cn=schema",scope=>"base",
                         filter=>"(objectclass=*)");
my $entry = $mesg->entry(0);

if (!$entry)
{
    print "Sorry, this server doesn't support schema discovery.\n";
    exit;
}

my @ldapsyntaxes = $entry->get_value("ldapsyntaxes"};

my (%syntaxes,%rules);

foreach my $ls (@ldapsyntaxes)
{
    $ls =~ /\( ([0-9\.]+) DESC '(.+)'/;
    $syntaxes{$1} = $2;
}

my @matchingrules = $entry->get_value("matchingrules"};

foreach my $mr (@matchingrules)
{
    $mr =~ /\( ([0-9\.]+) NAME '(.+)'/;
    $rules{$1} = $2;
}

my @attributetypes = $entry->get_value(attributetypes"};

foreach my $at (@attributetypes)
{
    my ($name,$desc,$sup,$syntax,$equality,$match,@name,$one_name);

    if ($at =~ /NAME '(\w+)'/ ||
        $at =~ /NAME \( ([\w\;\_\-\' ]+) \)/)
    {
        $name = $1;
        $name =~ s/'//g;
        @name = split(/ /,$name);
    }

    foreach $one_name (@name)
    {
```

```perl
            if (grep (/^$one_name$/i,@ARGV))
            {
                $match = 1;
            }
        }

        if ($match)
        {
            if ($at =~ /DESC '(.+)'/)
            {
                if ($1 =~ /\w+/)
                {
                    $desc = $1;
                }
            }

            if ($at =~ /SYNTAX ([0-9\.]+)/)
            {
                $syntax = $1;
            }

            if ($at =~ /EQUALITY ([0-9\.]+)/)
            {
                $equality = $1;
            }
        }

        print "Name:\t\t$name\n" if ($match || $#ARGV < 0 && $name);
        print "Desc:\t\t$desc\n" if $desc;
        print "Syntax:\t\t" . $syntaxes{$syntax} . "\n" if $syntax;
        print "Equality:\t" . $rules{$equality} . "\n" if $equality;
        print "\n" if ($match);
    }

    $conn->close;
```

Understanding the code

Your first order of business is opening a connection to the LDAP server:

```perl
use Net::LDAP;

my $conn = new Net::LDAP("localhost");
```

As in the previous example, you do a search on the cn=schema entry. This entry normally holds all schema information:

```perl
my $mesg = $conn->search(base=>"cn=schema",scope=>"base",
                         filter=>"(objectclass=*)");
my $entry = $mesg->entry(0);
```

If no entry is returned, the server you queried does not support schema discovery, or perhaps the entry is located elsewhere in the directory tree:

```
if (!$entry)
{
    print "Sorry, this server doesn't support schema discovery.\n";
    exit;
}
```

Before you rush for the attribute type definitions, you want to get the list of supported syntaxes from the server. Otherwise you'll only be able to display the OID for the syntaxes later in the program:

```
my @ldapsyntaxes = $entry->get_value("ldapsyntaxes"};

my (%syntaxes,%rules);

foreach my $ls (@ldapsyntaxes)
{
    $ls =~ /\( ([0-9\.]+) DESC '(.+)'/;
    $syntaxes{$1} = $2;
}
```

Similarly, you need to find the matching rules supported by this server. The server uses the matching rules to find attributes within an entry that match particular search filters:

```
my @matchingrules = $entry->get_value("matchingrules"};

foreach my $mr (@matchingrules)
{
    $mr =~ /\( ([0-9\.]+) NAME '(.+)'/;
    $rules{$1} = $2;
}
```

Finally, you get around to retrieving the multivalued `attributetypes` attribute from this entry. The format of this attribute is the same one mentioned in chapter 2 and defined in the LDAP standards:

```
my @attributetypes = $entry->get_value(attributetypes"};

foreach my $at (@attributetypes)
{
    my ($name,$desc,$sup,$syntax,$equality,$match,@name,$one_name);
```

Next, you basically do the same thing you did in the object class example (listing 9.2). The method for matching command-line arguments is a little more sophisticated because an attribute can have multiple names:

```
    if ($at =~ /NAME '(\w+)'/ ||
        $at =~ /NAME \( ([\w\;\_\-\' ]+) \)/)
    {
        $name = $1;
        $name =~ s/'//g;
        @name = split(/ /,$name);
    }
```

```
    foreach $one_name (@name)
    {
        if (grep (/^$one_name$/i,@ARGV))
        {
            $match = 1;
        }
    }

    if ($match)
    {
```

If match is true, you parse this attribute type. Let's begin with the long description, if the type has one defined:

```
        if ($at =~ /DESC '(.+)'/)
        {
            if ($1 =~ /\w+/)
            {
                $desc = $1;
            }
        }
```

The SYNTAX keyword marks the start of the syntax this attribute type follows. The format of the syntax is its dot-separated OID:

```
        if ($at =~ /SYNTAX ([0-9\.]+)/)
        {
            $syntax = $1;
        }
```

In this script you also parse out the EQUALITY matching rules that apply to this type. Other matching rules may exist, but this should give you a good idea how parsing can be done:

```
        if ($at =~ /EQUALITY ([0-9\.]+)/)
        {
            $equality = $1;
        }
    }
```

Everything is parsed, so it is now simply a matter of doing something with all this information. In this example, you print it to standard output:

```
    print "Name:\t\t$name\n" if ($match || $#ARGV < 0 && $name);
    print "Desc:\t\t$desc\n" if $desc;
    print "Syntax:\t\t" . $syntaxes{$syntax} . "\n" if $syntax;
    print "Equality:\t" . $rules{$equality} . "\n" if $equality;
    print "\n" if ($match);
}

$conn->close;
```

Combined with the previous example for object classes (listing 9.2), you could easily change this code to output HTML or other formats to provide a simple schema browser.

9.2 MONITORING WITH LDAP

Many servers offer information about the LDAP server through a special read-only LDAP entry, usually called `cn=monitor`. It is possible to get both the monitor distinguished name and entry with Net::LDAP. Such information can easily be used to watch a server over a period of time; doing so will let you adopt proactive measures to correct any potential problems.

> **NOTE**   The examples in this section cannot be used with Microsoft Active Directory, because the monitor entry used in this example is not a standard. Rather, it's a convention followed by a number of LDAP vendors.

Let's look at some examples of how you can script this kind of activity.

9.2.1 Getting the monitor's name

Rather than assume the monitor's distinguished name is `cn=monitor`, new servers include information in the root that will give you this information. As in listing 9.1, you look into the server's root entry to find the location of the monitor entry.

Let's begin by opening a connection to the server and searching for the root entry:

```
my $conn = new Net::LDAP("localhost");

my $mesg = $conn->search(base=>"",scope=>"base",
                         filter=>"objectclass=*");
my $entry = $mesg->entry(0);
```

If the entry doesn't exist, you use a default of `cn=monitor`, which exists on many servers:

```
if (!$entry) {
      $monitordn = "cn=monitor";
} else {
      $monitordn = $entry->get_value("monitor");
}
```

Once the monitor entry is found or set, you can begin to retrieve some of the server's basic operational information.

9.2.2 Reading the monitor information

So far, you've retrieved the monitor's distinguished name. It's time to put that information to good use. If you had simply listed the contents of the monitor entry, it might look something like this:

```
dn: cn=monitor
objectclass: top
objectclass: extensibleObject
```

```
cn: monitor
version: Netscape-Directory/4.13 B01.023.0000
threads: 20
connection: 576:20010713172253Z:2:1::cn=Directory Manager
currentconnections: 1
totalconnections: 1
dtablesize: 2003
readwaiters: 0
opsinitiated: 2
opscompleted: 1
entriessent: 0
bytessent: 14
currenttime: 20010713172253Z
starttime: 20010712012437Z
nbackends: 1
dataversion: cdonley-t21.:31389 020010712012436 0
ldapserverconfigdn: cn=ldap://:31389,dc=cdonley-t21,dc=
backendmonitordn: cn=monitor,cn=ldbm
```

Instead of dumping information, you will retrieve important information and use it
to determine whether to generate an alert. Listing 9.4 offers a basic example that
reads the monitor information from the server once and reports when the number of
concurrent connections exceeds 100.

Listing 9.4   get_monitor.pl

```perl
use Net::LDAP;

my $conn = new Net::LDAP("localhost");

my $entry = $conn->search(base=>"",scope=>"base",
                          filter=>"(objectclass=*)");

my $monitordn;

if (!$entry) {
     $monitordn = "cn=monitor";
} else {
     $monitordn = $entry->{"monitor"}[0];
}

$mesg = $conn->search(base=>$monitordn,scope=>"base",
                      Filter=>"objectclass=*");
my $monitor_entry = $mesg->entry(0);

print "Connections: " .
    $monitor_entry->get_value("connections") . "\n";

if ($monitor_entry->get_value("connections") > 100) {
    print "Warning: More than 100 concurrent connections.\n";
}
```

Understanding the code

After doing basic setup, the code needs to read the monitor once and spew out its contents:

```
$mesg = $conn->search(base=>$monitordn,scope=>"base",
                              filter=>"(objectclass=*)");
my $monitor_entry = $mesg->entry(0);

my $ldif = new Net::LDAP::LDIF("-","w");
$ldif->write_entry($monitor_entry);
$ldif->done;
```

Pretty easy, eh? This code gives output similar to the dump of cn=monitor shown earlier in this section. However, because you're considering doing some automated monitoring, perhaps you should output only the attribute you care about in a way that can be easily evaluated. You can look at the number of connections and print that information to the standard output. Simply replace the three previous lines as follows:

```
$mesg = $conn->search(base=>$monitordn,scope=>"base",
                            filter=>"objectclass=*");
my $monitor_entry = $mesg->entry(0);

print "Connections: " .
    $monitor_entry->get_value("connections") . "\n";
```

Or, simpler yet, you can have the program print an alarm if the connection count is over 100. Here you replace the last print statement with an expression to perform this evaluation:

```
if ($monitor_entry->get_value("connections") > 100) {
    print "Warning: More than 100 concurrent connections.\n";
}
```

9.2.3 Polling the monitor entry

Now let's see how you can vary your approach. You will either query the monitor once each time your script is run, as shown previously, or poll the monitor at a specified interval from within the script. In the latter case, you can wrap the core of the previous example within a while loop with a wait between queries (see listing 9.5).

> **Listing 9.5   poll_monitor.pl**

```
use Net::LDAP;

my $conn = new Net::LDAP("localhost");

my $entry = $conn->search(base=>"",scope=>"base",
                            filter=>"(objectclass=*)");

my $monitordn;

if (!$entry) {
    $monitordn = "cn=monitor";
} else {
```

```
    $monitordn = $entry->{"monitor"}[0];
}

while (1) {
    $mesg = $conn->search(base=>$monitordn,scope=>"base",
                          filter=>"objectclass=*");
    my $monitor_entry = $mesg->entry(0);

    print "Connections: " .
    $monitor_entry->get_value("connections") . "\n";

    if ($monitor_entry->get_value("connections") > 100) {
        print "Warning: More than 100 concurrent connections.\n";
    }
    sleep 30;
}
```

The bolded lines in listing 9.5 show how you can add this polling capability to the previous example. When run, the program will continue forever, checking the monitor entry every 30 seconds.

9.3   TESTING REPLICATION

In chapter 8, we discussed synchronization and migration techniques. We also mentioned replication, although each LDAP implementation handles it differently.

It is possible to test replication in a generic fashion through the use of a synthetic transaction. To test whether entries are being replicated on another server, you generate a dummy entry and store it on the master. After waiting a specified time period for replication, you query all the replicas to see if the change made it.

This approach allows you to ensure that replication takes place within an acceptable window of time. Such tests are important in an environment where password and policy changes must be propagated quickly to allow for proper application behavior.

Listing 9.6 shows a script that can perform this type of basic replication monitoring.

Listing 9.6   test_replication.pl

```
use Net::LDAP;
use Net::LDAP::Entry;

@replicas = ("server-a","server-b","server-c");

$master = "masterhostname";

$conn = new Net::LDAP($master_name);
$conn->bind(dn=>"cn=Admin",password=>"password");

$testentry_name =
    "cn=Sam Jones, ou=Test Branch, dc=domain, dc=com";

$master->delete($testentry_name);

$testentry = new Net::LDAP::Entry();
```

```
$testentry->dn($testentry_name);
$testentry->add("objectclass","inetOrgPerson");
$testentry->add("cn","Sam Jones");
$testentry->add("sn","Jones");

$conn->add($testentry);

sleep 10;

for ( $i = 1; $i <= $#replicas; $i++) {
    $replica_name = $replicas[$i];
    $replica = new Net::LDAP($replica_name);

    $mesg = $replica->search(base=>$testentry_name,scope=>"base",
                             filter=>"(objectclass=*)");
    $entry = $mesg->entry(0);

    if (!$entry) {
        print "$replica_name FAILED!\n";
    } else {
        print "$replica_name PASSED!\n";
    }
    $replica->unbind();
}

$conn->delete($testentry_name);

$conn->unbind();
```

Understanding the code

In the first few lines, you define the list of replicas and the name of your master server:

```
@replicas = ("server-a","server-b","server-c");
$master = "masterhostname";
```

Next you open a connection to the master server using an account with sufficient privileges to add an entry to the directory:

```
$conn = new Net::LDAP($master_name);
$conn->bind(dn=>"cn=Admin",password=>"password");
```

The entry you add should not be put in a branch of the directory tree that contains live data. It should, however, be in a branch of the tree that is part of the replication agreement:

```
$testentry_name =
    "cn=Sam Jones, ou=Test Branch, dc=domain, dc=com";
```

Before adding the entry to the server, you should first delete the entry if it already exists. It shouldn't exist, but there is the possibility that the script or final delete operation failed in a previous run:

```
$master->delete($testentry_name);
```

Now you create a dummy entry with the minimum amount of information. You may also want to add an additional attribute for use as a time stamp. Such a time stamp will ensure that you are looking at the same version of the entry:

```
$testentry = new Net::LDAP::Entry();
$testentry->dn($testentry_name);
$testentry->add("objectclass","inetOrgPerson");
$testentry->add("cn","Sam Jones");
$testentry->add("sn","Jones");
```

Finally, you add the entry to the directory server and wait a bit for replication to take place. The `sleep` function waits for the number of seconds you specify. In this case, you wait 10 seconds:

```
$conn->add($testentry);

sleep 10;
```

After this wait, you are ready to search each of your replicas. You begin by looping through each replica and opening a connection:

```
for ( $i = 0; $i <= $#replicas; $i++) {
    $replica_name = $replicas[$i];
    $replica = new Net::LDAP($replica_name);
```

Using a search scope of `base` and the test entry's name as the search base, you do a simple search in an attempt to retrieve the entry.

```
    $mesg = $replica->search(base=>$testentry_name,scope=>"base",
                             filter=>"(objectclass=*)");
    $entry = $mesg->entry(0);
```

If the entry doesn't exist, replication has not yet taken place and there may be a problem. If it does exist, the test has passed:

```
    if (!$entry) {
        print "$replica_name FAILED!\n";
    } else {
        print "$replica_name PASSED!\n";
    }
```

You are finished with this replica, so you unbind from it and continue to the next:

```
    $replica->unbind();
}
```

At the end of the test, you need to delete the entry from the master and unbind. Doing so ensures that the directory is in a good state to run this test again:

```
$conn->delete($testentry_name);

$conn->unbind();
```

9.4 SUMMARY

You can easily access important operational information with many commercial LDAP servers. All LDAPv3-compliant directory servers offer the ability to access server information, including available schemas and root-naming contexts, via the LDAP protocol. This ability is important in creating tools that can work from server to server without significant changes. In this chapter, we looked at examples for retrieving the naming context, extracting object class information, and getting attribute definitions.

Many servers also offer the ability to monitor activity via LDAP. We looked at a few examples of getting and reading monitor information.

In a multiserver environment, it is often important to go beyond what the server provides and perform synthetic transactions to test the entire directory environment. We discussed how to test the replication process.

Chapter 10 will move from discussing operational information to showcasing detailed information about DSML and its use from Perl. The chapter will allow you to tie together the information you've picked up so far with an emerging new standard for representing and sharing directory information.

CHAPTER 10

DSML:
getting under the hood

In chapter 5, we took a first look at DSML and how it can be used as an interchange format. This chapter examines DSML in more detail, providing a deeper view into how you can use DSML programmatically from Perl.

At the end of this chapter, you will better understand the answers to the following questions:

- How can DSML be parsed using the Simple API for XML (SAX)?

- What is the best way to create DSML documents?

- How can DSML be transformed using other standards, such as XSLT?

10.1 DSML PARSING WITH SAX

In chapter 5, you saw what DSML looks like. Now we will explore how to formulate a strategy for working with DSML documents.

If you are familiar with Perl, your first thought may be to use regular expressions to parse out elements, attributes, and characters. Although this approach is possible, you will be on a path toward reinventing the wheel.

In addition to a Perl module called XML::Parser, which will help you parse your XML documents, there are two standard APIs that are well documented and easy to use. One API DOM), is a full-featured interface for dealing with entire documents. The other API is SAX, which is useful for parsing most XML documents.

Both of these APIs are available in many development environments, including Perl, C, and Java. Their use in these environments is identical in many ways. In this chapter, we will deal exclusively with the Perl version of the SAX API, which can be found on the Comprehensive Perl Archive Network (CPAN; http://www.cpan.org/) in the `libxml-perl` package.

10.1.1 Basics of parsing XML with SAX

PerlSAX, as the SAX parser for Perl is known, may seem relatively useless out of the box. In fact, given a document implementing DSML or other XML document types, PerlSAX does little more than tell you whether the document has structural problems, such as improper element nesting. Looking beyond its simplicity, the important thing about PerlSAX is it allows you to create custom handlers that can perform whatever operations are necessary to use XML elements within a particular application.

10.1.2 A simple XML parser handler

The handler in listing 10.1 takes input from the PerlSAX parser and prints the name and attribute of each new element, any character data, and the name of each ending element.

> **Listing 10.1   SimpleHandler.pm**

```perl
package SimpleHandler;

sub new {
    my ($type) = @_;
    return bless {}, $type;
}

sub start_element {
    my ($self, $element) = @_;

    print "Start Element: " . $element->{Name} . "\n";

    my %attr_hash = %{$element->{Attributes}};

    foreach my $attr (keys %attr_hash)
    {
```

```perl
        print "Attribute: " . $attr .
            " = " . $attr_hash{$attr} . "\n";
    }
}

sub end_element {
    my ($self, $element) = @_;

    print "End element: $element->{Name}\n";
}

sub characters {
    my ($self, $characters) = @_;

    print "Characters: $characters->{Data}\n";
}

1;
```

Understanding the code

The package directive allows you to start a new Perl class:

```perl
package SimpleHandler;
```

The new() method creates a new object that is an instance of the SimpleHandler Perl class. You do not initialize any other structures:

```perl
sub new {
    my ($type) = @_;
    return bless {}, $type;
}
```

The variable $element is a hash reference containing the information about a new element. It is passed in by the SAX parser whenever the parser encounters a new element:

```perl
sub start_element {
    my ($self, $element) = @_;
```

In the next line, you simply print the name of the new element:

```perl
    print "Start Element: " . $element->{Name} . "\n";
```

The Attributes key of the $element hash reference includes a hash reference containing all the attributes associated with this element. As we will discuss shortly, XML attributes are different from LDAP attributes. The start_element() method is called by the parser whenever it sees a new element. As we already mentioned, the variable $element is a hash reference that contains two keys: Name and Attributes. The following code simply prints the name of each new element and cycles through and prints the attributes it contains:

```
    my %attr_hash = %{$element->{Attributes}};

    foreach my $attr (keys %attr_hash)
    {
        print "Attribute: " . $attr .
            " = " . $attr_hash{$attr} . "\n";
    }
}
```

The end_element() method is called when the parser meets a closing tag for a particular element—</dsml:dsml>, for example. The $element variable's Name key tells you which element has ended:

```
sub end_element {
    my ($self, $element) = @_;

    print "End element: $element->{Name}\n";
}
```

In this handler, you print the name of the element that ends:

```
sub characters {
    my ($self, $characters) = @_;

    print "Characters: $characters->{Data}\n";
}
```

The parser uses the character() method in your handler whenever characters are found outside angle brackets. The text can be found in the passed hash reference under the Data key. For example, in the janet.xml file you created in chapter 5, the text *Janet Smith* found between the start and end tags for the dsml:value element would be sent here.

In order to complete this package, you return a positive result in the main portion of your package outside the various subroutines:

```
1;
```

10.1.3   Parsing a simple document

Before you can use the SimpleHandler class created in the previous section, you need to create a program to call the SAX parser; listing 10.2 shows such a program. The parser also needs to know that it should use your particular handler.

Listing 10.2   SimpleHandler.pl

```
use XML::Parser::PerlSAX;
use SimpleHandler;

my $handler = new SimpleHandler;

my $parser = new XML::Parser::PerlSAX( Handler => $handler );

my $xmlfile = $ARGV[0];
$parser->parse(Source => { SystemId => $xmlfile });
```

First you use both the SAX parser and your simple handler:

```
use XML::Parser::PerlSAX;
use SimpleHandler;
```

Next you create a new instance of the `SimpleHandler` class created in the previous example as well as an instance of the PerlSAX parser that knows to use your handler:

```
my $handler = new SimpleHandler;

my $parser = new XML::Parser::PerlSAX( Handler => $handler );
```

You can now invoke the `parse()` method on the PerlSAX parser. In this example, you have it read the first argument passed to your program (`$ARGV[0]`):

```
my $xmlfile = $ARGV[0];
$parser->parse(Source => { SystemId => $xmlfile });
```

If you now run this program, giving it the path to your janet.xml file, you should see the following output:

```
Start Element: dsml:dsml
Attribute: xmlns:dsml = http://www.dsml.org/DSML
Characters:

Characters:
Start Element: dsml:directory-entries
Characters:

Characters:
Start Element: dsml:entry
Attribute: dn = cn=Janet Smith,dc=xyz,dc=com
Characters:

Characters:
Start Element: dsml:objectclass
Characters:

Characters:
Start Element: dsml:oc-value
Characters: top
End element: dsml:oc-value
Characters:
```

The output will continue through the end of the file if everything works. Remember that the `Attribute` lines in this example contain XML attributes, so don't be confused by the dn = cn=Janet Smith, dc=xyz, dc=com attribute—it does not mean dn is a directory entry attribute in LDAP.

10.1.4   PerlSAX's built-in error checking

As we mentioned previously, one of the benefits of using XML is the ability to avoid writing code to detect potential errors in the input file. For example, let's change the following line in janet.xml:

```
</dsml:directory-entries>
```

Delete the *y* in *directory*, changing the line to the following, and rerun the Simple-Handler.pl program:

```
</dsml:director-entries>
```

The parser should output an error message looking similar to this:

```
mismatched tag at line 11, column 3, byte 424 at
   .../XML/Parser.pm line 168
```

PerlSAX and the Expat parser on which it is built do not support document checking based on document type definitions (DTDs). So, if you also misspell the starting tag for the `dsml:directory-entries` element as follows, the parser will not complain:

```
<dsml:director-entries>
....some entries....
</dsml:director-entries>
```

Parsers available in other languages, such as IBM's XML4J parser for Java, will detect this error if they're told to check against the DSML definition. Without this functionality, you must do your own checking.

10.2 PARSING DSML INTO A PERL OBJECT

Although the `SimpleHandler` class is useful to understand how PerlSAX handlers work, the ability to print the elements in an XML file does not help you in your quest to do something useful with DSML. Let's leverage both Net::LDAP and PerlSAX to create a handler that will read a DSML file containing entries, making those entries available as Net::LDAP `Entry` objects that can be updated in the directory. The functionality you will use from Net::LDAP was explored in chapter 6. Listing 10.3 presents the entire handler; the following sections explain the code.

Listing 10.3   DSMLHandler.pm

```perl
use strict;

package DSMLHandler;
$VERSION = "1.00";

my @entries = ();
my $current_entry;
my @where = ();
my $cur_attr;

my $DSML_DSML = 0;
my $DSML_DIRECTORY_ENTRIES = 1;
my $DSML_ENTRY = 2;
my $DSML_OBJECTCLASS = 3;
my $DSML_OC_VALUE = 4;
my $DSML_ATTR = 5;
```

```perl
my $DSML_VALUE = 6;

sub new {
    my ($type) = @_;
    return bless {}, $type;
}

sub start_element {
    my ($self, $element) = @_;
    my %attr_hash = %{$element->{Attributes}};
    my $cur_tag = $where[$#where];

    $_ = $element->{Name};
    if (/dsml:entry/ && $cur_tag == $DSML_DIRECTORY_ENTRIES) {
        $current_entry = new Net::LDAP::Entry();
        # We can use the DN XML attribute to set the DN for this entry.
        $current_entry->dn($attr_hash{"dn"});
        push(@where,$DSML_ENTRY);
    } elsif (/dsml:oc-value/ && $cur_tag == $DSML_OBJECTCLASS) {
        push(@where,$DSML_OC_VALUE);
    } elsif (/dsml:objectclass/ && $cur_tag == $DSML_ENTRY) {
        push(@where,$DSML_OBJECTCLASS);
    } elsif (/dsml:attr/ && $cur_tag == $DSML_ENTRY) {
        # Here we set the current attribute for later use
        push(@where,$DSML_ATTR);
        $cur_attr = $attr_hash{"name"};
    } elsif (/dsml:value/ && $cur_tag == $DSML_ATTR) {
        push(@where,$DSML_VALUE);
    } elsif (/dsml:dsml/) {
        push(@where,$DSML_DSML);
    } elsif (/dsml:directory-entries/ && $cur_tag == $DSML_DSML) {
        push(@where,$DSML_DIRECTORY_ENTRIES);
    }
}

sub end_element {
    my ($self, $element) = @_;
    if ($element->{Name} =~ /^dsml/) {
        if ($element->{Name} =~ /dsml:entry/) {
            push(@entries,$current_entry);
        }
        pop(@where);
    }
}

sub characters {
    my ($self, $characters) = @_;

    my $cur_tag = $where[$#where];

    if ($cur_tag == $DSML_OC_VALUE) {
        $current_entry->add("objectclass",$characters->{"Data"});
    } elsif ($cur_tag == $DSML_VALUE) {
        $current_entry->add($cur_attr,$characters->{"Data"});
    }
```

```
}
sub get_entries {
    return @entries;
}

1;
```

◼

10.2.1 Beginnings of a useful DSML parser handler

As usual, you begin your new handler class with the `package` directive. Call this class `DSMLHandler`:

```
package DSMLHandler;
```

You need to keep state, because you will potentially be parsing multiple entries and need to know where you are at all times. The `@entries` array contains all the entries you parse out of this file. `$current_entry` holds the current entry, if there is one. You use the `@where` array as a stack containing the elements above you in the document tree. Finally, you need to track the current attribute when adding new attribute values; you use the scalar `$cur_attr` for this purpose:

```
my @entries = ();
my $current_entry;
my @where = ();
my $cur_attr;
```

For simplicity, you define constants for each of the major elements you plan to encounter:

```
my $DSML_DSML = 0;
my $DSML_DIRECTORY_ENTRIES = 1;
my $DSML_ENTRY = 2;
my $DSML_OBJECTCLASS = 3;
my $DSML_OC_VALUE = 4;
my $DSML_ATTR = 5;
my $DSML_VALUE = 6;
```

You use the same constructor as in the `SimpleHandler` class. If you needed to initialize any variables, you might do so here as well:

```
sub new {
    my ($type) = @_;
    return bless {}, $type;
}
```

This code allows you to create new `DSMLHandler` objects in Perl. The constructor requires two parameters and returns a new, empty handler. It will be called directly only by the SAX parser.

10.2.2 Handling elements in the DSML file

The `start_element()` method looks rather complicated, but is much simpler than it appears. You begin by putting XML attributes, if any, into the `%attr_hash` hash. The current element is then located at the end of your `@where` array and placed into `$cur_tag`:

```
sub start_element {
    my ($self, $element) = @_;
    my %attr_hash = %{$element->{Attributes}};
    my $cur_tag = $where[$#where];
```

Next you check to see what the previous element is (`$cur_tag`) and determine the name of the current element. If both criteria match, you add the current element to the `@where` stack. If there are XML attributes, you handle them appropriately:

```
    $_ = $element->{Name};
    if (/dsml:entry/ && $cur_tag == $DSML_DIRECTORY_ENTRIES) {
        $current_entry = new Net::LDAP::Entry();
        # We can use the DN XML attribute to set the DN for this entry.
        $current_entry->dn($attr_hash{"dn"});
        push(@where,$DSML_ENTRY);
    } elsif (/dsml:oc-value/ && $cur_tag == $DSML_OBJECTCLASS) {
        push(@where,$DSML_OC_VALUE);
    } elsif (/dsml:objectclass/ && $cur_tag == $DSML_ENTRY) {
        push(@where,$DSML_OBJECTCLASS);
    } elsif (/dsml:attr/ && $cur_tag == $DSML_ENTRY) {
        push(@where,$DSML_ATTR);
        # Here we set the current attribute for later use
        $cur_attr = $attr_hash{"name"};
    } elsif (/dsml:value/ && $cur_tag == $DSML_ATTR) {
        push(@where,$DSML_VALUE);
    } elsif (/dsml:dsml/) {
        push(@where,$DSML_DSML);
    } elsif (/dsml:directory-entries/ && $cur_tag == $DSML_DSML) {
        push(@where,$DSML_DIRECTORY_ENTRIES);
    }
}
```

While you check tags, you take a shortcut in the `end_element()` method. Here you check to see that the name of the ending element begins with `dsml`. Those elements that match will cause a value to be removed from the `@where` stack. If you are ending an entry, you add the entry to the `@entries` array:

```
sub end_element {
    my ($self, $element) = @_;
    if ($element->{Name} =~ /^dsml/) {
        if ($element->{Name} =~ /dsml:entry/) {
```

```
                push(@entries,$current_entry);
        }
        pop(@where);
    }
}
```

With both the start and end tags handled appropriately, you are almost finished.

10.2.3   Extracting characters between start and end tags

You only care if you receive characters when the current element is either dsml:
oc-value or dsml:value. In both cases, you add a new value to the appropriate
attribute within the current Entry object:

```
sub characters {
    my ($self, $characters) = @_;

    my $cur_tag = $where[$#where];

    if ($cur_tag == $DSML_OC_VALUE) {
        $current_entry->add("objectclass",$characters->{"Data"});
    } elsif ($cur_tag == $DSML_VALUE) {
        $current_entry->add($cur_attr,$characters->{"Data"});
    }
}
```

You can complete your class by adding a method that allows people to get the
@entries array after parsing the DSML file. As usual, you also return 1 at the end
of the package file to indicate that the class has loaded properly:

```
sub get_entries {
    return @entries;
}

1;
```

10.2.4   Preparing to use DSMLHandler

You have now created a fully usable SAX handler for converting DSML into
Net::LDAP::Entry objects that can be used directly with the Net::LDAP module.
With the DSMLHandler created, you are about ready to parse your first DSML file
into a useful Perl object. First, you can do a simple test to see if it works properly.
That test involves invoking the parser with your handler, and then cycling through
each of the returned Entry objects, printing each in LDIF format.

10.2.5   Invoking the SAX parser using DSMLHandler

Your next order of business is to create a new script that invokes the parser using your
handler. Listing 10.4 shows such an example.

Listing 10.4   testdsml.pl

```
use XML::Parser::PerlSAX;
use Net::LDAP;
use DSMLHandler;

my $handler = new DSMLHandler;
my $parser = new XML::Parser::PerlSAX( Handler => $handler );

my $xmlfile = $ARGV[0];
$parser->parse(Source => { SystemId => $xmlfile });
my @entries = $handler->get_entries();

my $conn = new Net::LDAP("localhost");
$conn->bind("cn=admin","password");
```

You begin, as usual, by using the necessary modules. In this example, you include
both the PerlSAX parser and the DSMLHandler class you just created:

```
use XML::Parser::PerlSAX;
use DSMLHandler;
```

Next you create a new instance of both your DSMLHandler and the parser. As in the
SimpleHandler, you use the input filename specified as an argument to this program and invoke the parser on the referenced file:

```
my $handler = new DSMLHandler;
my $parser = new XML::Parser::PerlSAX( Handler => $handler );

my $xmlfile = $ARGV[0];
$parser->parse(Source => { SystemId => $xmlfile });
```

Now that the file has been parsed, you can call the get_entries() method on
your handler to retrieve all the entries parsed from the input file. You then loop
through each of the Entry objects, calling the printLDIF() method on them to
do the dirty work of displaying the entry's LDIF representation:

```
my @entries = $handler->get_entries();

foreach my $entry (@entries) {
    $entry->printLDIF();
}
```

If you run the test program, passing your janet.xml file from chapter 5, you should
see the following results:

```
dn: cn=Janet Smith,dc=xyz,dc=com
objectclass: top
objectclass: person
cn: Janet Smith
sn: Smith
```

If you were importing entries from DSML, you could modify your test program slightly. The bold lines in listing 10.5 for testdsml2.pl show how you can use Net::LDAP to add the entry to the directory.

Listing 10.5   testdsml2.pl

```perl
use XML::Parser::PerlSAX;
use Net::LDAP;
use DSMLHandler;

my $handler = new DSMLHandler;
my $parser = new XML::Parser::PerlSAX( Handler => $handler );

my $xmlfile = $ARGV[0];
$parser->parse(Source => { SystemId => $xmlfile });
my @entries = $handler->get_entries();

my $conn = new Net::LDAP("localhost");
$conn->bind("cn=admin","password");

foreach my $entry (@entries) {
    print "Adding Entry: " . $entry->dn() . "\n";
    $conn->add($entry);
}
```

Why would you want to add these DSML entries to the directory? After all, they probably came from a directory, right?

There are many reasons, but one is to share information across organizational boundaries. This ability is especially useful because of DSML's ability to handle schemas in addition to entry data, as you learned in chapter 5. Such functionality makes it possible to safely share a subset of directory information plus metadata that provides the context necessary to use that information without forcing a direct-connect or highly invasive synchronization model.

10.3   GENERATING DSML

You can generate DSML two ways. The first is simply to write code that sequentially generates the appropriate XML tags. The other is to manipulate the DOM tree and then print the contents of the tree. The DOM tree is the hierarchy of XML attributes that can be manipulated using the XML DOM APIs.

For most simple scripts, the first approach is the way to go. However, applications that constantly update a DSML document may be better off using DOM, which allows the nodes in the XML document to be manipulated more freely.

10.3.1   Writing directory entries

To better understand how a DSML document can be created, let's walk through the creation of a DSML document containing an LDAP entry. Listing 10.6 shows the script. You'll use Net::LDAP to query the directory; the DSML structure will be generated manually using `print` statements.

Listing 10.6   entryToDSML.pl

```perl
use Net::LDAP;
use Net::LDAP::Entry;

$conn = new Net::LDAP("localhost");

$mesg = $conn->search(base=>"dc=xyz,dc=com",scope=>"sub",
                      filter=>"(sn=Smith)");

print "<dsml:dsml xmlns:dsml=\"http://www.dsml.org/DSML\">\n";
print "  <dsml:dsml-entries>\n";

for ($i = 0; $i = $mesg->count; $i++) {
    $entry = $mesg->entry($i);

    print "    <dsml:entry dn=\"" . $entry->dn() . "\">\n";
    print "      <dsml:objectclass>\n";

    foreach $oclass ($entry->get_value("objectclass")) {
        print "        <dsml:oc-value>" . $oclass .
            "</dsml:oc-value>\n";
    }
    print "      </dsml:objectclass>\n";

    foreach $attr ($entry->attributes) {
        if ($attr !~ /objectclass/i) {
            print "      <dsml:attr name=\"" . $attr . "\">\n";
            @vals = $entry->get_value($attr);
            foreach $val (@vals) {
                print "        <dsml:value>" . $val .
                    "</dsml:value>\n";
            }
            print "      </dsml:attr>\n";
        }
    }
    print "    </dsml:entry>\n";
}

print "  </dsml:directory-entries>\n";
print "</dsml:dsml>\n";
```

As expected, the following search returns any entry with the last name Smith within the dc=xyz,dc=com subtree. The first returned entry is placed in the $entry variable:

```perl
$conn = new Net::LDAP("localhost");

$mesg = $conn->search(base=>"dc=xyz,dc=com",scope=>"sub",
                      filter=>"(sn=Smith)");
```

The line that follows is needed at the beginning of the DSML file to indicate which type of XML document you are producing. It also provides a URL pointing to where the document's definition can be found:

```
print "<dsml:dsml xmlns:dsml=\"http://www.dsml.org/DSML\">\n";
```

Because you are creating LDAP entries, not schemas, you need to indicate the start of your entries with the dsml:dsml-entries tag. You can then begin cycling through each of the returned entries:

```
print " <dsml:dsml-entries>\n";

for ($i = 0; $i = $mesg->count; $i++) {
    $entry = $mesg->entry($i);
```

The entry's distinguished name is published as part of the dsml:entry element. This indicates the start of a DSML entry:

```
    print "    <dsml:entry dn=\"" . $entry->dn() . "\">\n";
```

In DSML, the values of the objectclass attribute are separated from the others. These values are instead wrapped within dsml:oc-value tags within the dsml:objectclass section of the entry:

```
    print "      <dsml:objectclass>\n";

    foreach $oclass ($entry->get_value("objectclass")) {
        print "        <dsml:oc-value>" . $oclass .
            "</dsml:oc-value>\n";
    }
    print "      </dsml:objectclass>\n";
```

Each LDAP attribute type, with the exception of the objectclass attribute, needs to be printed within a dsml:attr element. In the second line that follows, you ensure that you print only attributes other than the entry's objectclass:

```
    foreach $attr ($entry->attributes) {
        if ($attr !~ /objectclass/i) {
            print "      <dsml:attr name=\"" . $attr . "\">\n";
            @vals = $entry->get_value($attr);
```

The attribute values are wrapped within individual dsml:value tags. DSML, like LDAP, allows for multiple values for each attribute:

```
            foreach $val (@vals) {
                print "        <dsml:value>" . $val .
                    "</dsml:value>\n";
            }
            print "      </dsml:attr>\n";
        }
    }
```

At the end of each entry, you need to end the dsml:entry element:

```
    print "    </dsml:entry>\n";
}
```

When you are finished processing all entries, you print the end tags to note the end of both the list of entries and the DSML file:

```
print "  </dsml:directory-entries>\n";
print "</dsml:dsml>\n";
```

When run, the script in listing 10.6 prints out any number of entries returned from the LDAP server as a set of DSML-formatted entries in a single DSML document.

10.3.2 Converting RFC-style LDAP schemas to DSML LDAP schemas

In the previous example, you included only entry information in your DSML output. This is fine, as long as the recipient of the DSML document knows the schema you are using. In fact, even without knowing the LDAP schema you are using, the recipient could make some use of the DSML document, such as translating it for printout in a more human-readable format.

However, if you want to include the schema, you have work to do. The schema is commonly defined in standards using a fairly compressed format described in RFC 2252.

Here is an example of what the person object class looks like in this format:

```
( 2.5.6.6 NAME 'person' SUP top STRUCTURAL MUST ( sn $ cn )
    MAY ( userPassword $ telephoneNumber $ seeAlso
    $ description ) )
```

This code contains all the information related to the object class described in chapter 2, including OID, class name, superior class, type of class, and required and allowed attributes.

A similar format is defined for LDAP attribute types. The following is an example of what the telephoneNumber attribute looks like in this format:

```
( 2.5.4.20 NAME 'telephoneNumber' EQUALITY telephoneNumberMatch
    SUBSTR telephoneNumberSubstringsMatch
    SYNTAX 1.3.6.1.4.1.1466.115.121.1.50{32} )
```

DSML, as you've seen, uses a different format for representing both of these schema elements. Therefore, if you want to include schema information in your DSML documents, you need to convert from these RFC-style definitions to DSML style.

10.3.3 Conversion example for object classes

Because you will sometimes need to take an RFC 2252–style object class and write it out as DSML, the example in listing 10.7 does exactly that. You will expect input as formatted in the object class schema definition style shown in the previous section.

Listing 10.7   rfcToDSMLObjectClass.pl

```perl
print "<dsml:dsml xmlns:dsml=\"http://www.dsml.org/DSML\">\n";
print "  <dsml:directory-schema>\n";

open(AFILE,$ARGV[0]);

while ($def = <AFILE>)
{
    chop $def;

    $def =~ /([\d\.]+)\s+NAME\s+'([\w\d;-]+)'/;
    $oid = $1;
    $name = $2;
    $sup = "";
    if ($def =~ /SUP ([\w]+)/)
    {
        $sup = $1;
    }

    if ($def =~ /MUST [\(']+([$ \w]+)[\)']+/ ||
        $def =~ /MUST (\w+)/)
    {
        $must = $1;
        $must =~ s/ //g;
        @must = split(/\$/,$must);
    }

    if ($def =~ /MAY [\(']+([$ \w]+)[\)']+/ ||
        $def =~ /MAY (\w+)/)
    {
        $may = $1;
        $may =~ s/ //g;
        @may = split(/\$/,$may);
    }

    $type = "";

    if ($def =~ /ABSTRACT/) {
        $type = "abstract";
    }

    if ($def =~ /AUXILIARY/) {
        $type = "auxiliary";
    }

    if ($type eq "")
    {
        $type = "structural";
    }

    print "    <dsml:class\n";
    print "          id=\"" . $name . "\"\n";
    print "          type=\"" . $type . "\"";

    if ($sup ne "") {
```

```
        print "\n            superior=\"#" . $sup . "\"";
    }
    print ">\n";
    print "    <dsml:name>" . $name . "</dsml:name>\n";
    print "    <dsml:object-identifier>" . $oid .
        "</dsml:object-identifier>\n";

    foreach $must (@must) {
        print "    <dsml:attribute ref=\"#" . $must .
            "\" required=\"true\"/>\n";
    }

    foreach $may (@may) {
        print "    <dsml:attribute ref=\"#" . $may .
            "\" required=\"false\"/>\n";
    }

    print "  </dsml:class>\n";
}
print "  </dsml:dsml-schema>\n";
print "</dsml:dsml>\n";
```

As in the earlier DSML files, you print a line indicated the start of the DSML document and the URL for the XML document type. However, in this document you are producing a schema; you indicate that fact with the opening dsml:directory-schema element:

```
print "<dsml:dsml xmlns:dsml=\"http://www.dsml.org/DSML\">\n";
print "  <dsml:directory-schema>\n";
```

Note that it is possible, and likely, that you will include both a schema and entries in the same file. To do so, you simply ensure that you have only a single dsml:dsml tag, with both a dsml:directory-schema tag and a dsml:dsml-entries tag below it.

In some of the previous examples, you read from standard input. In this example you take the first argument passed from the command line as the name of the file containing RFC-style definitions. Once open, you read each line as an individual RFC-style definition:

```
open(AFILE, $ARGV[0]);

while ($def = <AFILE>)
{
```

You next remove the trailing linefeeds and use regular expressions to parse the OID and name of the attribute. The following regular expression looks for a dot-separated number, followed by one or more spaces, the word *NAME*, another space, and then a combination of letters, numbers, semicolons, and dashes—the characters that can make up an object class name. In the next two lines, $1 matches the first set of parentheses, and

$2 matches the second set. Because these two sets are around the OID and name of the object class, respectively, you assign them to appropriate variables:

```
chop $def;

$def =~ /([\d\.]+)\s+NAME\s+'([\w\d;-]+)'/;
$oid = $1;
$name = $2;
```

It is possible, but not required, for an object class to have a superior class. Here you see if the SUP keyword exists; if so, you assign its value to the $sup variable:

```
$sup = "";
if ($def =~ /SUP ([\w]+)/)
{
    $sup = $1;
}
```

Writing required and allowed attributes

MUST definitions are a little more complex, because the format of the definition changes depending on whether a single attribute type or multiple types are required. The following regular expressions will parse either style and then place the entire list of required attributes into the $must variable. You next remove any spaces that may occur in the definition. If multiple attributes exist, they are separated by the dollar sign ($), which you use in the final line to split the $must variable into the @must array:

```
if ($def =~ /MUST [\(']+([$ \w]+)[\)']+/ ||
   $def =~ /MUST (\w+)/)
{
    $must = $1;
    $must =~ s/ //g;
    @must = split(/\$/,$must);
}
```

The MAY keyword is parsed identically to the MUST keyword, except that you put the list into the @may array:

```
if ($def =~ /MAY [\(']+([$ \w]+)[\)']+/ ||
   $def =~ /MAY (\w+)/)
{
    $may = $1;
    $may =~ s/ //g;
    @may = split(/\$/,$may);
}
```

Handling the object class's type

If the object class type is undefined, it is structural by default. Here you check to see if the type is either abstract or auxiliary:

```
$type = "";

if ($def =~ /ABSTRACT/) {
```

```
        $type = "abstract";
    }

    if ($def =~ /AUXILIARY/) {
        $type = "auxiliary";
    }

    if ($type eq "")
    {
        $type = "structural";
    }
```

Printing the parsed information as DSML

Having parsed the entire definition, you are now ready to print the definition as DSML. You begin with the dsml:class tag, which initiates each new class, specifying the class's id, type, and optional superior class as XML attributes. It is common to use the class name as its DSML id:

```
print "    <dsml:class\n";
print "            id=\"" . $name . "\"\n";
print "            type=\"" . $type . "\"";

if ($sup ne "") {
    print "\n            superior=\"#" . $sup . "\"";
}

print ">\n";
```

Next you need to print out the class name and object identifier using the dsml:name and dsml:object-identifier, respectively. You could also print a dsml:description here if you had one available:

```
print "    <dsml:name>" . $name . "</dsml:name>\n";
print "    <dsml:object-identifier>" . $oid .
      "</dsml:object-identifier>\n";
```

You now cycle through each of the required attributes in the @must array, printing each one as a reference to its attribute type definition. In this example, you assume that the attribute type definitions follow later in the file:

```
foreach $must (@must) {
    print "    <dsml:attribute ref=\"#" . $must .
          "\" required=\"true\"/>\n";
}
```

You use the same logic for the @may array that lists optional attribute types, but for these you set the required XML attribute to false:

```
foreach $may (@may) {
    print "    <dsml:attribute ref=\"#" . $may .
          "\" required=\"false\"/>\n";
}
```

Finally, you end each class by issuing the closing tag for the dsml:class element and continue on to the next object class:

```
    print "  </dsml:class>\n";
}
```

When run, this example gives output that looks something like the following partial output for the top object class:

```
<dsml:dsml xmlns:dsml="http://www.dsml.org/DSML">
    <dsml:directory-schema>
        <dsml:class id="top" type="abstract">
            <dsml:name>top</dsml:name>
            <dsml:object-identifier>2.5.6.0</dsml:object-identifier>
            <dsml:attribute ref="#objectClass" required="true" />
        </dsml:class>
...
```

This output conforms to the DSML standard for schema representation; the segment here shows the definition of the standard top object class.

10.3.4 Converting attribute types

The conversion of attribute types is similar in some ways to the conversion of object classes shown in the previous section. Listing 10.8 shows a full program that takes a file with RFC 2252–formatted attributes as input and generates compliant DSML.

Listing 10.8 rfcToDSMLAttrTypes.pl

```
print "<dsml:dsml xmlns:dsml=\"http://www.dsml.org/DSML\">\n";
print "  <dsml:directory-schema>\n";

open(AFILE,$ARGV[0]);

while ($def = <AFILE>)
{
    chop $def;

    $def =~ /([\d\.]+)\s+NAME\s+'([\w\d;-]+)'/;
    $oid = $1;
    $name = $2;
    $sup = "";
    $syntax = "";
    $equality = "";
    $substr = "";

    if ($def =~ /SYNTAX ([\w\d\.\{\}]+)/) {
        $syntax = $1;
    }

    if ($def =~ /EQUALITY (\w+)/) {
        $equality = $1;
    }

    if ($def =~ /SUBSTR (\w+)/) {
```

CHAPTER 10 DSML: GETTING UNDER THE HOOD

```
            $substr = $1;
    }

    if ($def =~ /SUP ([\w\d;-]+)/) {
        $sup = $1;
    }

    if ($def =~ /SINGLE-VALUE/) {
        $multival = 0;
    } else {
        $multival = 1;
    }

    if ($def =~ /NO-USER-MODIFICATION/) {
        $usermod = 0;
    } else {
        $usermod = 1;
    }

    print "<dsml:attribute-type id=\"$name\"";
    if ($sup) {
        print " superior=\"#$sup\"";
    }
    print ">\n";

    print "    <dsml:name>$name</dsml:name>\n";
    print "    <dsml:object-identifier>$oid" .
        "</dsml:object-identifier>\n";

    if ($syntax ne "") {
        $syntax =~ /([\d\.]+)/;
        $oidsyntax = $syntax{$1};
        print "    <dsml:syntax>$oidsyntax</dsml:syntax>\n";
    }

    if ($equality ne "") {
        print "    <dsml:equality>" . $equality .
            "</dsml:equality>\n";
    }

    if ($substr ne "") {
        print "    <dsml:substring>" . $substr .
            "</dsml:substring>\n";
    }

    if ($multival == 0 {
        print "    <dsml:single-value>true</dsml:single-value>\n";
    }

    if ($usermod == 0) {
        print "    <dsml:user-modification>false" .
            "</dsml:user-modification>";
    }
}
```

Understanding the code

As in the previous example, you print the DSML header and DSML schema tag. You also open the input file specified by the first command-line argument to the script and cycle through each of the attribute types listed in this file:

```
print "<dsml:dsml xmlns:dsml=\"http://www.dsml.org/DSML\">\n";
print "  <dsml:directory-schema>\n";

open(AFILE,$ARGV[0]);

while ($def = <AFILE>)
{
    chop $def;
```

In the RFC format, the name and OID of an attribute type are formatted the same way as in an object class. You can use the same regular expression to perform this match:

```
$def =~ /([\d\.]+)\s+NAME\s+'([\w\d;-]+)'/;
$oid = $1;
$name = $2;
```

Next, you need to ensure that you do not carry over any of the values parsed from the previous attribute type. To do so, you empty these variables before you continue parsing:

```
$sup = "";
$syntax = "";
$equality = "";
$substr = "";
```

The first part of the definition you parse out is the syntax. It can be either an OID or a textual syntax definition. It is typically an OID in the standards documents:

```
if ($def =~ /SYNTAX ([\w\d\.\{\}]+)/) {
    $syntax = $1;
}
```

Similarly, you parse out equality and substring matching rules. Servers use these to determine how different types of searches should be performed against the attribute:

```
if ($def =~ /EQUALITY (\w+)/) {
    $equality = $1;
}

if ($def =~ /SUBSTR (\w+)/) {
    $substr = $1;
}
```

Like object classes, attribute types may have superiors from which they inherit. This inheritance may include matching rules, as well as other information, including syntax. Here you simply need to find the name of the superior type, if it exists:

```
if ($def =~ /SUP ([\w\d;-]+)/) {
    $sup = $1;
}
```

Not all attributes are multivalued. RFC-style attribute definitions with the SINGLE-VALUE flag allow only a single value. By default, a type allows multiple values:

```
if ($def =~ /SINGLE-VALUE/) {
    $multival = 0;
} else {
    $multival = 1;
}
```

Some attribute types are operational in nature, meaning that they are reserved for modification by the directory server process itself, rather than by users connected via the LDAP protocol. These types are designated in the RFCs by the NO-USER-MODIFICATION flag:

```
if ($def =~ /NO-USER-MODIFICATION/) {
    $usermod = 0;
} else {
    $usermod = 1;
}
```

Having parsed all the important information from the RFC-style attribute type, you can now print it in DSML. You begin by printing the dsml:attribute-type element, which includes the id of the type, as well as superior (if it exists):

```
print "    <dsml:attribute-type id=\"$name\"";
if ($sup) {
    print " superior=\"#$sup\"";
}
print ">\n";
```

Next you must print both the name and OID of the type using the dsml:name and dsml:object-identifier elements:

```
print "        <dsml:name>$name</dsml:name>\n";
print "        <dsml:object-identifier>$oid" .
    "</dsml:object-identifier>\n";
```

The dsml:syntax tag is used to detail the syntax of the type. Here you filter out anything other than the syntax's OID. You could later extend this code to check for any bounds information, which is sometimes specified:

```
if ($syntax ne "") {
    $syntax =~ /([\d\.]+)/;
    $oidsyntax = $syntax{$1};
    print "        <dsml:syntax>$oidsyntax</dsml:syntax>\n";
}
```

Equality and substring matching rules are printed as they are found within the appropriate tags:

```
if ($equality ne "") {
    print "        <dsml:equality>" . $equality .
        "</dsml:equality>\n";
```

```
    }
    if ($substr ne "") {
        print "        <dsml:substring>" . $substr .
            "</dsml:substring>\n";
    }
```

If the attribute is single-valued, you need to note it using the dsml:single-value element. You could optionally set this tag to false, but because that is the default value, it does not need to be set explicitly:

```
    if ($multival == 0) {
        print "        <dsml:single-value>true</dsml:single-value>\n";
    }
```

The same goes for the dsml:user-modification element. By default, this value is set to true. If it is not to be modified by end users, you need to change the value within this tag to false:

```
    if ($usermod == 0) {
        print "        <dsml:user-modification>false" .
            "</dsml:user-modification>";
    }
}
```

When you run this program with sample input from one of the RFCs, you will see output something like the following lines:

```
...
    <dsml:attribute-type id="createTimestamp">
      <dsml:name>createTimestamp</dsml:name>
      <dsml:object-identifier>2.5.18.1</dsml:object-identifier>
      <dsml:syntax>1.3.6.1.4.1.1466.115.121.1.24</dsml:syntax>
      <dsml:single-value>true</dsml:single-value>
      <dsml:user-modification>false</dsml:user-modification>
      <dsml:equality>generalizedTimeMatch</dsml:equality>
    </dsml:attribute-type>
...
```

This output shows the createTimestamp attribute type, which is explicitly defined in RFC 2252. You see that it allows only a single value and does not allow user modification; the output also provides other information that directly matches the type's standard definition.

10.4 USING PERL TO CONVERT DSML WITH XSLT

As discussed in chapter 5, XSLT is a very popular, standard way of transforming an XML document into other forms. It allows you to do things like convert DSML into HTML or even non-XML–style documents based on a set of rules.

In chapter 5, we gave an example of a stylesheet and showed how the output of a DSML file looks after being run through the stylesheet. In this section, you'll generate the Perl code necessary to perform this conversion.

10.4.1 Converting DSML to HTML

Because HTML is a commonly used general encoding format for documents, this example uses Perl and XSLT to convert DSML into HTML. A stylesheet for doing this conversion is shown in listing 10.9. Even if you aren't familiar with XSLT, you can read through the stylesheet and see that it basically lists HTML tags around DSML elements.

Listing 10.9 simple.xsl

```
<xsl:stylesheet version="1.0"
    xmlns:xsl="http://www.w3.org/1999/XSL/Transform">
  <xsl:template match="/">
    <html>
      <head>
        <title>Results</title>
      </head>
      <body>
        <h1>Results</h1>
        <xsl:for-each select=
            "dsml:dsml/dsml:directory-entries/dsml:entry">
          <h4>
            <xsl:value-of select="@dn"/>
          </h4>
          <table border="1">
            <xsl:for-each select="dsml:attr">
              <tr>
                <th>
                  <xsl:value-of select="@name"/>
                </th>
                <xsl:for-each select="dsml:value">
                  <td>
                    <xsl:value-of select="."/>
                  </td>
                </xsl:for-each>
              </tr>
            </xsl:for-each>
          </table>
        </xsl:for-each>
      </body>
    </html>
  </xsl:template>
</xsl:stylesheet>
```

This stylesheet can be invoked in Perl by the XML::XSLT module. The code to do this is in the short code segment dsmlxslt.pl (listing 10.10).

Listing 10.10   dsmlxslt.pl

```
use XML::XSLT;

$xslfile = $ARGV[0];
$xmlfile = $ARGV[1];

my $parser = new XML::XSLT($xslfile);
$parser->transform_document($xmlfile);
$parser->print_result;
$parser->dispose();
```

Executing the dsmlxslt.pl script transforms the janet.xml DSML file from chapter 5 into the HTML shown in listing 10.11.

Listing 10.11   janet.html

```
<html>
  <head>
    <title>Results</title>
  </head>
  <body>
    <h1>Results</h1>
    <h4>cn=Janet Smith,dc=xyz,dc=com</h4>
    <table border="1">
      <tr>
        <th>cn</th>
        <td>Janet Smith</td>
      </tr>
      <tr>
        <th>sn</th>
        <td>Smith</td>
      </tr>
    </table>
  </body>
</html>
```

Converting to a format other than HTML only requires a different stylesheet. Thus you can change the document's presentation without changing the contents of the original data found in the janet.xml file.

10.5 SUMMARY

This chapter expanded on the basic understanding of DSML provided in chapter 5 by showing real examples for generating and parsing DSML documents. We covered both entry and schema information. We also discussed XML transformations with XSLT using Perl examples that automatically convert documents from DSML into HTML.

The next part of the book moves from covering data integration and server management to using LDAP from applications. In making this transition, the examples will shift from Perl to Java.

Application integration

It is possible to deploy a directory without considering the applications that will need to directly interface with it. However, keeping an eye on specific applications needed in your environment that will impact directories will ensure that both directory and application deployments go more smoothly.

The examples in this part of the book use Java. In chapter 11, we walk through the use of the JNDI to access and manipulate information in an LDAP directory.

Chapter 12 tackles using DSML, the XML standard for directory services. Because this standard can be used with web-based, component-based, and even directory synchronization applications, it is an important one to understand. Our examples include both parsing and creation of DSML documents as well as the creation of DSMLv2 operations.

Chapter 13 moves to one of the most important uses of directories: security. Security is critical for applications, and directories are becoming the point of storage for credentials and policies. In this chapter, we discuss how you can use directories to provide these services, and we look at directory dependencies from PKI and other technologies.

C H A P T E R   1 1

Accessing LDAP directories with JNDI

Integrating support for directory services based on the standards described in this book requires an understanding of both what needs to be done as well as the actual interfaces for doing it. Multiple interfaces are available for accessing LDAP-enabled directories in Java. One interface was originally designed and developed by Netscape; the other, JNDI, was developed by Sun as part of the core Java environment. This chapter introduces the basics of using JNDI to access LDAP-enabled directories and provides several JNDI-based examples.

In this chapter we will answer the following questions:

- What is JNDI? What alternatives are there, and why was JNDI selected for this book versus those alternatives?

- How can JNDI be used to open and close connections to directories? What is the `DirContext` object?

- How can `DirContext` be used to search the directory? How can the results be abstracted for easier access?

- What is the best way to add entries to the directory with JNDI? What about other types of changes to the directory?

11.1 INTRODUCTION TO JNDI

JNDI began its life a few years ago as an optional Java package, but it is now part of the core Java 2 Platform Standard Edition (J2SE) and Java 2 Platform Enterprise Edition (J2EE) distributions. Although you will be using it to access LDAP-enabled directories, JNDI is also quite capable of accessing naming services such as DNS as well as non-LDAP directory services.

11.1.1 JNDI versus the LDAP Java SDK

Other LDAP software development kits (SDKs) exist from Sun and Novell, but with new standards like DSML emerging, JNDI offers a better level of abstraction that ensures your applications can fit into a broader array of directory environments. Additionally, JNDI is a core part of the J2SE and J2EE standards.

This is not to say that the LDAP-specific APIs do not offer any benefits. Many benefits exist, with most relating to their close mapping to LDAP operations. However, this close mapping can mean that applications written using these LDAP-specific APIs will not map well to web services or other non-LDAP directory access mechanisms as they surface. As we'll show in chapter 13 with DSML, JNDI faces no such limitations.

11.2 JNDI ARCHITECTURE

JNDI's architecture assures its long-term extensibility as new directory standards emerge and gain acceptance. The architecture consists of two layers. The bottom layer contains service provider interfaces (SPIs) that know how to talk directly to a specific kind of directory. Those providers plug directly into a more abstract layer, which consists of the user-accessible JNDI classes that reside in the `javax.naming` hierarchy.

User code talks directly to the exposed JNDI classes to access and manipulate directories and name services. As shown in figure 11.1, existing lower-level providers include NIS and DSML in addition to LDAP. Several other providers are available from Sun and third parties.

This architecture allows relatively seamless movement from one type of connected directory to another without substantial changes to code.

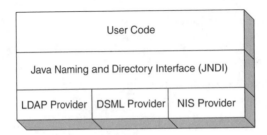

Figure 11.1
JNDI provides a standard interface to various directory and name services through its extensible provider architecture.

11.2.1 JNDI providers

Like JDBC and other Java APIs, JNDI has an architecture that provides for a high-level API implemented by any number of low-level drivers. In JNDI's case, these drivers can connect to everything from LDAP servers to NIS servers.

Two JNDI drivers are commonly available for LDAP:

- *Sun LDAP provider for JNDI*—com.sun.jndi.ldap.LdapCtxFactory
- *IBM LDAP provider for JNDI*—com.ibm.jndi.LDAPCtxFactory

The Sun provider is included as part of the main J2SE distribution. The other is available from IBM as part of its directory server client development kit. Both of these drivers provide the same basic functionality and work with nearly every LDAP-enabled directory server on the market.

In the examples in this chapter you will use Sun's driver, because it tends to be used more frequently. However, as you will see, changing drivers is not difficult.

11.2.2 The JNDI package

JNDI functionality is part of the `javax.naming` hierarchy. The classes in `javax.naming` are most useful when handling simple name services, whereas the classes in `javax.naming.directory` extend the base naming classes to handle complex directory services, such as LDAP. You will frequently need to import the classes from these packages in the examples.

11.3 JNDI OPERATIONS: THE DIRCONTEXT CLASS

All operations in JNDI are performed by creating an object called a `DirContext`. You can create these objects by specifying a set of properties that define the way the application should communicate with the server.

The following example creates a `DirContext` object that is connected to the LDAP server and can be used for subsequent operations:

```
Properties env = new Properties();
env.put(DirContext.INITIAL_CONTEXT_FACTORY,
        "com.sun.jndi.ldap.LdapCtxFactory");
env.put(DirContext.PROVIDER_URL,"ldap://localhost:389");
DirContext dirContext = new InitialDirContext(env);
```

The class specified by `INITIAL_CONTEXT_FACTORY` is the factory within the low-level driver that creates new `DirContext` objects appropriate for handling the desired type of directory. In this case you are using the Sun LDAP provider for JNDI, so you specify `"com.sun.jndi.ldap.LdapCtxFactory"`. You could use the IBM provider without altering more than a single line of code by simply changing that factory name.

11.3.1 Handling basic exceptions

The previous snippet of code will not compile, because creating a new `DirContext` object has the potential to throw a Java exception called `NamingException`. You can handle it easily using a typical Java `try`/`catch` block as shown:

```
try {
    Properties env = new Properties();
    env.put(DirContext.INITIAL_CONTEXT_FACTORY,
            "com.sun.jndi.ldap.LdapCtxFactory");
    env.put(DirContext.PROVIDER_URL,"ldap://localhost:389");
    DirContext dirContext = new InitialDirContext(env);
} catch (NamingException ne) {
    System.err.println("Exception when connecting, " +
                       "printing stack trace.");
    ne.printStackTrace();
}
```

All exceptions in JNDI are derived from `NamingException`. As we move through the various examples, we will cover some of the more important specializations of `NamingException`.

11.3.2 Closing the connection

Once you have completed all desired operations with the `DirContext` object, you should close it to disconnect from the server and free up any associated resources. In JNDI, you can do so easily by calling the `close()` method on the open `DirContext` object.

Like most other operations in JNDI, closing a connection has the ability to throw a `NamingException`, which you catch:

```
try {
    dirContext.close();
} catch (NamingException ne) {
    System.err.println("Exception disconnecting, " +
                       "printing stack trace.");
    ne.printStackTrace();
}
```

In real-world code, you would obviously put in whatever code was necessary to handle these exceptions rather than simply dump stack traces. However, this code does give you everything you need to open and close connections to the LDAP server at will.

11.3.3 Binding to the directory

You may not have noticed it in the previous sections, but when you connect to the directory, you're actually letting the directory know who you are. You didn't notice in the previous examples because you authenticated as the default user—anonymous.

Unlike other LDAP APIs that have separate methods or functions for explicitly binding to the directory as specific users, JNDI does not separate the creation of the `DirContext` object from authentication. Thus if you want to authenticate as a particular user, you need to specify that user's distinguished name and password as part of the environment passed when creating the initial DirContext.

What follows is an example of the creation of an authenticated DirContext:

```
Properties env = new Properties();
env.put(DirContext.INITIAL_CONTEXT_FACTORY,
        "com.sun.jndi.ldap.LdapCtxFactory");
env.put(DirContext.PROVIDER_URL,"ldap://localhost:389");
env.put(DirContext.SECURITY_PRINCIPAL,"cn=Admin");
env.put(DirContext.SECURITY_CREDENTIALS,"manager");
DirContext dirContext = new InitialDirContext(env);
```

Note that you add two extra properties to the original code for opening the connection. The first of these lines specifies a SECURITY_PRINCIPAL. This is the distinguished name you want to use to identify yourself to the directory. SECURITY_CREDENTIALS in this instance is a password associated with the selected identity.

Now, if the distinguished name and password are correct, you will receive an authenticated DirContext object. Otherwise, creation of the DirContext object will throw an exception and fail.

11.3.4   A reusable LDAP connection handler

From this point on, every example that connects to an LDAP server will need to create and close these DirContext objects. Rather than repeat this code for every example, you should create a reusable class that does most of the grunt work for you and allows you to focus on the task at hand.

Listing 11.1 does exactly this. You will use this class in many of the examples throughout this chapter.

Listing 11.1   LDAPConnection.java

```
import javax.naming.directory.DirContext;
import javax.naming.directory.InitialDirContext;
import javax.naming.NamingException;
import java.util.Properties;

public class LDAPConnection {

    private String host = "localhost";
    private int port = 389;
    private String dn = null;
    private String password = null;

    public LDAPConnection() {
    }

    public LDAPConnection(String dn, String password) {
        this.dn = dn;
        this.password = password;
    }
```

```java
    public LDAPConnection(String host, int port,
                          String dn, String password) {
        this.host = host;
        this.port = port;
        this.dn = dn;
        this.password = password;
    }

    public DirContext open() throws NamingException {
        Properties env = new Properties();                          // Set
        env.put(DirContext.INITIAL_CONTEXT_FACTORY,                 // provider
                "com.sun.jndi.ldap.LdapCtxFactory");

        env.put(DirContext.PROVIDER_URL,"ldap://" + host
                + ":" + port);
        if (dn != null) {                                          // Optionally
            env.put(DirContext.SECURITY_PRINCIPAL,dn);             // set DN and
            env.put(DirContext.SECURITY_CREDENTIALS,password);     // password
        }                                                          // for bind
        DirContext dirContext = new InitialDirContext(env);        // Create
        return dirContext;                                         // DirContext
    }

    public void close(DirContext dc) {
        try {
            dc.close();
        } catch (NamingException ne) {
            // Ignore exceptions when closing connection...
        }
    }
}
```

The LDAPConnection class reuses some of the code you developed earlier, but adds a few constructors that allow you to set some defaults for the connections you open in the examples. Because in many cases you will open multiple connections, sometimes with different credentials, these constructors simplify the task of creating and destroying connections while at the same time allowing you to change your connection information in a central place.

A more sophisticated LDAPConnection class used in a server environment might be extended to pool anonymous DirContext objects that can be used to do many common tasks we will discuss. We leave such improvements as an exercise for you, because there are many good ways to do basic object pooling in Java.

11.4 SEARCHING WITH JNDI

Searching is both the most common and most complex operation that can be performed with LDAP. However, most of the complexity is related to the search criteria, which chapter 4 describes in great detail.

Once you understand search criteria, the actual coding is quite simple. The following code segment shows how you can search the directory using a connection opened with the `LDAPConnection` class created in the previous section:

```
try {
    LDAPConnection lc = new LDAPConnection();
    DirContext dc = lc.open();

    SearchControls sc = new SearchControls();
    sc.setSearchScope(SearchControls.SUBTREE_SCOPE);

    NamingEnumeration ne = dc.search("dc=manning,dc=com",sc,
                                     "(objectclass=*)");
    while (ne.hasMore()) {
        SearchResult sr = ne.next();
        System.out.println(sr.toString());
    }
} catch (NamingException ne) {
    System.err.println("Error Searching: " + ne.getMessage());
}
```

In this code snippet, you use a few new classes, including `SearchControls` and `NamingEnumeration`. The `setSearchScope()` method on the `SearchControls` class sets the search scope, which is part of the search criteria. In this example you indicate that you will be searching the entire subtree.

You call the `search()` method on the open `DirContext`, which returns a `NamingEnumeration`. JNDI makes extensive use of `NamingEnumeration` objects, which behave similarly to a standard Java `Enumeration` object. You can test whether the `NamingEnumeration` has more results by using the `hasMore()` method and retrieve the next result with the `next()` method.

The printed output of this example is anything but pretty. The next section walks through how you can extract information from the search results and make those results more useful.

11.4.1 Abstracting the entry

Before you create a generalized class for simplifying the activity of searching an LDAP-enabled directory from JNDI, let's look at the way you might want to work with LDAP-sourced information in Java. Most applications will not be solely focused on directory activity, and passing a directory-centric object like `NamingEnumeration` to other parts of the application may not make much sense. Abstracting the returned entry into something that can be easily manipulated and accessed makes it easier to handle the directory information in the parts of the code that do not depend heavily on directories.

As we discussed in chapter 2, LDAP information is stored in entries, and each entry has a name, class, and associated attributes. Let's create a simple class (listing 11.2) that is easy to manipulate and gives you instant access to a particular piece of information retrieved from an LDAP server.

Listing 11.2   Entry.java

```
import java.util.Hashtable;

public class Entry extends Hashtable {

    // Keys and Values will be in the hashtable, but
    // we will store the DN separately.
    private String dn = null;

    public Entry() {
        super();
    }

    public Entry(Entry entry) {
        super((Hashtable)entry);
        setDN(entry.getDN());
    }

    public void setDN(String dn) {
        this.dn = dn;
    }

    public String getDN() {
        return dn;
    }
}
```

Because an LDAP entry in its most basic form contains a list of keys and values, you can make manipulation simpler by using a `Hashtable`. It gives you random access into a particular key or value without having to make the `Entry` class terribly complicated:

```
public class Entry extends Hashtable {
```

The only information you store outside the key/value pairs associated with attribute types and values will be the distinguished name.

Although you include a basic constructor that simply initializes the object, another useful method is to make a copy of an existing `Entry` object. As you see here, the constructor is quite simple because you let the `Hashtable` handle the grunt work:

```
public Entry(Entry entry) {
    super((Hashtable)entry);
    setDN(entry.getDN());
```

Finally you add a getter and setter to simplify setting and getting the name of the entry:

```
public void setDN(String dn) {
    this.dn = dn;
}

public String getDN() {
    return dn;
}
```

11.4.2 A search class

You use searches throughout this book. In some cases it is important to remind yourself of the semantics of communicating using JNDI. In others, the process is more important than the semantics. In these latter cases, it makes sense to have a class that can do a search and return the results as something easily reusable, such as the Entry class described in the previous section. Listing 11.3 provides this functionality.

Listing 11.3   LDAPSearch.java

```java
import javax.naming.directory.*;
import javax.naming.*;
import java.util.Vector;
import java.util.Enumeration;

public class LDAPSearch {

    public static Vector search(String base, String scope,
                                String filter,
                                String[] attributes) {

        Vector results = new Vector();

        LDAPConnection lc = new LDAPConnection();

        DirContext dc = null;
        try {
            dc = lc.open();
        } catch (NamingException ne) {
            System.err.println("Error Opening Connection: " +
                               ne.getMessage());
            return results;
        }

        SearchControls sc = new SearchControls();

        if (scope.equals("base")) {
            sc.setSearchScope(SearchControls.OBJECT_SCOPE);
        } else if (scope.equals("one")) {
            sc.setSearchScope(SearchControls.ONELEVEL_SCOPE);
        } else {
            sc.setSearchScope(SearchControls.SUBTREE_SCOPE);
        }

        // Reduce data provided by the LDAP server by listing
        // only those attributes we want to return.

        if (attributes.length > 0) {
            sc.setReturningAttributes(attributes);
        }

        NamingEnumeration ne = null;
        try {
            ne = dc.search(base, filter, sc);
            Entry entry = new Entry();
```

```
    // Use the NamingEnumeration object to cycle through
    // the result set.
    while (ne.hasMore()) {

        SearchResult sr = (SearchResult) ne.next();
        String name = sr.getName();
        if (base != null && !base.equals("")) {
            entry.setDN(name + "," + base);
        } else {
            entry.setDN(name);
        }

        Attributes at = sr.getAttributes();
        NamingEnumeration ane = at.getAll();
        while (ane.hasMore()) {
            Attribute attr = (Attribute) ane.next();
            String attrType = attr.getID();
            NamingEnumeration values = attr.getAll();
            Vector vals = new Vector();
            //Another NamingEnumeration object, this time
            // to iterate through attribute values.
            while (values.hasMore()) {
                Object oneVal = values.nextElement();
                if (oneVal instanceof String) {
                    vals.addElement((String) oneVal);
                } else {
                    vals.addElement(new String(
                                    (byte[]) oneVal));
                }
            }

            entry.put(attrType, vals);
        }
        results.addElement(entry);
    }
    lc.close(dc);

// The search() method can throw a number of exceptions.
// Here we just handle and print the exception.
// In real life we might want to pass the exception along
// to a piece of the software that might have a better
// context for correcting or presenting the problem.
} catch (InvalidSearchFilterException isfe) {
    System.err.println("Search Filter Invalid: " + filter);
    lc.close(dc);
} catch (NameNotFoundException nnfe) {
    System.err.println("Object Not Found: " + base);
    lc.close(dc);
} catch (NoPermissionException npe) {
    System.err.println("Search Failed: Permission Denied");
    lc.close(dc);
} catch (CommunicationException ce) {
    System.err.println("Error Communicating with Server");
```

```
        lc.close(dc);
    } catch (NamingException nex) {
        System.err.println("Error: " + nex.getMessage());
        lc.close(dc);
    }

    return results;
  }
}
```

In chapter 4, we talk about search scopes. It is important to note that JNDI has abstracted the names of these scopes from the ones you have used before. A search scope of OBJECT is equal to an LDAP BASE search, whereas ONELEVEL and SUB-TREE retain their name from LDAP:

```
if (scope.equals("base")) {
    sc.setSearchScope(SearchControls.OBJECT_SCOPE);
} else if (scope.equals("one")) {
    sc.setSearchScope(SearchControls.ONELEVEL_SCOPE);
} else {
    sc.setSearchScope(SearchControls.SUBTREE_SCOPE);
}
```

Now that you have all the search criteria, you can pass them to the search() method on your DirContext object:

```
ne = dc.search(base, filter, sc);
```

As you saw in the earlier example, the name of the entry returned does not include the search base. This result can be confusing to people who have used other LDAP APIs that return the full name. It is also usually not the desired behavior, because the full distinguished name is needed in most cases to change an entry:

```
entry.setDN(name + "," + base);
```

The getID() method on individual attributes returns the attribute type of the current attribute:

```
String attrType = attr.getID();
```

Some attributes are binary and will be returned as byte arrays. The instanceof query helps you determine that attributes that reach this line are in fact binary and lets you handle them specially. In this case, you turn such attributes into strings. If this program displayed images, it might keep the values as byte arrays. If you expected an object, you might use the byte array for serialization:

```
if (oneVal instanceof String) {
    vals.addElement((String) oneVal);
} else {
    vals.addElement(new String(
                    (byte[]) oneVal));
}
```

Now you place both the attribute type and values into the `Entry` object you created earlier. Doing so allows other bits and pieces of your code to use the information you just collected on a random-access basis without having to walk through scores of enumerations:

```
entry.put(attrType, vals);
```

11.5 ADDING ENTRIES

Adding entries to an LDAP-enabled directory using JNDI is relatively straightforward. However, unlike the search operation, the add operation almost universally requires the connection to be authenticated.

11.5.1 A simple add example

Fortunately, you already have the `LDAPConnection` class devised earlier in the chapter for retrieving an authenticated connection from the server. You can easily do this by setting the appropriate environment variables:

```
LDAPConnection lc = new LDAPConnection("cn=Admin","manager");
try {
    DirContext dc = lc.open();
```

Now that you've set up the context, you can focus on creating the set of attributes that will be added to this entry. Let's create a short example that creates an LDAP entry that looks like the following snippet of LDIF:

```
dn: cn=Janet Smith, dc=manning, dc=com
cn: Janet Smith
sn: Smith
objectclass: person
```

JNDI makes this easy. To create the attributes, you first create a new instance of the `BasicAttributes` class:

```
Attributes attrs = new BasicAttributes();
```

Next, for each attribute you want included in the new entry, you create a new `BasicAttribute` object. You then add the desired value or values to each attribute:

```
Attribute cn = new BasicAttribute("cn");
cn.add("Janet Smith");

Attribute sn = new BasicAttribute("sn");
sn.add("Smith");

Attribute objectclass =
    new BasicAttribute("objectclass");
objectclass.add("person");
```

Next, you simply add each attribute individually to the `BasicAttributes` object you created earlier:

```
attrs.put(cn);
attrs.put(sn);
attrs.put(objectclass);
```

Now that you've built your list of attributes, you can call the `createSubcontext()` method to add the entry to the directory. Note that the first argument is the distinguished name of the entry. When you're done, you close the connection, handling any exceptions that might have been thrown in the creation of attributes or communication with the directory:

```
dc.createSubcontext(
    "cn=Janet Smith,dc=manning,dc=com", attrs);
lc.close(dc);
} catch (NamingException ne) {
    System.err.println("Error: " + ne.getMessage());
}
```

Done! You now have a short example that shows the general pattern for adding entries to the directory.

11.5.2 A generalized add example

The previous example offered the ability to add a specific entry. What if you simply want a class that will take care of all the dirty work involved in adding an entry, without mucking with the `Attributes` object? In the final search example, you put data into an `Entry` object. There are many cases where you might want to use a similarly simple object to create entries in the directory.

Let's create a simple class that will take an `Entry` object as defined in section 11.4.1 and add it to the directory (see listing 11.4).

Listing 11.4   LDAPAdd.java

```
import javax.naming.directory.*;
import javax.naming.*;
import java.util.Vector;
import java.util.Enumeration;

public class LDAPAdd {

    public static void add(Entry entry) {
        LDAPConnection lc = new LDAPConnection();
        DirContext dc = null;
        try {
            dc = lc.open();
            Attributes attrs = new BasicAttributes();
            Enumeration attrEnum = entry.keys();
            while (attrEnum.hasMoreElements()) {
                String type = (String) attrEnum.nextElement();
                Attribute oneAttr = new BasicAttribute(type);

                Vector vals = (Vector) entry.get(type);

                Enumeration valEnum = vals.elements();
```

```
            while (valEnum.hasMoreElements()) {
                oneAttr.add((String) valEnum.nextElement());
            }
            attrs.put(oneAttr);
        }
        dc.createSubcontext(entry.getDN(), attrs);
    } catch (SchemaViolationException sve) {
        System.err.println("Schema Violation: " +
                            sve.getMessage());
    } catch (InvalidAttributesException iae) {
        System.err.println("Invalid Attributes: " +
                            iae.getMessage());
    } catch (NameAlreadyBoundException nabe) {
        System.err.println("Entry Already Exists: " +
                            entry.getDN());
    } catch (NoPermissionException npe) {
        System.err.println("Access Denied to Add: " +
                            entry.getDN());
    } catch (CommunicationException ce) {
        System.err.println(
            "Error communicating with the server");
    } catch (NamingException ne) {
        System.err.println("Error: " + ne.getMessage());
    }
    if (dc != null) {
        lc.close(dc);
    }
    }
}
```

In the previous example, you created each attribute individually. Here you walk through each of the attributes in your `Entry` object, creating new `Basic-Attribute` objects for each attribute:

```
Attribute oneAttr = new BasicAttribute(type);
```

Next you must get the values for this attribute. Because attributes can be multivalued, you store these values in a `Vector` within the `Entry` object. Here you get an enumeration of these values and walk through them:

```
Vector vals = (Vector) entry.get(type);
```

Each value you encounter must be added to the `BasicAttribute` object you created earlier in the code:

```
oneAttr.add((String) valEnum.nextElement());
```

Once you've completed all the values for a particular attribute, you add that attribute to the `Attributes` object that will contain the full list of attributes to be added:

```
attrs.put(oneAttr);
```

11.6   MANIPULATING ENTRIES

Up to this point, we have discussed searching the directory and adding entries to it. LDAP supports other operations that cover modification, deletion, and renaming of entries in the directory. Because you've already seen some general patterns, this section will help you quickly use what you've learned about the Attribute and Dir-Context objects to perform these remaining operations.

11.6.1   Modifying entries

Like adding entries, modifying entries almost always requires an authenticated connection to the server. This process also uses attributes that determine the values that are added, replaced, and deleted from the specified entry.

The short bit of code in listing 11.5 follows the pattern of the previous full examples. This code modifies the directory entry you created in the add example from listing 11.4.

Listing 11.5   SimpleModify.java

```java
import javax.naming.directory.*;
import javax.naming.*;
import java.util.Vector;
import java.util.Enumeration;

public class SimpleModify {

    public static void main(String[] args) {
        LDAPConnection lc = new LDAPConnection();
        try {
            DirContext dc = lc.open();

            ModificationItem[] mods = new ModificationItem[2];

            Attribute description = new BasicAttribute("description",
                "Janet Smith Description");
            Attribute sn = new BasicAttribute("sn","Smith");

            mods[0] = new ModificationItem(DirContext.ADD_ATTRIBUTE,
                description);
            mods[1] = new ModificationItem(DirContext.REPLACE_ATTRIBUTE,
                sn);
            dc.modifyAttributes("cn=Janet Smith,dc=manning,dc=com",
                mods);

            lc.close(dc);
        } catch (NamingException ne) {
            System.err.println("Error: " + ne.getMessage());
        }
    }

}
```

In this code you make two modifications. Because the `modifyAttributes()` method takes an array of `ModificationItem` objects, you need to allocate the number of changes you'll be submitting:

```
ModificationItem[] mods =
            new ModificationItem[2];
```

Now you create `BasicAttribute` objects exactly as you did in the previous section. The difference here is how you use these attributes, not how they are created:

```
Attribute description =
    new BasicAttribute("description",
                        "Janet Smith Description");
Attribute sn =
    new BasicAttribute("sn","Smith");
```

Note that you create a `ModificationItem` for each change. This is where the code gets interesting. Each item associates a particular change type with the `Attribute` objects you just created. The three types of changes available are add, replace, and delete. The first change you perform is an add:

```
mods[0] =
    new ModificationItem(DirContext.ADD_ATTRIBUTE,
                        description);
```

Now you do a replace, which has the effect of removing any existing attributes prior to adding the value you just assigned. If you had selected to delete the attribute value, you would have specified `DirContext.DELETE_ATTRIBUTE` instead:

```
mods[1] =
    new ModificationItem(DirContext.REPLACE_ATTRIBUTE,
                        sn);
```

Finally, you actually make the modification. The `modifyAttributes()` method takes two arguments. The first is the distinguished name, and the second is your array of `ModificationItems`:

```
dc.modifyAttributes("cn=Janet Smith,dc=manning,dc=com",
                        mods);
```

When you run the code, it adds values to the `description` attribute and replaces any values in the `sn` attribute. It does so by creating an array of `Modification-Item` objects. A `ModificationItem` holds both an attribute and the type of change being made to that attribute.

11.6.2   Deleting entries

Entries can be deleted from the LDAP server quite easily. Restrictions in some products prevent the deletion of entries that have children, because the deletion of such entries would cause a break in the namespace between the deleted entry's parent and children. Other than that, there are few issues.

Listing 11.6 is a short example that shows how to delete an entry.

Listing 11.6   SimpleDelete.java

```java
import javax.naming.directory.*;
import javax.naming.*;
import java.util.Vector;
import java.util.Enumeration;

public class SimpleDelete {

    public static void main(String[] args) {
        LDAPConnection lc = new LDAPConnection();
        try {
            DirContext dc = lc.open();

            dc.destroySubcontext("cn=Janet Smith,dc=manning,dc=com");

            lc.close(dc);
        } catch (NamingException ne) {
            System.err.println("Error: " + ne.getMessage());
        }
    }

}
```

In this example, the `destroySubcontext()` method takes an argument that specifies the distinguished name of the entry to delete. If the entry exists and you have permission, the entry is deleted. Otherwise an exception is thrown.

11.6.3   Renaming entries

LDAP servers have varying degrees of capability when it comes to renaming entries. Some servers, such as Microsoft Active Directory, have no problems even when renaming entire subtrees. Many other directory products have restrictions that permit only the renaming of leaf nodes—those entries that have no children.

The rename operation is one of the few completely new operations with LDAPv3; earlier versions of the protocol only supported a rename in which the entry did not change its location in the directory tree.

You can perform a rename with only a few lines of code. The first and last few lines set up and tear down an authenticated connection; a single line actually performs the modification. In listing 11.7, the bolded lines show how to rename an entry from `Janet Smith` to `Janet Jones`.

Listing 11.7   SimpleRename.java

```java
import javax.naming.directory.*;
import javax.naming.*;
import java.util.Vector;
import java.util.Enumeration;

public class SimpleRename {
```

```
public static void main(String[] args) {
    LDAPConnection lc = new LDAPConnection();
    try {
        DirContext dc = lc.open();

        dc.rename("cn=Janet Smith,dc=manning,dc=com",
                  "cn=Janet Jones,dc=manning,dc=com");

        lc.close(dc);
    } catch (NamingException ne) {
        System.err.println("Error: " + ne.getMessage());
    }
}

}
```

This example renames an entry under the `dc=manning,dc=com` branch of the directory. If you try to move the entry `dc=manning,dc=com` while the `cn=Janet Smith` user is present in the directory, it is possible that the directory will refuse, resulting in a `NamingException`. The standards do not require that servers be capable of renaming entries that have leaf nodes.

You can get around this limitation by reading individual entries from one part of the tree, adding them to another part of the tree, and deleting the entry from its original place. Unfortunately, without standardized relational integrity or transactions, both of these options permit situations that might cause the entry to exist in multiple locations, with references to the entries in groups and other similar types of entries being broken as well. For this reason, it is most important that you look back at the discussion of namespace design in chapter 3 to ensure that such full subtree renaming will not happen, or will happen very infrequently.

11.7 SUMMARY

JNDI is our interface of choice for accessing LDAP directories because it supports a wide array of directory protocols, including LDAP, DNS, and NIS. As new directory access mechanisms (such as DSML over SOAP) become more prevalent in web services types of environments, JNDI's layer of abstraction will be very useful. For example, JNDI can help ensure that applications quickly adapt to these standards without requiring substantial modification to do so.

JNDI uses `DirContext` objects to perform operations against the directory. All LDAP operations are supported and, in this chapter, we looked at examples of search, add, modify, delete, and rename functionality. We examined LDAP operations throughout this chapter using a few example classes; we will return to these examples.

In the next chapter, you will use what you've learned about JNDI to access and manipulate LDAP directory information in XML. The combination of Java and DSML will simplify integration of LDAP directory information into XML-aware applications.

C H A P T E R   1 2

Java programming with DSML

In chapter 5, we introduced the DSML. In chapter 10, we looked at how you can parse and create DSML files in Perl, which can be an important way of sharing directory information.

This chapter covers some of the basics of DSML manipulation in Java. However, we'll go beyond simply parsing and creating DSML documents and discuss the new DSML operation capabilities in the latest DSML draft (DSMLv2).

By the end of this chapter, you will better understand the answers to the following questions:

- What is the simplest way to create a DSML document in Java?

- How can DSML entries and schemas be retrieved using JNDI?

- In what ways can DOM be used instead of SAX to manipulate a large DSML file?

- What is new with DSMLv2 and how DSMLv2 operations are performed in Java?

12.1 WRITING DSML WITH JAVA

One way you can use DSML is to write it directly. This is by far the simplest way when you're dealing with new documents, because it does not require learning any new APIs.

You can create such a DSML document by extending the `Entry` class you wrote in chapter 11 to output DSML as its string representation; listing 12.1 shows this new `DSMLEntry` class. This approach allows you to write out any entry as DSML relatively easily. When you run the code, the output will look something like the following:

```
<dsml:entry dn="cn=Janet Smith, dc=manning,dc=com">
  <dsml:objectclass>
    <dsml:oc-value>person</dsml:oc-value>
    <dsml:oc-value>top</dsml:oc-value>
  </dsml:objectclass>
  <dsml:attr name="sn">
    <dsml:value>Smith</dsml:value>
  </dsml:attr>
  <dsml:attr name="cn">
    <dsml:value>Janet Smith</dsml:value>
  </dsml:attr>
</dsml:entry>
```

Listing 12.1   DSMLEntry.java

```java
import javax.naming.directory.Attribute;
import java.util.Enumeration;
import java.util.Vector;

public class DSMLEntry extends Entry {          Extend Entry
                                                class from
    public DSMLEntry() {                        chapter II
    }

    public DSMLEntry(Entry entry) {
        super(entry);
    }

    public String toString() {
        StringBuffer dsmlString = new StringBuffer();

        dsmlString.append("<dsml:entry dn=\"");      Write
        dsmlString.append(getDN());                  distinguished
        dsmlString.append("\">\n");                  name

        Vector ocs = (Vector) get("objectclass");
        if (ocs != null) {
            dsmlString.append("  <dsml:objectclass>\n");      Special
            Enumeration enumOcs = ocs.elements();             care for
            while (enumOcs.hasMoreElements()) {               objectclass
                dsmlString.append("    <dsml:oc-value>");     values
                dsmlString.append((String) enumOcs.nextElement());
                dsmlString.append("</dsml:oc-value>\n");
```

```
            }
            dsmlString.append("   </dsml:objectclass>\n");
        }

        Enumeration enumAttrs = keys();                     Filter out objectclass
        while (enumAttrs.hasMoreElements()) {                         attribute
            String nextAttr = (String) enumAttrs.nextElement();
            if (!nextAttr.equalsIgnoreCase("objectclass")) {
                dsmlString.append("   <dsml:attr name=\"");
                dsmlString.append(nextAttr);
                dsmlString.append("\">\n");
                Enumeration valEnum = ((Vector)
                        get(nextAttr)).elements();
                                                                   Cycle through
                while (valEnum.hasMoreElements()) {              and print values
                    dsmlString.append("     <dsml:value>");
                    dsmlString.append(valEnum.nextElement());
                    dsmlString.append("</dsml:value>\n");
                }
                dsmlString.append("   </dsml:attr>\n");
            }
        }
        dsmlString.append("</dsml:entry>\n");

        return dsmlString.toString();
    }
}
```

The DSMLEntry class can be instantiated by passing in a normal Entry object to the constructor and manipulated using the same methods as the Entry class you created in chapter 11. The difference is that the toString() method now returns a string representation in DSML, rather than in an LDIF-like format.

You can add DSML output to your search code in chapter 11 by simply adding the following line after retrieving an entry:

```
System.out.println(new DSMLEntry(entry).toString());
```

This piece of code causes the DSML version of the entry to be written directly to the console. Doing so is useful if you are creating a file of DSML entries that will be shared with other applications that are DSML aware.

12.2   DSML WITH JNDI

We covered JNDI in considerable detail in chapter 11. This interface allows you to perform all the important LDAP operations from Java in a way that is somewhat abstract from LDAP itself. JNDI offers the important ability to plug in different providers that support protocols other than LDAP without having to make structural changes to your applications.

Sun has released an early access version of a JNDI provider that can handle some DSML natively. This provider allows direct JNDI access to DSML-formatted files and direct DSML output from an LDAP URL. Thus, rather than having to query using LDAP and then transform the returned information into DSML, the provider takes care of substituting DSML for LDAP.

For example, suppose you have an application that uses JNDI with the LDAP provider, and you would like it to be able to access a server that is providing DSML information via HTTP, rather than a server that exposes information natively with LDAP. Thanks to the provider, you do not need to rewrite many of the key components of the application to take advantage of the DSML service. This benefit is particularly important in software that needs to plug into enterprise environments, because it is often nearly impossible to predict how an enterprise will expose its directory information.

12.2.1 Automatic DSML output from LDAP URLs

In the first example in this chapter, we looked at how to manually generate XML. You could easily have used various XML APIs to generate such a file manually, as well. However, the DSML provider for JNDI offers a way to generate DSML entries and schemas automatically. Listing 12.2 takes advantage of this capability by retrieving all the entries in the LDAP server under the `dc=manning,dc=com` branch and printing them as valid DSML entries.

Listing 12.2 JNDIDSMLSearch.java

```java
import javax.naming.directory.InitialDirContext;
import javax.naming.directory.DirContext;
import javax.naming.Context;
import javax.naming.NamingException;
import java.util.Hashtable;

public class JNDIDSMLSearch {

    public JNDIDSMLSearch() {
        Hashtable env = new Hashtable();
        env.put(Context.INITIAL_CONTEXT_FACTORY,          DSML provider
                "com.sun.jndi.dsml.DsmlCtxFactory");        context factory

        env.put(Context.PROVIDER_URL,                      LDAP URL
                "ldap://localhost/dc=manning,dc=com??sub");  to query

        env.put(Context.SECURITY_PRINCIPAL,"cn=Admin");    Credentials
        env.put(Context.SECURITY_CREDENTIALS, "manager");  forwarded to
                                                           LDAP server
        try {
            DirContext ctx = new InitialDirContext(env);
            String dsmlresults = ctx.lookup("").toString();
            System.out.println(dsmlresults);               Returns entries
            ctx.close();                                   as DSML
        } catch (NamingException ne) {
```

```
                System.err.println("Error: " + ne.getMessage());
            }
        }

    public static void main(String[] args) {
        new JNDIDSMLSearch();
    }
}
```

This example creates output that looks something like the following DSML:

```
<dsml:directory-entries>
  <dsml:entry dn="cn=Janet Smith,dc=manning,dc=com">
    <dsml:objectclass>
      <dsml:oc-value>person</dsml:oc-value>
      <dsml:oc-value>top</dsml:oc-value>
    </dsml:objectclass>
    <dsml:attr name="sn">
      <dsml:value>Smith</dsml:value>
    </dsml:attr>
    <dsml:attr name="cn">
      <dsml:value>Janet Smith</dsml:value>
    </dsml:attr>
  </dsml:entry>
  <dsml:entry dn="dc=manning,dc=com">
    <dsml:objectclass>
      <dsml:oc-value>domain</dsml:oc-value>
      <dsml:oc-value>top</dsml:oc-value>
    </dsml:objectclass>
    <dsml:attr name="dc">
      <dsml:value>manning</dsml:value>
    </dsml:attr>
  </dsml:entry>
</dsml:directory-entries>
```

Notice that the results contain multiple entries wrapped in `dsml:directory-entries` tags. The first entry listed is the same one that appeared earlier in the chapter—but in this example you have not written a single line of XML by hand.

12.3   WORKING WITH SCHEMAS IN DSML

As you learned in chapter 5, DSML represents schemas as well as entries. The DSML provider for JNDI lets you take advantage of this functionality in much the same way that you queried for entries natively with LDAP in chapter 11.

As with many aspects of working with DSML in Java, you have many choices about how to build this functionality. The main choices are between the SAX-, DOM-, and the DSML-handling capabilities of the DSML JNDI provider (which uses XML handling under the covers).

Clearly, it is also possible to do this kind of parsing manually by writing custom code to scan lines for opening and closing angle brackets. But with such great APIs that do this kind of heavy lifting automatically, this approach doesn't warrant discussion.

Generally, if you are reading in a large document and do not want to keep it all in memory, you'll use SAX. You might also use SAX if you're looking to build your own custom objects while you read the XML file and have little intention of making changes to the file.

DOM's strength is its ability to manage the XML/DSML document as if it were a tree of Java objects. This approach makes it easier to change the DSML object.

Using the DSML provider for JNDI, you can spend more time focusing on the information and less time worrying about the fact that the information is in DSML format. In many cases, this is preferable when the provider offers enough functionality to get the job done. Otherwise you may still need to use the other two APIs for acting on the DSML document directly.

In this section, we'll focus primarily on using the SAX parser. Listings 12.6 and 12.9 show some basics of using the DSML provider for JNDI and the DOM APIs respectively, although not specifically with schema information.

12.3.1 Reading schemas with SAX

As we just discussed, the SAX APIs tend to be the best approach when you're handling very large documents or when you're parsing documents into custom objects as they are read in. In this section, we'll look at an example of how you can use the SAX APIs in Java to automatically parse and print information from a DSML schema file.

Listing 12.3 shows the DSML file you will be parsing. It contains a definition of the standard person object class.

Listing 12.3 DSMLSchema.xml

```
<dsml:dsml xmlns:dsml="http://www.dsml.org/DSML">
  <dsml:directory-schema>
   <dsml:class
        id="person"
        type="structural"
        superior="#top">
    <dsml:name>person</dsml:name>
    <dsml:description></dsml:description>
    <dsml:object-identifier>2.5.6.6</dsml:object-identifier>
    <dsml:attribute ref="#sn" required="true"/>
    <dsml:attribute ref="#cn" required="true"/>
    <dsml:attribute ref="#userPassword" required="false"/>
    <dsml:attribute ref="#telephoneNumber" required="false"/>
    <dsml:attribute ref="#seeAlso" required="false"/>
    <dsml:attribute ref="#description" required="false"/>
   </dsml:class>
  </dsml:directory-schema>
</dsml:dsml>
```

When the test program is run, it displays a simple textual representation of the contents of important fields in the DSML schema definition; following is a sample of the type of output generated. You can easily forego printing in favor of populating an appropriate type of Java object that will let you use this information programmatically:

```
Superior: top
Structural Class

Object Class: person
OID: 2.5.6.6
Must Have Attribute: sn
Must Have Attribute: cn
May Have Attribute: userPassword
May Have Attribute: telephoneNumber
May Have Attribute: seeAlso
May Have Attribute: description
```

Now that you have a basic DSML file and the desired output defined, let's look at the code that drives the DSML parsing. Listing 12.4 shows the DSMLSchema class, which is responsible for setting up the SAX parser and passing in the DSML schema file to be parsed as well as a handler that knows how to parse DSML schemas.

Listing 12.4   DSMLSchema.java

```java
import org.xml.sax.SAXException;

import javax.xml.parsers.SAXParserFactory;
import javax.xml.parsers.SAXParser;
import javax.xml.parsers.ParserConfigurationException;
import java.io.FileInputStream;
import java.io.FileNotFoundException;
import java.io.IOException;

public class DSMLSchema {

    public static void main(String[] args) {
        new DSMLSchema().read(args[0]);
    }

    public DSMLSchema() {
    }

    public void read(String filename) {

      SAXParser parser = null;

        try {
          SAXParserFactory spf = SAXParserFactory.newInstance();
          spf.setNamespaceAware(true);
          spf.setValidating(true);
          parser = spf.newSAXParser();

          SchemaXMLHandler handler = new SchemaXMLHandler();

          FileInputStream fis = new FileInputStream(filename);
          parser.parse(fis,handler,filename);
```

```
        } catch (ParserConfigurationException pce) {
            System.err.println("Parser Configuration Error: " +
                                pce.getMessage());
        } catch (FileNotFoundException fnfe) {
            System.err.println("File Not Found: " + filename);
        } catch (IOException ioe) {
            System.err.println("Error reading XML file: " +
                                ioe.getMessage());
        } catch (SAXException se) {
            System.err.println("SAX Error: " + se.getMessage());
        }
    }
}
```

Notice that this listing needs a handler. You specify one called SchemaXMLHand-
ler, which you now need to create. This handler will be called every time a new
XML element or text element is found. It will be responsible for keeping state information necessary to properly parse the DSML file, as well as performing any desired
actions when a particular element is found.

12.3.2 Designing a basic SAX handler

One possible version of a SAX handler is shown in listing 12.5. This handler parses
both object class and attribute type information. Although it only prints the information as it is parsed, it can easily be extended to populate other objects or perform
other actions as desired.

Listing 12.5   SchemaXMLHandler.java

```
import org.xml.sax.Attributes;              Need to extend
import org.xml.sax.helpers.DefaultHandler;   DefaultHandler

public class SchemaXMLHandler extends DefaultHandler {   ◄──

    // Since some DSML elements are common between object classes
    // and attribute types, we need to maintain state about which
    // type of element we are currently parsing.
    private static final int DSML_OC = 0;
    private static final int DSML_AT = 1;       State variable for
    private int currentType = DSML_OC;   ◄──    class/attribute

    // Various states that can exist within an object class or
    // attribute type definition.
    private static final int OP_IGNORE = 0;
    private static final int OP_NAME = 1;
    private static final int OP_DESC = 2;
    private static final int OP_OID = 3;
    private static final int OP_SYNTAX = 4;
    private static final int OP_SINGLEVAL = 5;
    private static final int OP_USERMOD = 6;
    private static final int OP_EQUALITY = 7;
```

```
      private static final int OP_ORDERING = 8;
      private static final int OP_SUBSTRING = 9;
                                                       State variable for
      private int currentOp = OP_IGNORE;    ⟵――――   current operation

    public void characters(char[] ch, int start,      Receives characters
int length) {                                          that are not part of
                                                       an element definition
        String text = new String(ch, start, length);

        // Name, OID, and description are places within an object
        // class definition where we care about character text.
        if (currentType == DSML_OC && text != null) {
            if (currentOp == OP_NAME) {
                System.out.println("\nObject Class: " + text);
            }
            if (currentOp == OP_DESC) {
                System.out.println("Description: " + text);
            }
            if (currentOp == OP_OID) {
                System.out.println("OID: " + text);
            }
        }

        // These characters occur within attribute type definitions

        if (currentType == DSML_AT && text != null) {
            if (currentOp == OP_NAME) {
                System.out.println("\nAttribute Type: " +text);
            }
            if (currentOp == OP_DESC) {
                System.out.println("Description: " + text);
            }
            if (currentOp == OP_OID) {
                System.out.println("OID: " + text);
            }
            if (currentOp == OP_EQUALITY) {
                System.out.println("Matching Rule (Equality): "
                                   + text);
            }
            if (currentOp == OP_USERMOD) {
                if (text.equalsIgnoreCase("false")) {
                    System.out.println("NO User Modifications");
                }
            }
            if (currentOp == OP_SINGLEVAL) {
                if (text.equalsIgnoreCase("true")) {
                    System.out.println("Single Valued");
                }
            }

            if (currentOp == OP_SYNTAX) {
                System.out.println("Syntax: " + text);
            }

            if (currentOp == OP_ORDERING) {
```

```
            System.out.println("Matching Rule (Ordering): " +
                                text);
        }

        if (currentOp == OP_SUBSTRING) {
            System.out.println("Matching Rule (Substring): " +
                                text);
        }
    }
    currentOp = OP_IGNORE;
}

public void endElement(String scratch1, String scratch2,
String name) {
    if (name.equals("dsml:class") ||
        name.equals("dsml:attribute-type")) {
        System.out.println("\n");
    }
    currentOp = OP_IGNORE;
}

public void startElement(String scratch1, String scratch2,
                    String name, Attributes atts) {
    // Check for the start of a new object class definition
    if (name.equals("dsml:class")) {
        currentType = DSML_OC;

        String superior = atts.getValue("superior");
        if (superior != null) {
            System.out.println("Superior: " +
                                superior.substring(1));
        }
        String ocType = atts.getValue("type");
        if (ocType != null) {
            if (ocType.equals("abstract")) {
                System.out.println("Abstract Class");
            } else if (ocType.equals("auxiliary")) {
                System.out.println("Auxiliary Class");
            } else {
                System.out.println("Structural Class");
            }
        }
    }

    // Check for elements that occur within an
    // object class definition
    if (name.equals("dsml:name")) {
        currentOp = OP_NAME;
    }

    if (name.equals("dsml:description")) {
        currentOp = OP_DESC;
    }
```

Called when an XML element ends

Called when an XML element begins

```
if (name.equals("dsml:object-identifier")) {
    currentOp = OP_OID;
}

// The attribute element within an object class definition
if (name.equals("dsml:attribute") &&
    currentType == DSML_OC) {
    String ref = atts.getValue("ref");
    String req = atts.getValue("required");
    if (req != null && ref != null && req.equals("true")) {
        System.out.println("Must Have Attribute: " +
                            ref.substring(1));
    } else if (ref != null) {
        System.out.println("May Have Attribute: " +
                            ref.substring(1));
    }
}

// Check to see if we're starting a new
// attribute type definition
if (name.equals("dsml:attribute-type")) {
    currentType = DSML_AT;

    String superior = atts.getValue("superior");
    if (superior != null) {
        System.out.println("Superior: " +
                            superior.substring(1));
    }
}

// The rest of these checks check to see if we're within an
// attribute type definition and the element name is set to
// a particular value.

if (name.equals("dsml:name") && currentType == DSML_AT) {
    currentOp = OP_NAME;
}

if (name.equals("dsml:description") &&
    currentType == DSML_AT) {
    currentOp = OP_DESC;
}

if (name.equals("dsml:syntax") && currentType == DSML_AT) {
    currentOp = OP_SYNTAX;
}

if (name.equals("dsml:object-identifier") &&
        currentType == DSML_AT) {
    currentOp = OP_OID;
}

if (name.equals("dsml:single-value") &&
    currentType == DSML_AT) {
    currentOp = OP_SINGLEVAL;
}
```

```
        if (name.equals("dsml:user-modification") &&
            currentType == DSML_AT) {
            currentOp = OP_USERMOD;
        }

        if (name.equals("dsml:equality") &&
            currentType == DSML_AT) {
            currentOp = OP_EQUALITY;
        }

        if (name.equals("dsml:ordering") &&
            currentType == DSML_AT) {
            currentOp = OP_ORDERING;
        }

        if (name.equals("dsml:substring") &&
            currentType == DSML_AT) {
            currentOp = OP_SUBSTRING;
        }
    }
}
```

■

If you now start the DSMLSchema class with this handler, you will see the output just as it was defined earlier in this section.

12.4 TRANSFORMATION WITH *XSLT* IN *JAVA*

In chapter 5, we discussed the ability to transform XML documents, including those using the DSML specification, using XSLT. In chapter 11, we looked at an example of doing this from the command line in Perl. In this section, we'll look at how using DSML can make it easier to programmatically create new documents, such as the one shown in figure 12.1.

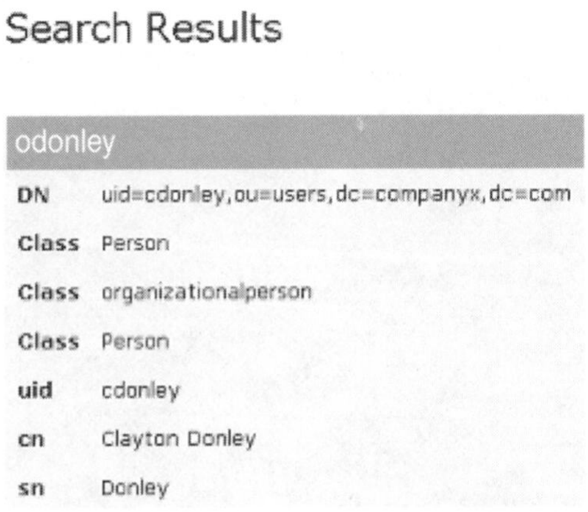

Search Results

odonley	
DN	uid=cdonley,ou=users,dc=companyx,dc=com
Class	Person
Class	organizationalperson
Class	Person
uid	cdonley
cn	Clayton Donley
sn	Donley

Figure 12.1
Potential output of DSML when transformed via XSLT into HTML and viewed with a web browser

You can achieve many output variations based on the same DSML data by using XML stylesheets that are used by XSLT-processing APIs. Listing 12.6 contains a Java servlet that can be run on most web servers. This servlet reads a stylesheet file and provides the translated version of a query as output to client applications. This example takes advantage of the DSML provider for JNDI to do the actual query using an LDAP URL and get DSML-formatted results.

Listing 12.6 DSMLXSLT.java

```java
import javax.xml.transform.stream.StreamResult;
import javax.xml.transform.stream.StreamSource;
import javax.xml.transform.Transformer;
import javax.xml.transform.Source;
import javax.xml.transform.TransformerFactory;
import javax.naming.Context;
import javax.naming.NamingException;
import javax.naming.directory.DirContext;
import javax.naming.directory.InitialDirContext;
import java.util.StringTokenizer;
import java.util.Vector;
import java.util.Enumeration;
import java.util.Hashtable;
import java.net.URL;
import java.io.ByteArrayInputStream;
import java.io.PrintWriter;
import java.io.ByteArrayOutputStream;

public class DSMLXSLT extends javax.servlet.http.HttpServlet {

    // Change this path as necessary to the XSL file
    public String myxsl = "file:d:\\Manning\\html.xsl";

    // If we do an HTTP GET or POST operation, send the request
    //to the performTask method.

    public void doGet(
            javax.servlet.http.HttpServletRequest request,
            javax.servlet.http.HttpServletResponse response)
            throws javax.servlet.ServletException,
                java.io.IOException {
        performTask(request, response);
    }

    public void doPost(
            javax.servlet.http.HttpServletRequest request,
            javax.servlet.http.HttpServletResponse response)
            throws javax.servlet.ServletException,
                java.io.IOException {
        performTask(request, response);
    }

    public String getServletInfo() {
        return super.getServletInfo();
```

```
}

// If we were doing searches rather than
// reading from a file, we might
// initialize connection information or a connection pool here.
public void init() {
}

// This is the method that does the heavy lifting.
public void performTask(
        javax.servlet.http.HttpServletRequest request,
        javax.servlet.http.HttpServletResponse response) {

    try {

        String base = request.getParameter("base");
        String filter = request.getParameter("filter");
        String scope = request.getParameter("scope");
        String attrs = request.getParameter("attrs");
        String xsl = request.getParameter("xsl");

        if (scope == null) {
            scope = "base";
        }
        if (filter == null) {
            filter = "(objectclass=*)";
        }
        if (base == null) {
            base = "";
        }

        if (attrs == null) {
            attrs = "";
        }

        // We'll be creating an HTML document
        response.setContentType("text/html");

        PrintWriter out = response.getWriter();
        ByteArrayOutputStream baos =
                    new ByteArrayOutputStream();

        baos.write(
          "<dsml:dsml xmlns:dsml=\"http://www.dsml.org/DSML\">"
            .getBytes());

        Hashtable env = new Hashtable();

        env.put(Context.INITIAL_CONTEXT_FACTORY,
                    "com.sun.jndi.dsml.DsmlCtxFactory");

        env.put(Context.PROVIDER_URL,
                    "ldap://localhost/" + base +
                    "?" + attrs +
                    "?" + scope + "?" + filter);

        env.put(Context.SECURITY_PRINCIPAL, "cn=Admin");
```

Create LDAP URL for query

```
                env.put(Context.SECURITY_CREDENTIALS, "manager");

                String dsmlresults = null;

                try {
                    DirContext ctx = new InitialDirContext(env);       ⎤ Perform
                    dsmlresults = ctx.lookup("").toString();      ◁──⎦ lookup
                    ctx.close();
                } catch (NamingException ne) {
                    System.err.println("Error: " + ne.getMessage());
                    System.exit(0);
                }                                                 ⎤ Dump DSML output
                baos.write(dsmlresults.getBytes());          ◁──⎦ to output stream

                baos.write("</dsml:dsml>".getBytes());
                byte[] dsmlbytes = baos.toByteArray();
                baos.close();

                ByteArrayInputStream bais =
                        new ByteArrayInputStream(dsmlbytes);
                TransformerFactory tFactory =
                        TransformerFactory.newInstance();
                                                                 ⎤ Specify XML
                Source xmlSource = new StreamSource(bais);    ◁─⎦ source

                Source xslSource =
                        new StreamSource(new URL(myxsl).openStream()); ◁─
                                                                    ⎤ Open
                Transformer transformer =                           ⎦ stylesheet
                        tFactory.newTransformer(xslSource);

                transformer.transform(xmlSource,    │ Perform
                        new StreamResult(out));      │ transformation
            } catch (Throwable theException) {
                theException.printStackTrace();
            }
        }
    }
}
```

With the servlet coded, the only thing missing is a working stylesheet. In listing 12.6, you can specify the stylesheet using a query string in the HTTP GET or POST operation; the example will default to a stylesheet called html.xsl. Listing 12.7 shows a working stylesheet that will do basic conversion of DSML into HTML.

Listing 12.7   html.xsl

```
<?xml version="1.0"?>

<xsl:stylesheet xmlns:xsl="http://www.w3.org/1999/XSL/Transform"
        version="1.0"
        xmlns="http://www.w3.org/TR/REC-html40"
        xmlns:dsml="http://www.dsml.org/DSML">

<xml:output method="html" indent="yes"/>
```

```
<xsl:template match="/">
  <html>
    <head>
      <title>Results</title>
    </head>
    <body>
      <h1>Results</h1>
      <xsl:for-each
          select="dsml:dsml/dsml:directory-entries/dsml:entry">
        <h4>
          <xsl:value-of select="@dn"/>
        </h4>
        <table border="1">
          <xsl:for-each select="dsml:attr">
            <tr>
              <th>
                <xsl:value-of select="@name"/>
              </th>
              <xsl:for-each select="dsml:value">
                <td>
                  <xsl:value-of select="."/>
                </td>
              </xsl:for-each>
            </tr>
          </xsl:for-each>
        </table>
      </xsl:for-each>
    </body>
  </html>
</xsl:template>
</xsl:stylesheet>
```

12.5   ENHANCEMENTS WITH DSMLv2

Up until now, our discussion has focused primarily on functionality described in
DSMLv1. That version discusses only the representation of directory entry and
schema information in XML.

DSMLv2 is a newer standard that has emerged to take integration between XML
and directories to the next level. It does so by providing the ability to perform nearly
all LDAP operations in XML. These operations can then be transmitted via messages
or RPCs to another DSMLv2-aware application, extending the reach of directory information along the way.

DSMLv2 operations are based completely on LDAP counterparts; all arguments
to DSMLv2 operation elements mirror those in LDAP. Thus everything you've
learned about LDAP's information model and operations applies directly to
DSMLv2 operations.

Why bother with DSMLv2 operations when LDAP already exists and has much
broader acceptance? The answer is web services. Although many applications will

continue to use LDAP as their primary means of accessing directory information, the advent of formal web services around HTTP, SOAP, XML, and other standards makes it easier to use a standard like DSML, because DSMLv2 is based on those same standards.

12.5.1 Implementing interapplication communication

It is becoming impossible to talk about RPCs in Java without bringing up the SOAP standard. SOAP has emerged as the most widely advocated, if not accepted, standard for enabling the kind of interapplication communication that will form the basis for web services.

DSMLv2 lists SOAP as one possible avenue for transmitting these new DSML operations. It is equally possible to simply send the operations in email or via messaging-oriented middleware (MOM), but we will focus our energy on SOAP over HTTP in this section.

12.5.2 Creating DSMLv2 SOAP requests

Because DSMLv2 operations are encoded as SOAP requests, it makes sense to take a quick peek at what these operations look like once they've been encoded. Listing 12.8 shows an add request in DSMLv2.

> **Listing 12.8 DSML SOAP Add.xml**

```
<?xml version="1.0" encoding="UTF-8"?>
<SOAP-ENV:Envelope xmlns:SOAP-ENV=
    http://schemas.xmlsoap.org/soap/envelope/
    xmlns:xsd=http://www.w3.org/2001/XMLSchema
    xmlns:xsi="http://www.w3.org/2001/XMLSchema-instance">
 <SOAP-ENV:Body>
  <dsml:batchRequest xmlns:dsml="urn:oasis:names:tc:DSML:2:0:core">
   <dsml:addRequest dn="cn=George Smith,dc=manning,dc=com">
   <dsml:attr name="objectclass">
    <dsml:value>person</dsml:value>
   </dsml:attr>
   <dsml:attr name="cn">
    <dsml:value>George Smith</dsml:value>
   </dsml:attr>
   <dsml:attr name="sn">
    <dsml:value>Smith</dsml:value>
   </dsml:attr>
   </dsml:addRequest>
  </dsml:batchRequest>
 </SOAP-ENV:Body></SOAP-ENV:Envelope>
```

If you look carefully at this add request, you'll see that it can be divided into two main parts. First is the SOAP envelope: this information wraps the dsml:addRequest. element and gives the context needed by the recipient to direct to the correct service.

The second part begins with the dsml:addRequest element and specifies the distinguished name and attributes associated with the add operation. This is exactly the information required to do an LDAP add operation—but instead of the underlying system encoding the operation as ASN.1 structures, per the LDAP standards, you encode this same information as XML.

Listing 12.9 for the DSMLSOAPAdd class posts a properly formatted DSMLv2 add request to a hypothetical DSMLv2 service. It requires the Apache AXIS API package for handling SOAP messages and uses DOM (discussed earlier in the chapter) to build the request.

Listing 12.9   DSMLSOAPAdd.java

```
import org.apache.axis.client.ServiceClient;
import org.apache.axis.AxisFault;
import org.apache.axis.utils.QName;
import org.apache.axis.message.RPCParam;
import org.apache.axis.message.SOAPEnvelope;
import org.apache.axis.message.SOAPBodyElement;
import org.w3c.dom.Element;
import org.w3c.dom.Document;

import javax.xml.parsers.ParserConfigurationException;
import javax.xml.parsers.DocumentBuilder;
import javax.xml.parsers.DocumentBuilderFactory;

public class DSMLSOAPAdd {

    public static void main(String[] args) {
        // We would change this to point to a real server capable of
        // processing this request.
        String endpoint = "http://localhost/dsml2service";

        // Some sample entry data to add.
        String dn = "cn=George Smith,dc=manning,dc=com";
        String cnvalue = "George Smith";
        String snvalue = "Smith";                           Create SOAP client
                                                            connected to endpoint
        try {
            ServiceClient client = new ServiceClient(endpoint);     ◄┘
            SOAPEnvelope se = new SOAPEnvelope();

            DocumentBuilderFactory factory = DocumentBuilderFactory
                                        .newInstance();
            Document document = null;

            try {
                DocumentBuilder builder =
                    factory.newDocumentBuilder();
                                                            Build new DOM
                document = builder.newDocument();     ◄┘   document

            } catch (ParserConfigurationException pce) {
                System.err.println("Parse Error: " +
                                pce.getMessage());
```

```
            System.exit(0);
    }

Element br =
   (Element) document.createElement("dsml:batchRequest");
br.setAttribute("xmlns:dsml",
                "urn:oasis:names:tc:DSML:2:0:core");

Element ar = (Element) document          │ Beginning of
    .createElement("dsml:addRequest");   │ add request
ar.setAttribute("dn",   dn);
ar.appendChild(document.createTextNode("\n"));
br.appendChild(ar);

Element oc = (Element)
    document.createElement("dsml:attr");
oc.setAttribute("name","objectclass");

Element ocval = (Element)
    document.createElement("dsml:value");
ocval.appendChild(document.createTextNode("person"));
oc.appendChild(ocval);

Element cn = (Element)
    document.createElement("dsml:attr");
cn.setAttribute("name","cn");

Element cnval = (Element)
    document.createElement("dsml:value");
cnval.appendChild(document.createTextNode(cnvalue));
cn.appendChild(cnval);

Element sn = (Element)
    document.createElement("dsml:attr");
sn.setAttribute("name","sn");

Element snval = (Element)
    document.createElement("dsml:value");
snval.appendChild(document.createTextNode(snvalue));
sn.appendChild(snval);

ar.appendChild(oc);
ar.appendChild(cn);
ar.appendChild(sn);

SOAPBodyElement sb = new SOAPBodyElement(br);

se.addBodyElement(sb);   ◄─────────────────   Add document to
                                              SOAP envelope
client.invoke(se);   ◄──── Send request to
} catch (AxisFault af) {  connected endpoint
    System.err.println("Error: " + af.getMessage());
    }
  }
}
```

When run, this class creates a DSMLv2 add request and transmits it to the connected endpoint. At the time of this writing, no DSMLv2 services are available to process such requests; however, these types of services will likely arise primarily as front-ends to information that currently exists in LDAP-enabled directories.

You can currently check the code output for general validity by using the various SOAP proxy services available that can intercept a SOAP request and print its contents. Doing so demonstrates that the proper message is being transmitted.

Until more DSMLv2 services are available, the DSMLv2 standard offers little beyond the features we've discussed as being available in the DSMLv1 specification.

12.5.3 Creating DSMLv2 SOAP requests with JNDI

Just as this book was going to press, an early-access DSMLv2 provider was released that allows JNDI-enabled applications to make DSMLv2 requests as easily as they make LDAP requests. Thanks to the magic of JNDI abstraction, most of our JNDI examples work with almost no modification.

The example from section 11.3 that creates an LDAP connection could be easily changed to the following lines of code:

```
Properties env = new Properties();
env.put(DirContext.INITIAL_CONTEXT_FACTORY,
        "com.sun.jndi.dsmlv2.soap.DsmlSoapCtxFactory");
env.put(DirContext.PROVIDER_URL,"ldap://localhost:8080");
DirContext dirContext = new InitialDirContext(env);
```

Assuming a server was listening for DSMLv2 requests over HTTP on port 8080, any further JNDI requests on the `dirContext` object would be performed using DSML rather than LDAP.

12.6 SUMMARY

In this chapter, you discovered new ways to access and manipulate documents using DSML. We covered using JNDI to access both DSMLv1- and DSMLv2-compliant servers, as well as techniques for using the DOM APIs for XML to manipulate potentially large DSML files. We provided Java code for using XSLT to transform DSML into HTML, as an example of the power that existing XML APIs can provide to directory-enabled applications. Finally, we discussed improvements with DSMLv2 and used Java to create an example SOAP message that encapsulates a DSMLv2 operation.

In chapter 13, we take a detailed look at enterprise information security as it relates to and uses LDAP-enabled directory services.

C H A P T E R   1 3

Application security and directory services

Security is a vast topic that means many things to many people. In this chapter, we will look at how applications can leverage directories to provide security services. We'll also explore the relationship between directories and security services.

By the end of this chapter, you will have learned the answers to these questions:

- What is security, and how does it relate to directories?
- How can directories most effectively enable different types of security?
- How can an LDAP server be used for authentication?
- What are the limitations of private keys when used for authentication? How can certificates help?
- How can certificates be generated and stored in the directory?
- What is necessary to enable session encryption in JNDI?

13.1 THE RELATIONSHIP BETWEEN SECURITY AND DIRECTORIES

There are many misconceptions about the role directories play in securing an environment. To avoid these pitfalls, we will briefly look at what security really entails and then explore the relationship between security and directory services.

13.1.1 What is security?

In computing, *security* is a broad term. It tends to imply that information and functionality are available to those who should be able to access them and unavailable to those who shouldn't have access. Although this is true, application security can be summed up as comprising several components: authentication, authorization, privacy, availability, and integrity. Table 13.1 briefly summarizes these security-related components.

Table 13.1 Security involves a number of important components

Security component	Definition
Authentication	The process of identifying who is attempting to access a particular set of resources. When you connect to the directory and do a bind, you let the server know who you are by passing an identity and credentials that prove your identity.
Authorization	The process of evaluating whether the authenticated entity is authorized to do something to a particular resource under a defined set of circumstances. For example, after you authenticate to a bank ATM using a plastic card and matching PIN number, the machine uses a set of predefined rules to determine that you can only access the two accounts associated with your authenticated identity.
Privacy	The anonymity and secrecy of information. When you fill out a form on the Internet with personal information, you expect that data to remain private. Similarly, when you're transmitting a credit card number or password over the Internet, you need to ensure that it remains a secret from anyone who might be spying on Internet data.
Availability	Continuous, uninterrupted service. When hackers deface a web site or use denial-of-service (DOS) attacks to make a service unreachable, the availability of the information provided by that service is affected while the site is repaired.
Integrity	The assurance that information has not been changed or corrupted by an unauthorized party. Viruses can affect the integrity of a system by adding information to a document that can produce undesired, potentially damaging, results.

Figure 13.1 shows how all these components come together to form a secure computing environment.

Note that from a user's perspective, the end goal is to get access to the desired application functionality or information. What happens in between is merely overhead that allows access to happen in a way that reduces the risk of unauthorized individuals gaining access to inappropriate resources.

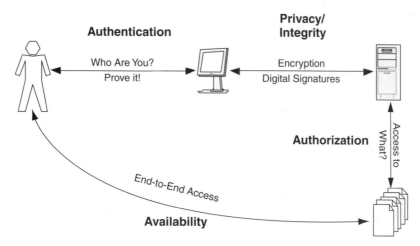

Figure 13.1 An environment that includes all the security elements

Assessing security risks to your environment

Although security includes many components, it's important to keep in mind that security is rarely perfect and should never be viewed as an all-or-nothing proposition. For example, an application that allows people to look at general-purpose news on a subscription basis will suffer little damage if a hacker finds a password and looks at the site for free. On the other hand, an application that allows someone to make financial transactions is a more enticing target and susceptible to greater damage.

The differences noted are linked directly to risk. The single most important aspect of security is risk evaluation and reduction. Different environments have different levels of need for the types of security we've defined. In the two examples we just gave, the first situation might need simple logins and passwords with few control processes, and the second might require biometric authentication mechanisms for high value transactions.

The actual level to which the various components of application security are required is also dependent on risk. Consider the following scenarios:

- A public web site that provides general-purpose news for free may only be interested in knowing that someone accessed the site, not who that person is. In this instance, authentication and authorization are fairly low needs; a much higher need exists for ensuring availability and integrity of the news service to the public.

- Two CEOs communicating about a possible merger need privacy and integrity, as well as basic levels of availability. Privacy ensures that competitors and investors cannot eavesdrop on this information, and integrity assures each CEO that they are not speaking with an impostor.

Certain top-secret information may be so sensitive that all other factors are given higher priority than availability. In some cases, the risk associated with the unauthorized access is so high that complete service interruption or self-destruction is preferable.

13.1.2 How LDAP provides security

LDAP is not an authentication service, nor is it an authorization service. LDAP also does not directly affect availability, provide any layer of privacy, or ensure data integrity outside the directory itself. Why is it, then, that people so often find their way to directory services when trying to implement solutions related to security?

Although LDAP is not an authentication service, it stores the identities and credentials used by those services, and many applications can use LDAP as an authentication service if one is not available. LDAP aids in authorization because it acts as a network-accessible data store for access control lists and policies that can be used to authorize access to resources.

Public key cryptography allows applications and people to authenticate and secure information without either party having previously shared the secret code that is used in the process. Strong data privacy and integrity are made possible by public key cryptography, and directories play a vital role in distributing the information needed to make many aspects of public key cryptography work on a large scale. We will discuss public key cryptography and the critical role directories play with this technology in section 13.2.

Finally, a properly distributed directory, when used for storing and providing access to information, can increase overall availability of the applications that depend on it.

Figure 13.2 shows how some off-the-shelf authentication and authorization services use directories to store credentials, policies, and access controls.

It is important to note that it is not necessary to have those services if the application itself is sufficiently aware of how to use that information. Using the information in the directory this way is perfectly acceptable, and applications that do so in a few

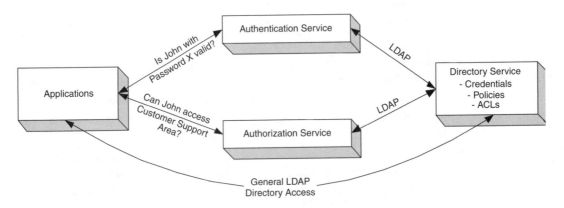

Figure 13.2 Directories provide information to external authentication and authorization services.

standard ways will be compatible with off-the-shelf variants to a great degree. We will walk through using the directory directly from your applications later in the chapter.

LDAP authentication support

Just because LDAP directories are not external authentication services does not mean they do not perform authentication. In fact, much of the recent work related to LDAP has been to strengthen the authentication mechanisms available.

The bind operation allows an LDAP client to authenticate. This in turn allows the LDAP server to authorize access to a set of entries and attributes based on any access control lists it may be using. Figure 13.3 shows this process.

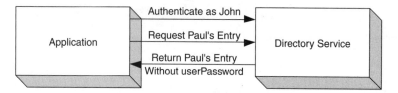

Figure 13.3   The directory service knows that the application user is John, based on an LDAP bind request. It determines that John is not allowed to see Paul's password.

LDAP has long supported anonymous and simple authentication. *Anonymous* means exactly what it sounds like, and *simple authentication* means that passwords are transmitted in the clear over the network.

Earlier LDAP vendors added a level of security in the form of SSL encryption, which allows passwords to be encrypted by the virtue of having encryption for the entire session. SSL also adds the ability to authenticate the server using certificates.

More recent standards have required support for the SASL, which allows client and server to negotiate and use different mechanisms to authenticate each other.

Using LDAP as an authentication service

Applications presenting valid credentials to an LDAP server via the LDAP bind operation are informed that the credentials passed were valid. This bit of functionality has long been used to allow applications to check the password presented by a user against the one stored in the directory. Thus, although LDAP is not a true authentication service, applications can use it to provide this service as shown in figure 13.4.
Most applications that offer to use LDAP as an authentication service do so exactly as we've just described. By using the bind operation instead of comparing the value stored in the `userPassword` attribute or other locations, the application can check the validity of credentials provided by a user without needing to worry about the lack of password encryption standards.

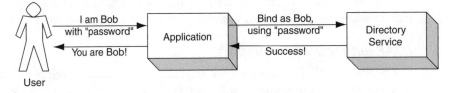

Figure 13.4   Using LDAP as an authentication service

The example in listing 13.1 shows how LDAP can be used to check the validity of a password.

Listing 13.1   LDAPLogin.java

```java
import javax.naming.directory.DirContext;
import javax.naming.NamingException;
import java.util.Vector;

public class LDAPLogin {

    private static final String USERID_ATTRIBUTE = "uid";
    private static void main(String args[]) {
        if (args.length != 2) {
            System.err.println("Must give userid and password");
        }
        boolean result = LDAPLogin.login(args[0],args[1]);

        if (result) {
            System.out.println("Login as " +
                                args[0] + " was successful!");
        } else {
            System.out.println("Login as " +
                                args[0] + " was incorrect!");
        }
    }

    public static boolean login(String username, String password) {
        LDAPConnection lc = new LDAPConnection();
        String dn = null;
        //Filter construction for search on UID
        String filter = new String("(" + USERID_ATTRIBUTE + "=" +
                                username + ")");

        try {
            DirContext dc = lc.open();
            // Perform the search
            Vector results = LDAPSearch.search("","sub",filter,
                        new String[0]);
            // If we get more than one result, the userid given was
            // not unique. If no result is returned, the userid
            // given was invalid.
            if (results.size() != 1) {
                return false;
```

Set attribute for UserID comparison

Take two arguments: login and password

```
        }
        Entry entry = (Entry)results.elementAt(0);      ⎤ Get DN from
        dn = entry.getDN();                              ⎬ only returned
        lc.close(dc);                                    ⎦ entry
    } catch (NamingException ne) {
        // Error getting initial anonymous connection
        System.err.println("Error connecting to server.");
        return false;
    }

    lc = new LDAPConnection(dn,password);      ⎤ Open connection
    try {                                       ⎬ using DN and
        DirContext dc = lc.open();              ⎦ password
        lc.close(dc);
    } catch (NamingException ne) {
        // Error Logging in
        return false;              ⎤ Failed connection indicates incorrect
    }                              ⎬ password; successful connection
    return true;                   ⎦ indicates correct password
    }
}
```

This technique allows passwords to be checked against the contents of a Novell directory or an IBM directory, even though both of these directories use different password encryption techniques. The limitation of this technique is that many authentication mechanisms cannot be supported this way. For example, a web server does not have a person's private key, so it is unable to bind to the directory server on the user's behalf if it wants to authenticate using public key infrastructure. So, it is up to the web server or a trusted authentication service to perform the validation.

13.2   STORING KEY AND CERTIFICATE DATA

Storage of user credentials is one of the most popular uses of directory services. As we discussed earlier in the chapter, these credentials form the basis for many aspects of security, but are particularly important for authentication and authorization. Many types of credentials can be stored in an LDAP-enabled directory. The types we will discuss here include preshared secret keys and the digital certificates used in public key cryptography.

13.2.1   Preshared secret keys

The most common credentials used today are preshared secret keys. These keys include passwords that both parties need to know in advance for successful authentication to occur.

The userPassword attribute type is used to associate a password with an entry. However, the value of this attribute may be in any format, because the syntax is simply defined as being a binary string.

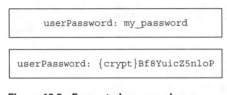

Figure 13.5 Encrypted passwords are prefixed by the algorithm used.

Such ambiguity makes it difficult for an external authentication service to compare the password provided by an end user with an encrypted password in the directory. To mitigate this potential issue, convention dictates that a password is stored in plain text unless it is prefixed by the encryption algorithm used. Figure 13.5 shows how this process works.

Of course, the application may not be familiar with the type of encryption algorithm used to store the password. In other instances, a comparison cannot be performed using the LDAP compare operation because the client does not have access to the entire context necessary to generate the encrypted version of the shared secret. For instance, in the "crypt" example in figure 13.5, the first two characters are a salt—random characters—that impacts the final encrypted value.

Problems with secret keys

The problem with preshared secret keys is that both parties need to know the secret. Consider a situation involving two applications. The same users participate in both applications and want to use the same password for every application they use. Doing so may be fine if both applications are written and operated by the same group, but such an environment cannot be guaranteed in most instances. Where such a closed environment is not possible, trust becomes an issue.

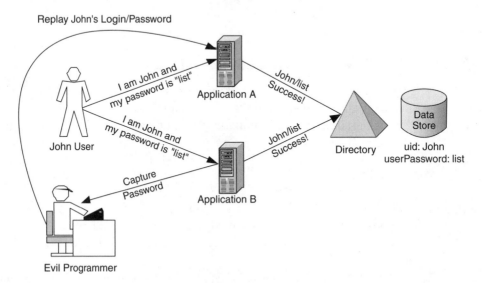

Figure 13.6 An evil developer of application B knows that he can replay passwords given to his application to application A.

It is possible that the developer of one of the two applications may decide to capture passwords provided to users of that application and relay them to the second application, gaining access via the captured accounts. Figure 13.6 shows this risk.

Although this risk has existed for some time, it has been amplified as directory environments have become more integrated. Directories that are integrated beyond organizational boundaries, such as those directory environments used in extranets, are at a higher degree of risk from these kinds of attacks. True authentication services, such as Kerberos, can mitigate some of these risks, but they are often difficult to deploy across organizational boundaries.

13.2.2   Public/private key pairs

Public key cryptography solves many of the problems that secret keys pose. Unlike secret keys, public key cryptography removes the need to preshare any private information used in the authentication process.

Instead, a user generates a pair of keys: one private, the other public. The private key is secret; only the user should ever know what it is. The public key, on the other hand, can and should be shared with the world.

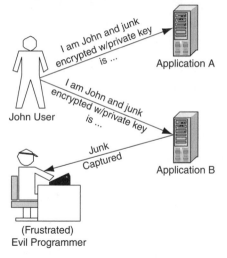

Only the private key can decrypt information the public key encrypts. Similarly, only the public key can decrypt information the private key encrypts. The latter instance may seem odd, considering that anyone can have access to the public key. However, if the public key is guaranteed to have been generated by John User, you can also guarantee that only John User has encrypted a piece of data. As a result, you know with certainty that it is in fact John User who is attempting to access your application.

Figure 13.7 shows that even though John is using the same private key as part of the authentication process, the information that goes over the wire and is received by the application is useless in the type of replay attack shown in the previous section.

Figure 13.7   With public key cryptography, an evil programmer cannot use information sent to his application to access another application.

Because it is theoretically possible for anyone to have the public key, it is now possible for anyone to authenticate John User without divulging secret information.

Problems with key pairs

The problem with this scenario is that it is often difficult to guarantee that John User really owns a particular public key. After all, if Evil Hacker forges an email to Sally Jones using John User's email address, he can tell Sally about his "new public key."

Without proper verification, Sally will have the false sense that the information sent by Evil Hacker is from John. In the next section, we look at how digital certificates can solve this problem, particularly when used with a directory.

13.3 USING DIGITAL CERTIFICATES

Digital certificates attempt to solve part of the public key distribution problem mentioned in the previous section. Together with the rest of public key cryptography, digital certificates greatly enhance many of the security components we discussed at the beginning of the chapter.

A digital certificate is basically a signed public key. By *signed*, we mean that some entity has encrypted a public key with its private key. This signing process is a guarantee by a third party that the signed public key is valid.

Consider the scenario depicted in figure 13.8. Paul knows John. Additionally, Sally knows Paul's public key. Rather than John simply sending his public key to Sally, he instead asks Paul to sign the key and generate a certificate. Now it is possible for John, Paul, or anyone else to forward this certificate to Sally. Sally can verify that it has not been changed because she trusts the validity of the signing key (Paul).

Although digital certificates solve much of the trust problem associated with using public/private key pairs for authentication, they still involve a few issues:

- Certificates require wide distribution.
- Certificates need to be associated with identity information.
- Private keys may be compromised.

Directories can be used to help resolve or mitigate all of these issues.

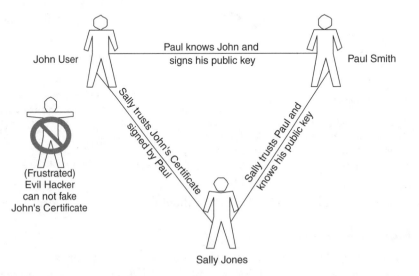

Figure 13.8 Sally trusts Paul and knows his public key. She also trusts certificates signed by Paul, including John's.

13.3.1 Creating a digital certificate in Java

In Java, a standard tool called `keytool` exists for creating public/private key pairs and managing certificates. The following command generates a public/private key pair:

```
$ keytool -genkey -alias jdoe -keyalg rsa
        -dname "cn=John Doe,dc=manning,dc=com"
Enter keystore password:  password
Enter key password for <jdoe>
        (RETURN if same as keystore password):  password
```

That's it. You now have a set of keys associated with jdoe. You can see them using keytool's `list` command:

```
$ keytool -list
Enter keystore password:  password

Keystore type: jks
Keystore provider: SUN

Your keystore contains 1 entry:

jdoe, Fri Dec 07 07:34:23 CST 2001, keyEntry,
Certificate fingerprint (MD5):
46:1D:C8:96:95:C4:E1:B5:07:C8:48:4F:EA:7F:C6:62
```

However, you still don't have a certificate. In order to generate a certificate, you need to do one of two things: self-sign or submit for signing. Because much of the point of having a certificate is to be able to share it and help people authenticate you, it doesn't help to self-sign unless everyone plans to trust you explicitly. The exception is during testing.

Self-signing a certificate

To self-sign a certificate, use the `selfcert` argument to `keytool`, as follows:

```
$ keytool -selfcert -alias jdoe -keyalg rsa
    -dname "cn=John Doe,dc=manning,dc=com"
    -validity 365
Enter keystore password:  password
```

Now notice that when you list the certificates, the fingerprint is different:

```
$ keytool -list
Enter keystore password:  password

Keystore type: jks
Keystore provider: SUN

Your keystore contains 1 entry:

jdoe, Fri Dec 07 07:46:28 CST 2001, keyEntry,
Certificate fingerprint (MD5):
65:30:7E:43:EE:DD:19:91:33:91:F0:96:F5:1D:CD:10
```

Submitting to a signing authority

If, instead of self-signing, you want to submit your key to a signing authority such as Thawte or VeriSign, you can do the following:

```
$ keytool -certreq -alias jdoe -file jdoe.csr
Enter keystore password:  password
```

You can now submit the file jdoe.csr to a signing authority (the CSR extension identifies it as a certificate signing request). That authority will return a fully signed certificate. You store that certificate in a file called jdoe.cer, and import it into your Java keystore using the following command:

```
$ keytool -import -alias jdoe -file jdoe.cer -v
Enter keystore password:  password
```

As you can see, working with certificates using the Java command-line tools isn't too difficult. These certificates can, in turn, be used by the Java Cryptography Extensions (JCE). With the few exceptions that we'll discuss in a moment, JCE is out of the scope of this book.

13.3.2   Storing and distributing digital certificates

Directories are a network storage point for digital certificates. Such a storage point offers applications a place to easily find a digital certificate for communications partners.

   With shared secret keys, the risk rises as keys are used by more applications. In contrast, distributing digital certificates adds immense value by allowing credentials to be shared across administrative domains and even organizations without adding risk. Because LDAP-based directories can be highly distributed, storing certificates in such a directory lets you distribute certificates in a relatively standard way.

   Digital certificates are commonly stored within LDAP servers in a format called X.509v3. Such a certificate includes the name of the certificate's owner, arbitrary key/value assertions, the public key of the owner, and an expiration time (see figure 13.9). Like LDAP, X.509v3 is defined using ASN.1, although it is encoded using a subset of Basic Encoding Rules (BERs) called Distinguished Encoding Rules (DERs). This encoding ensures that the same information is encoded identically each time, whereas BER allows for multiple encodings, particularly related to value length representations.

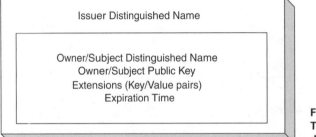

Figure 13.9
The contents of an X.509v3
digital certificate

The standard attribute type defined for storing certificates in an LDAP directory service is called `userCertificate`. The attribute is always stored in its DER-encoded, binary representation.

Let's look at what it takes to store the certificate you generated in the last section in the directory, rather than in Java's local keystore. To do so, you can use the JCE mentioned in the last section along with your existing knowledge of the JNDI.

Begin by exporting a certificate from your Java keystore—perhaps the jdoe certificate you issued in the last section, although any DER-formatted certificate will do. Place the exported certificate into a file called test.cer:

```
keytool -export -alias jdoe -file test.cer
```

Now that you have a certificate file, create the Java code in listing 13.2, which takes the contents of this file and publishes it to an appropriate entry within the directory. Note that it is possible with the JCE kit to read the certificate directly from the keystore, but this code deals with the more common occurrence of processing externally generated certificates. The output of your small program will look something like the following:

```
Found Certificate -
  Issuer : CN=John Doe, DC=manning, DC=com
  Subject: CN=John Doe, DC=manning, DC=com
  Expires: Sat Dec 07 07:46:27 CST 2002
Storing Certificate in Directory.
```

Listing 13.2   PublishCert.java

```java
import java.io.InputStream;
import java.io.FileInputStream;
import java.security.cert.CertificateFactory;
import java.security.cert.X509Certificate;
import java.security.cert.CertificateEncodingException;
import java.util.Vector;

public class PublishCert {

    private static String certFile = "test.cer";

    public static void main(String[] args) {
        X509Certificate cert = null;
        try {
            InputStream inStream =
                new FileInputStream(certFile);
            CertificateFactory cf =
                CertificateFactory.getInstance("X.509");

            // Generate a certificate from the information
            // in the open file
            cert = (X509Certificate)cf                      ⎤ Create
                    .generateCertificate(inStream);         ⎬ certificate
                                                            ⎦ from file
            inStream.close();
```

```
        } catch (Exception e) {
            System.err.println("Failed to Read Certificate: " +
                                e.getMessage());
        }

        System.out.println("Found Certificate -");
        System.out.println("  Issuer : " + cert.getIssuerDN());
        System.out.println("  Subject: " + cert.getSubjectDN());
        System.out.println("  Expires: " + cert.getNotAfter());

        System.out.println("Storing Certificate in Directory.");

        // Get the certificate in its DER-encoded form
        // as a string of bytes.
        byte[] certbytes = null;
        try {
            certbytes = cert.getEncoded();
        } catch (CertificateEncodingException cee) {
            System.err.println("Unable to encode certificate: " +
                                cee.getMessage());
        }

        // Use our Entry class from chapter 11
        Entry entry = new Entry();                          Set DN of
                                                        ◄──┘ new entry
        entry.setDN("cn=John Doe,dc=manning,dc=com");

        // Add the certificate value to the entry's userCertificate
        // using the ;binary attribute tag
        Vector certvals = new Vector();
        certvals.addElement(certbytes);
        entry.put("userCertificate",certvals);

        // We'll use the same value for CN and SN attributes
        Vector cnsnvals = new Vector();
        cnsnvals.addElement("John Doe");
        entry.put("cn",cnsnvals);
        entry.put("sn",cnsnvals);

        Vector ocvals = new Vector();
        ocvals.addElement("inetOrgPerson");
        entry.put("objectclass",ocvals);

        // Call the LDAPAdd.add() method from chapter 11
        LDAPConnection lc =
            new LDAPConnection("cn=admin","manager");
        LDAPAdd.add(lc,entry);
    }

}
```

You can verify that the program added the certificate to the directory entry by using the following ldapsearch command:

```
> ldapsearch -b "cn=Test User,dc=manning,dc=com" -s
    base objectclass=*
```

The returned entry in LDIF format looks something like this:

```
dn: cn=John Doe,dc=manning,dc=com
objectclass: inetOrgPerson
objectclass: organizationalPerson
objectclass: person
objectclass: top
userCertificate:: MIIB+DCCAWECBDwQyDMwDQYJKoZIhvcNAQ...
sn: Doe
cn: John Doe
```

The userCertificate attribute can now easily be read using the search code you developed in chapter 11. You can use it to create a certificate from the directory, rather than from a file as you did in this example.

Associating certificates with related directory information

A digital certificate, once issued, cannot be changed. This means the certificate is a poor choice to store information about roles and other potentially dynamic information. Instead, the directory can be used to map the distinguished name of the certificate owner to additional information that can be used for authorization and other services.

Revoking compromised certificates

Digital certificates have a fixed expiration time. However, in some cases, you'll need to cancel a digital certificate before its expiration time. Certificates can be revoked for a number of reasons, such as the following:

- Someone was terminated or left a project where he or she is authorized to have a certificate from a particular issuer.
- The holder of the certificate changed his or her legal name and requires a new certificate to be issued with the new name.
- A private key has been compromised, in which case it must be revoked to prevent unauthorized users from gaining access with compromised credentials.

The need to revoke certificates is a real issue, because there is no way to know how far a particular certificate has propagated. Additionally, this need is not uncommon. Consider the number of people who have left your organization in the last year. Now add any cases in which a private key may have been compromised. Each of those situations would require that a certificate be expired prior to its noted expiration date.

You can resolve this problem a number of ways, including revocation lists and special services that focus on providing certificate validity information. Certificate authorities (the services that issue certificates) can create a CRL of certificate serial numbers that have prematurely expired for one reason or another. Once created, this list is stored in a directory so that applications and validation services can verify the certificate being used continues to be valid.

More recently, protocols such as Online Certificate Status Protocol (OCSP) have played a more prominent role and have displaced direct lookup of CRLs in the directory. This change is the equivalent of merchants moving from using lists of bad or stolen credit card numbers to using real-time authorization systems when performing a typical credit card validation. Some of these OCSP services still perform queries against LDAP directories to locate expired certificates.

13.4 MANAGING AUTHORIZATION INFORMATION

Although we have touched on the need for directories as a storage point for authorization information, most of our focus has been on authentication. In this section, we take a closer look at authorization on two levels: directory and application.

13.4.1 Understanding access control rules

At its most basic level, authorization is the process of answering the question, "Does entity x have access to perform action y on resource z?" The answer to this question is always yes or no, given enough context.

Servers and applications use access control rules to evaluate these authorization questions. Rules usually take this form: "Set of entities x has access to perform set of actions y on set of resources z when the following conditions are met." The first three criteria map closely to the elements in the authorization question, but the final element is also important.

Take the following rule, for example: "Anyone who owns a record can update it." The people allowed to update a record are not fulfilling a global role of "owner." Instead, "owner" is a role that is associated with a particular resource.

Another example might say that "Managers can view salary information for any people they manage." This common situation also requires that someone fulfill a role relative to the resource being changed. Just knowing that someone has the title "manager" does not mean he or she can view anyone's salary: he or she must be the manager of the person whose information is being viewed.

If you're familiar with basic Unix file permissions, you know that three basic roles are associated with each file:

- Owner
- Group owner
- Other

By being assigned one of these roles relative to a particular file, you can be authorized to read, write, and execute exactly the same way as others who might fulfill that role.

How these types of access control rules are evaluated depends on whether you are protecting a data store (such as a directory) or an application.

13.4.2 Directory authorization

The need to protect information in the directory from being viewed or changed by unauthorized individuals is a type of authorization necessary in virtually every directory services environment. Unfortunately, no current standard exists for setting access control on information in an LDAP-enabled directory. There is also no current way for applications to determine in advance whether a desired operation will be allowed prior to an actual request.

Although no standard exists, most implementations provide some of the same types of access controls. These access controls include the ability to restrict certain parts of the directory tree to particular users and groups. Administrators can also restrict the attributes that directory users can access or update, in some cases based on their own relation to the entry being accessed or modified. For example, a user might authenticate to the server as a manager and be given special rights to manage entries in which the `manager` attribute is set to the authenticated user's distinguished name. Server documentation is the best source for server-specific access control information.

13.4.3 Application authorization

Applications use directory information for authorization as well as authentication. This is an excellent way to reuse information about people, groups, and accounts within the directory to enhance security. For example, if the directory entries about people contain a flag that indicates whether a person is a contractor or permanent employee, an application could allow or disallow access to parts of the application based on that information.

Such access control would be done within the application at some point following authentication by the user. With the distinguished name of the user known from the authentication process, it is only necessary to read that user's information to determine whether they are authorized to perform a particular action. If the test is to determine whether a user is a member of a group, you may need to search on the group to determine if the user is a member. Each of these options can be performed easily using the search techniques explored in this chapter and chapter 11.

It has become very popular to not only use the directory as an external source of authentication and authorization, but also to externalize considerable authentication and authorization logic from the application by using access management products. These products allow both user and policy information to be stored outside the application, often in a directory service, so that this information can be reused across multiple applications. The idea is to reduce the amount of security-related programming necessary in enterprise applications and portals.

Be aware that although these policies are often stored in a standards-based repository, such as an LDAP-enabled directory, the content of the policies is often proprietary and usable only by a particular access management product. However, user and group information that follows standard schemas is not proprietary and usually reusable.

13.5 ENCRYPTING LDAP SESSIONS USING JNDI AND SSL

Encryption is important to protect the privacy of the data being transmitted. For the most part, SSL is the standard for encrypting data sessions over the Internet. Most directories support LDAPS, which is basically LDAP encapsulated within an SSL session. Using Sun's Java Secure Socket Extension (JSSE) toolkit, JNDI allows an LDAP server to connect securely over a network using SSL. Figure 13.10 shows how these pieces fit together.

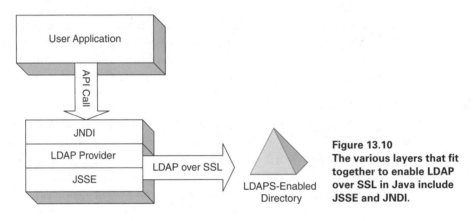

Figure 13.10
The various layers that fit together to enable LDAP over SSL in Java include JSSE and JNDI.

Wonderfully, you can do all this by simply changing a few lines of code when you create the initial `DirContext` object. Make the change shown in bold in listing 13.3 to the `LDAPConnection` class (from listing 11.1) to encrypt the sessions for all the examples in part 3 that use the class to open connections. No other code changes are necessary, because the fundamental LDAP operations are unchanged.

Listing 13.3 LDAPConnection.java

```
public DirContext open() throws NamingException {
    Properties env = new Properties();
    env.put(DirContext.INITIAL_CONTEXT_FACTORY,
            "com.sun.jndi.ldap.LdapCtxFactory");
    env.put(DirContext.PROVIDER_URL,"ldap://" + host +
            ":" + port);
    if (dn != null) {
        env.put(DirContext.SECURITY_PRINCIPAL,dn);
        env.put(DirContext.SECURITY_CREDENTIALS,password);
    }
```

```
env.put(Context.SECURITY_PROTOCOL, "ssl");
DirContext dirContext = new InitialDirContext(env);
return dirContext;
}
```

Note that all you have to do is add a line indicating that you want to use the `ssl` security protocol, and JNDI takes care of the rest. All your directory operations will now be private.

13.6 SUMMARY

In this chapter, you learned a considerable amount about application security and how it relates to directories. We discussed authentication using LDAP as a service for verifying passwords, and we presented an example that lets you validate a login and password against a server. You also saw how you can use Java to create and publish digital certificates. Finally, we explored how easy it is to enable SSL with Sun's LDAP provider for JNDI.

A P P E N D I X A

Standard schema reference

This appendix offers a detailed summary of commonly used, industry-standard schemas that have been defined by the IETF.

A.1 STANDARD OBJECT CLASSES

The object classes listed in this section are defined in three separate standards documents. Those defined in RFCs 2252 and 2256 are implemented by virtually every directory vendor. Those defined in RFC 2798 are supported by nearly every vendor, with Microsoft as a major exception.

alias

Some directories support entry aliases. The `alias` object class lets you create entries that reference other entries within the directory.

Type	Structural
Superior	top
OID	2.5.6.1
Required	aliasedObjectName
Defined	RFC 2256

certificationAuthority

This object class defines information about a certificate authority. It may be used in some PKI environments.

Type	Auxiliary
Superior	top
OID	2.5.6.16
Required	authorityRevocationList, certificateRevocationList, cACertificate
Allowed	crossCertificatePair
Defined	RFC 2256

country

The country object class is relatively straightforward. It mandates a country attribute. In older directories, a country entry is the first object below the root of the directory.

Type	Structural
Superior	top
OID	2.5.6.2
Required	c
Allowed	searchGuide, description
Defined	RFC 2256

cRLDistributionPoint

This object class defines a distribution point for CRLs in a PKI environment.

Type	Structural
Superior	top
OID	2.5.6.19
Required	cn
Allowed	certificateRevocationList, authorityRevocationList, deltaRevocationList
Defined	RFC 2256

device

The device object class is a generic object class for representing devices, such as modems and printers.

Type	Structural
Superior	top
OID	2.5.6.14

Required cn
Allowed serialNumber, seeAlso, owner, ou, o, l, description
Defined RFC 2256

dmd

The dmd object class defines a directory management domain. It is rarely used in most LDAP implementations.

Type Structural
Superior top
OID 2.5.6.20
Required dmdName
Allowed certificateRevocationList, authorityRevocationList, deltaRevocationList
Defined RFC 2256

extensibleObject

The extensibleObject object class, if present in an entry, permits that entry to optionally hold any attribute. It allows an entry to be constructed with arbitrary attribute types and values. Not all directory servers support this class. In addition, keep in mind that indexing issues may keep any arbitrary attributes from being searchable in implementations that do support this class.

Type Auxiliary
Superior top
OID 1.3.6.1.4.1.1466.101.120.111
Defined RFC 2252

groupOfNames

This object class makes it possible to create groups that contain a set of people or things. Typically, the member and owner attributes are populated with the distinguished names of other entries within the directory.

Type Structural
Superior top
OID 2.5.6.9
Required member, cn
Allowed businessCategory, seeAlso, owner, ou, o, description
Defined RFC 2256

groupOfUniqueNames

This object class is commonly used to reference a list of users or entries that belong to a common group. These groups can then be used for everything from mailing lists to access control.

Type	Structural
Superior	top
OID	2.5.6.17
Required	uniqueMember, cn
Allowed	businessCategory, seeAlso, owner, ou, o, description
Defined	RFC 2256

inetOrgPerson

The inetOrgPerson represents people who are associated with an organization in some way. It is a structural class derived from the organizationalPerson class.

Type	Structural
Superior	organizationalPerson
OID	2.16.840.1.113730.3.2.2
Allowed	audio, businessCategory, carLicense, departmentNumber, displayName, employeeNumber, employeeType, givenName, homePhone, homePostalAddress, initials, jpegPhoto, labeledURI, mail, manager, mobile, o, pager, photo, roomNumber, secretary, uid, userCertificate, x500uniqueIdentifier, preferredLanguage, userSMIMECertificate, userPKCS12
Defined	RFC 2798

locality

This object class typically defines a city, and in some cases a more specific location. It is most useful when you're adding a regional hierarchy to a directory tree.

Type	Structural
Superior	top
OID	2.5.6.3
Allowed	street, seeAlso, searchGuide, st, l, description
Defined	RFC 2256

organization

An organization is typically a company or other similar type of entity. Although you can use this class to simply represent a list of organizations for lookup, its most common purpose is as a high-level naming component in the directory tree that allows organization-style naming. The difference between organization-style and domain-style naming is discussed in chapter 3.

Type	Structural
Superior	top
OID	2.5.6.4
Required	o
Allowed	userPassword, searchGuide, seeAlso, businessCategory, x121Address, registeredAddress, destinationIndicator, preferredDeliveryMethod, telexNumber, teletexTerminalIdentifier, telephoneNumber, internationaliSDNNumber, facsimileTelephoneNumber, street, postOfficeBox, postalCode, postalAddress, physicalDeliveryOfficeName, st, l, description
Defined	RFC 2256

organizationalPerson

The organizationalPerson object class is a structural class that can be used to hold information about people. In Active Directory, the person object class is abstract, so person entries should be members of this class.

Type	Structural
Superior	person
OID	2.5.6.7
Required	sn, cn
Allowed	userPassword, telephoneNumber, seeAlso, description
Defined	RFC 2256

organizationalRole

Roles can be many things. For example, "accounts receivable clerk" and "customer support technician" might be roles. Defining such roles lets you define policies around them and add people to them, rather than policies being tied to individuals.

Type	Structural
Superior	top
OID	2.5.6.8
Required	cn
Allowed	x121Address, registeredAddress, destinationIndicator, preferredDeliveryMethod, telexNumber, teletexTerminalIdentifier, telephoneNumber, internationaliSDNNumber, facsimileTelephoneNumber, seeAlso, roleOccupant, preferredDeliveryMethod, street, postOfficeBox, postalCode, postalAddress, physicalDeliveryOfficeName, ou, st, l, description
Defined	RFC 2256

organizationalUnit

This class typically represents a division or part of an organization. However, it is also commonly used as a general-purpose class for nodes that divide the tree. For example, in chapter 3, we show how you can use this class to divide a directory into people and groups using `organizationalUnit` entries as containers.

Type	Structural
Superior	top
OID	2.5.6.5
Required	ou
Allowed	userPassword, searchGuide, seeAlso, businessCategory, x121Address, registeredAddress, destinationIndicator, preferredDeliveryMethod, telexNumber, teletexTerminalIdentifier, telephoneNumber, internationaliSDNNumber, facsimileTelephoneNumber, street, postOfficeBox, postalCode, postalAddress, physicalDeliveryOfficeName, st, l, description
Defined	RFC 2256

person

This is the simplest class for representing a person in a directory. It doesn't have many associated attributes, but it is often the superclass from which other people-related classes inherit. Most applications looking for people-like objects will look for entries containing this object class.

Type	Structural
Superior	top
OID	2.5.6.6
Required	sn, cn
Allowed	userPassword, telephoneNumber, seeAlso, description
Defined	RFC 2256

residentialPerson

The `residentialPerson` object class can be used to represent people who are not based in a particular organization. Generally, `inetOrgPerson` is a better alternative and more commonly used to represent all types of people.

Type	Structural
Superior	person
OID	2.5.6.10

| **Allowed** | businessCategory, x121Address, registeredAddress, destinationIndicator, preferredDeliveryMethod, telexNumber, teletexTerminalIdentifier, telephoneNumber, internationaliSDNNumber, facsimileTelephoneNumber, street, postOfficeBox, postalCode, postalAddress, physicalDeliveryOfficeName, st, l |
| **Defined** | RFC 2256 |

strongAuthenticationUser

The `strongAuthenticationUser` object class can be used to add supplemental certificate information to entries that are also members of other classes.

Type	Auxiliary
Superior	top
OID	2.5.6.15
Required	userCertificate
Defined	RFC 2256

subschema

This object class is used in the subschema entry. Subschema entries are used to hold information about the server's schema. The `objectClasses` and `attribute-Types` attributes would allow you to see whether the schemas listed in this appendix are supported on the server.

Type	Auxiliary
OID	2.5.20.1
Allowed	dITStructureRules, nameForms, ditContentRules, object-Classes, attributeTypes, matchingRules, matchingRuleUse
Defined	RFC 2252

top

The `top` object class is the root of all other object classes. This class specifically states that the `objectClass` attribute is required in all entries.

Type	Abstract
OID	2.5.6.0
Required	objectClass
Defined	RFC 2256

A.2 STANDARD ATTRIBUTE TYPES

This section details the attribute types defined by RFC 2252, RFC 2256, and the latest `inetOrgPerson` draft.

aliasedObjectName

The `aliasedObjectName` attribute is used by the directory service if the entry containing this attribute is an alias.

OID	2.5.4.1
Syntax	DN
Equality	`distinguishedNameMatch`
Multivalued	No
User modify	Yes
Defined	RFC 2256

altServer

The values of this attribute are URLs of other servers that may be contacted when this server becomes unavailable. If the server does not know of any other servers that can be used, this attribute is absent. Clients can cache this information in case their preferred LDAP server later becomes unavailable.

OID	1.3.6.1.4.1.1466.101.120.6
Syntax	IA5 String
Usage	`dSAOperation`
Multivalued	Yes
User modify	Yes
Defined	RFC 2252

attributeTypes

This attribute is typically located in the subschema entry.

OID	2.5.21.5
Syntax	Attribute Type Description
Usage	`directoryOperation`
Equality	`objectIdentifierFirstComponentMatch`
Multivalued	Yes
User modify	Yes
Defined	RFC 2252

authorityRevocationList

This attribute must be stored and requested in the binary form, as `authorityRevocationList;binary`.

OID	2.5.4.38
Syntax	Certificate List
Multivalued	Yes
User modify	Yes
Defined	RFC 2256

businessCategory

This attribute describes the kind of business performed by an organization.

OID	2.5.4.15
Syntax	Directory String{128}
Equality	`caseIgnoreMatch`
Substring	`caseIgnoreSubstringsMatch`
Multivalued	Yes
User modify	Yes
Defined	RFC 2256

c

This attribute contains a two-letter ISO 3166 country code; for example, US or CA.

Superior	name
OID	2.5.4.6
Multivalued	No
User modify	Yes
Defined	RFC 2256

cACertificate

This attribute must be stored and requested in the binary form, as `cACertificate;binary`.

OID	2.5.4.37
Syntax	Certificate
Multivalued	Yes
User modify	Yes
Defined	RFC 2256

carLicense

This multivalued field is used to record the values of the license or registration plate associated with an individual.

OID	2.16.840.1.113730.3.1.1
Syntax	Directory String
Equality	`caseIgnoreMatch`
Substring	`caseIgnoreSubstringsMatch`
Multivalued	Yes
User modify	Yes
Defined	RFC 2798

certificateRevocationList

This attribute must be stored and requested in the binary form, as `certificate-RevocationList;binary`.

OID	2.5.4.39
Syntax	Certificate List
Multivalued	Yes
User modify	Yes
Defined	RFC 2256

cn

This is the X.500 `commonName` attribute, which contains a name of an object. If the object corresponds to a person, it is typically the person's full name.

Superior	`name`
OID	2.5.4.3
Multivalued	Yes
User modify	Yes
Defined	RFC 2256

createTimestamp

This attribute should automatically appear in entries created on the directory server. It is an operational attribute maintained by the server.

OID	2.5.18.1
Syntax	Generalized Time
Usage	`directoryOperation`
Equality	`generalizedTimeMatch`
Multivalued	No
User modify	No
Defined	RFC 2252

creatorsName

This attribute should appear in entries created on the directory server. It is an operational attribute maintained by the server.

OID	2.5.18.3
Syntax	DN
Usage	directoryOperation
Equality	distinguishedNameMatch
Multivalued	No
User modify	No
Defined	RFC 2252

crossCertificatePair

This attribute must be stored and requested in the binary form, as `crossCertificatePair;binary`.

OID	2.5.4.40
Syntax	Certificate Pair
Multivalued	Yes
User modify	Yes
Defined	RFC 2256

dITContentRules

This attribute is used in some X.500-based implementations to define the content of the directory information tree. It is not generally useful outside that context.

OID	2.5.21.2
Syntax	DIT Content Rule Description
Usage	directoryOperation
Equality	objectIdentifierFirstComponentMatch
Multivalued	Yes
User modify	Yes
Defined	RFC 2252

dITStructureRules

This attribute is used in some X.500-based implementations to define the content of the directory information tree. It is not used by most pure LDAP directories.

OID	2.5.21.1
Syntax	DIT Structure Rule Description
Usage	directoryOperation
Equality	integerFirstComponentMatch
Multivalued	Yes

| **User modify** | Yes |
| **Defined** | RFC 2252 |

deltaRevocationList

This attribute must be stored and requested in the binary form, as `deltaRevocationList;binary`.

OID	2.5.4.53
Syntax	Certificate List
Multivalued	Yes
User modify	Yes
Defined	RFC 2256

departmentNumber

This attribute contains a code for the department to which a person belongs. It can also be strictly numeric (such as `1234`) or alphanumeric (such as `ABC123`).

OID	2.16.840.1.113730.3.1.2
Syntax	Directory String
Equality	`caseIgnoreMatch`
Substring	`caseIgnoreSubstringsMatch`
Multivalued	Yes
User modify	Yes
Defined	RFC 2798

description

This attribute contains a human-readable description of the object.

OID	2.5.4.13
Syntax	Directory String{1024}
Equality	`caseIgnoreMatch`
Substring	`caseIgnoreSubstringsMatch`
Multivalued	Yes
User modify	Yes
Defined	RFC 2256

destinationIndicator

This attribute is used for the telegram service.

OID	2.5.4.27
Syntax	Printable String{128}
Equality	`caseIgnoreMatch`
Substring	`caseIgnoreSubstringsMatch`

Multivalued	Yes
User modify	Yes
Defined	RFC 2256

displayName

When you're displaying an entry, especially within a one-line summary list, it is useful to be able to identify a name to be used. Because other attribute types such as `cn` are multivalued, an additional attribute type is needed. The `displayName` attribute is defined for this purpose.

OID	2.16.840.1.113730.3.1.241
Syntax	Directory String
Equality	`caseIgnoreMatch`
Substring	`caseIgnoreSubstringsMatch`
Multivalued	No
User modify	Yes
Defined	RFC 2798

distinguishedName

This attribute type is not used as the name of the object itself, but is instead a base type from which attributes with DN syntax inherit. It is unlikely that values of this type will occur in an entry.

OID	2.5.4.49
Syntax	DN
Equality	`distinguishedNameMatch`
Multivalued	Yes
User modify	Yes
Defined	RFC 2256

dmdName

The value of this attribute specifies a directory management domain (DMD), the administrative authority that operates the directory server.

Superior	`name`
OID	2.5.4.54
Multivalued	Yes
User modify	Yes
Defined	RFC 2256

dnQualifier

The `dnQualifier` attribute type specifies disambiguating information to add to the relative distinguished name of an entry. It is intended for use when you're merging data from multiple sources, in order to prevent conflicts between entries that would otherwise have the same name. It is recommended that the value of the dnQualifier attribute be the same for all entries from a particular source.

OID	2.5.4.46
Syntax	Printable String
Equality	caseIgnoreMatch
Substring	caseIgnoreSubstringsMatch
Multivalued	Yes
User modify	Yes
Defined	RFC 2256

employeeNumber

This single-valued attribute is a numeric or alphanumeric identifier assigned to a person, typically based on the order of hire or association with an organization.

OID	2.16.840.1.113730.3.1.3
Syntax	Directory String
Equality	caseIgnoreMatch
Substring	caseIgnoreSubstringsMatch
Multivalued	No
User modify	Yes
Defined	RFC 2798

employeeType

This attribute is used to identify the employer-to-employee relationship. Typical values are Contractor, Employee, Intern, Temp, External, and Unknown, but any value may be used.

OID	2.16.840.1.113730.3.1.4
Syntax	Directory String
Equality	caseIgnoreMatch
Substring	caseIgnoreSubstringsMatch
Multivalued	Yes
User modify	Yes
Defined	RFC 2798

enhancedSearchGuide

This attribute is for use by X.500 clients in constructing search filters.

OID	2.5.4.47
Syntax	Enhanced Guide
Multivalued	Yes

| User modify | Yes |
| Defined | RFC 2256 |

facsimileTelephoneNumber

This attribute represents a fax number.

OID	2.5.4.23
Syntax	Facsimile Telephone Number
Multivalued	Yes
User modify	Yes
Defined	RFC 2256

generationQualifier

The `generationQualifier` attribute contains the part of the name that typically is the suffix, such as `Jr.` or `III`.

Superior	name
OID	2.5.4.44
Multivalued	Yes
User modify	Yes
Defined	RFC 2256

givenName

The `givenName` attribute is used to hold the part of a person's name that is neither their surname nor middle name.

Superior	name
OID	2.5.4.42
Multivalued	Yes
User modify	Yes
Defined	RFC 2256

houseIdentifier

This attribute is used to identify a building within a location.

OID	2.5.4.51
Syntax	Directory String{32768}
Equality	caseIgnoreMatch
Substring	caseIgnoreSubstringsMatch
Multivalued	Yes
User modify	Yes
Defined	RFC 2256

initials

The `initials` attribute contains the initials of some or all of an individual's names, but not the surname(s).

Superior	name
OID	2.5.4.43
Multivalued	Yes
User modify	Yes
Defined	RFC 2256

internationalISDNNumber

This attribute stores the ISDN telephone number for the entry with which it is associated.

OID	2.5.4.25
Syntax	Numeric String{16}
Equality	numericStringMatch
Substring	numericStringSubstringsMatch
Multivalued	Yes
User modify	Yes
Defined	RFC 2256

jpegPhoto

This attribute is used to store one or more images of a person using the JPEG File Interchange Format (JFIF).

OID	0.9.2342.19200300.100.1.60
Syntax	JPEG
Multivalued	Yes
User modify	Yes
Defined	RFC 2798

l

This attribute contains the name of a locality, such as a city, county, or other geographic region (`localityName`).

Superior	name
OID	2.5.4.7
Multivalued	Yes
User modify	Yes
Defined	RFC 2256

ldapSyntaxes

Servers *may* use this attribute to list the syntaxes that are implemented. Each value corresponds to one syntax.

OID	1.3.6.1.4.1.1466.101.120.16
Syntax	LDAP Syntax Description
Usage	`directoryOperation`
Equality	`objectIdentifierFirstComponentMatch`
Multivalued	Yes
User modify	Yes
Defined	RFC 2252

matchingRules

This attribute is typically located in the subschema entry.

OID	2.5.21.4
Syntax	Matching Rule Description
Usage	`directoryOperation`
Equality	`objectIdentifierFirstComponentMatch`
Multivalued	Yes
User modify	Yes
Defined	RFC 2252

matchingRuleUse

This attribute is typically located in the subschema entry.

OID	2.5.21.8
Syntax	Matching Rule Use Description
Usage	`directoryOperation`
Equality	`objectIdentifierFirstComponentMatch`
Multivalued	Yes
User modify	Yes
Defined	RFC 2252

member

This attribute is used to represent a member of a group or group-like entry. It is designed to contain a distinguished name.

Superior	`distinguishedName`
OID	2.5.4.31
Multivalued	Yes
User modify	Yes
Defined	RFC 2256

modifiersName

This attribute should appear in entries that have been modified using the `Modify` operation. It is automatically updated by the directory server if the server supports the operational use of this attribute.

OID	2.5.18.4
Syntax	DN
Usage	`directoryOperation`
Equality	`distinguishedNameMatch`
Multivalued	No
User modify	No
Defined	RFC 2252

modifyTimestamp

This attribute should appear in entries that have been modified using the `Modify` operation. If the server supports this operational attribute, it will maintain the value automatically when an entry is updated.

OID	2.5.18.2
Syntax	Generalized Time
Usage	`directoryOperation`
Equality	`generalizedTimeMatch`
Multivalued	No
User modify	No
Defined	RFC 2252

name

The `name` attribute type is the attribute supertype from which string attribute types typically used for naming may be formed. It is unlikely that values of this type will occur in an entry.

OID	2.5.4.41
Syntax	Directory String{32768}
Equality	`caseIgnoreMatch`
Substring	`caseIgnoreSubstringsMatch`
Multivalued	Yes
User modify	Yes
Defined	RFC 2256

nameForms

This attribute is used by some X.500 servers as a way to define the content of the DIT.

OID	2.5.21.7
Syntax	Name Form Description
Usage	directoryOperation
Equality	objectIdentifierFirstComponentMatch
Multivalued	Yes
User modify	Yes
Defined	RFC 2252

namingContexts

The values of this attribute correspond to naming contexts that this server masters or shadows. If the server does not master any information (for example, if it is an LDAP gateway to a public X.500 directory), this attribute will be absent. If the server believes it contains the entire directory, the attribute will have a single value, and that value will be the empty string (indicating the null DN of the root). This attribute allows a client to choose suitable base objects for searching when it has contacted a server.

OID	1.3.6.1.4.1.1466.101.120.5
Syntax	DN
Usage	dSAOperation
Multivalued	Yes
User modify	Yes
Defined	RFC 2252

o

This attribute contains the name of an organization (organizationName).

Superior	name
OID	2.5.4.10
Multivalued	Yes
User modify	Yes
Defined	RFC 2256

objectClass

The values of the objectClass attribute describe the kind of object that an entry represents. The objectClass attribute is present in every entry, with at least two values. One of the values is either top or alias.

OID	2.5.4.0
Syntax	OID
Equality	objectIdentifierMatch

Multivalued	Yes
User modify	Yes
Defined	RFC 2256

objectClasses

This attribute is typically located in the subschema entry.

OID	2.5.21.6
Syntax	Object Class Description
Usage	`directoryOperation`
Equality	`objectIdentifierFirstComponentMatch`
Multivalued	Yes
User modify	Yes
Defined	RFC 2252

ou

This attribute contains the name of an organizational unit (`organizationalUnitName`).

Superior	`name`
OID	2.5.4.11
Multivalued	Yes
User modify	Yes
Defined	RFC 2256

owner

This attribute is normally used to define the distinguished name of the owner of an entry. For example, a `groupOfUniqueEntries` entry contains a list of members, but it also may list an owner that is allowed to make changes to the group using this attribute.

Superior	`distinguishedName`
OID	2.5.4.32
Multivalued	Yes
User modify	Yes
Defined	RFC 2256

physicalDeliveryOfficeName

This attribute contains a free-form name for a particular office to which a person may be assigned.

OID	2.5.4.19
Syntax	Directory String{128}
Equality	`caseIgnoreMatch`

Substring	caseIgnoreSubstringsMatch
Multivalued	Yes
User modify	Yes
Defined	RFC 2256

postalAddress

This attribute generally contains the full postal address (for example, 101 North Maple Street) minus city, state, and postal/ZIP code.

OID	2.5.4.16
Syntax	Postal Address
Equality	caseIgnoreListMatch
Substring	caseIgnoreListSubstringsMatch
Multivalued	Yes
User modify	Yes
Defined	RFC 2256

postalCode

This attribute contains a postal or ZIP code.

OID	2.5.4.17
Syntax	Directory String{40}
Equality	caseIgnoreMatch
Substring	caseIgnoreSubstringsMatch
Multivalued	Yes
User modify	Yes
Defined	RFC 2256

postOfficeBox

This attribute can contain a post office box number or similar information.

OID	2.5.4.18
Syntax	Directory String{40}
Equality	caseIgnoreMatch
Substring	caseIgnoreSubstringsMatch
Multivalued	Yes
User modify	Yes
Defined	RFC 2256

preferredDeliveryMethod

This attribute may specify whether a person prefers email, postal mail, FedEx, or some other delivery method. It is generally a free-form value, which limits its general usefulness.

OID	2.5.4.28
Syntax	Delivery Method
Multivalued	No
User modify	Yes
Defined	RFC 2256

preferredLanguage

This attribute is used to indicate an individual's preferred written or spoken language. It is useful for international correspondence or human-computer interaction. Values for this attribute type must conform to the definition of the `Accept-Language` header field defined in RFC 2068, with one exception: the sequence `Accept-Language:` should be omitted. This is a single-valued attribute type.

OID	2.16.840.1.113730.3.1.39
Syntax	Directory String
Equality	`caseIgnoreMatch`
Substring	`caseIgnoreSubstringsMatch`
Multivalued	No
User modify	Yes
Defined	RFC 2798

presentationAddress

This attribute contains an OSI presentation address.

OID	2.5.4.29
Syntax	Presentation Address
Equality	`presentationAddressMatch`
Multivalued	No
User modify	Yes
Defined	RFC 2256

protocolInformation

This attribute is used in conjunction with the `presentationAddress` attribute to provide additional information to the OSI network service.

OID	2.5.4.48
Syntax	1.3.6.1.4.1.1466.115.121.1.42
Equality	`protocolInformationMatch`

Multivalued	Yes
User modify	Yes
Defined	RFC 2256

registeredAddress

This attribute holds a postal address suitable for reception of telegrams or expedited documents, where it is necessary to have the recipient accept delivery.

Superior	postalAddress
OID	2.5.4.26
Syntax	Postal Address
Multivalued	Yes
User modify	Yes
Defined	RFC 2256

roleOccupant

An organizationalRole entry is associated with people who fill that role. This attribute is used to contain the distinguished names of those role-fillers.

Superior	distinguishedName
OID	2.5.4.33
Multivalued	Yes
User modify	Yes
Defined	RFC 2256

searchGuide

This attribute is used by X.500 clients when constructing search filters. It is made obsolete by enhancedSearchGuide.

OID	2.5.4.14
Syntax	1.3.6.1.4.1.1466.115.121.1.25
Multivalued	Yes
User modify	Yes
Defined	RFC 2256

seeAlso

This attribute can be used to point to the distinguished name of a related entry.

Superior	distinguishedName
OID	2.5.4.34
Multivalued	Yes
User modify	Yes
Defined	RFC 2256

serialNumber

This attribute contains the serial number of a device.

OID	2.5.4.5
Syntax	Printable String{64}
Equality	`caseIgnoreMatch`
Substring	`caseIgnoreSubstringsMatch`
Multivalued	Yes
User modify	Yes
Defined	RFC 2256

sn

This is the X.500 `surname` attribute, which contains a person's family name.

Superior	`name`
OID	2.5.4.4
Multivalued	Yes
User modify	Yes
Defined	RFC 2256

st

This attribute contains the full name of a state or province (`stateOrProvince-Name`).

Superior	`name`
OID	2.5.4.8
Multivalued	Yes
User modify	Yes
Defined	RFC 2256

street

This attribute contains the physical address of the object to which the entry corresponds, such as an address for package delivery (`streetAddress`).

OID	2.5.4.9
Syntax	Directory String{128}
Equality	`caseIgnoreMatch`
Substring	`caseIgnoreSubstringsMatch`
Multivalued	Yes
User modify	Yes
Defined	RFC 2256

subschemaSubentry

The value of this attribute is the name of a subschema entry (or subentry if the server is based on X.500(93)) in which the server makes available attributes specifying the schema.

OID	2.5.18.10
Syntax	DN
Usage	`directoryOperation`
Equality	`distinguishedNameMatch`
Multivalued	No
User modify	No
Defined	RFC 2252

supportedAlgorithms

This attribute must be stored and requested in the binary form, as `supportedAlgorithms;binary`.

OID	2.5.4.52
Syntax	Supported Algorithm
Multivalued	Yes
User modify	Yes
Defined	RFC 2256

supportedApplicationContext

This attribute contains the identifiers of OSI application contexts.

OID	2.5.4.30
Syntax	OID
Equality	`objectIdentifierMatch`
Multivalued	Yes
User modify	Yes
Defined	RFC 2256

supportedControl

The values of this attribute are the OIDs identifying controls the server supports. If the server does not support any controls, this attribute is absent.

OID	1.3.6.1.4.1.1466.101.120.13
Syntax	OID
Usage	`dSAOperation`
Multivalued	Yes
User modify	Yes
Defined	RFC 2252

supportedExtension

The values of this attribute are OIDs identifying the extended operations that the server supports. If the server does not support any extensions, this attribute is absent.

OID	1.3.6.1.4.1.1466.101.120.7
Syntax	OID
Usage	dSAOperation
Multivalued	Yes
User modify	Yes
Defined	RFC 2252

supportedLDAPVersion

The values of this attribute are the versions of the LDAP protocol that the server implements.

OID	1.3.6.1.4.1.1466.101.120.15
Syntax	Integer
Usage	dSAOperation
Multivalued	Yes
User modify	Yes
Defined	RFC 2252

supportedSASLMechanisms

The values of this attribute are the names of supported SASL mechanisms that the server supports. If the server does not support any mechanisms, this attribute is absent.

OID	1.3.6.1.4.1.1466.101.120.14
Syntax	Directory String
Usage	dSAOperation
Multivalued	Yes
User modify	Yes
Defined	RFC 2252

telephoneNumber

This attribute contains the telephone number associated with a particular entry.

OID	2.5.4.20
Syntax	Telephone Number{32}
Equality	telephoneNumberMatch
Substring	telephoneNumberSubstringsMatch
Multivalued	Yes
User modify	Yes
Defined	RFC 2256

teletexTerminalIdentifier

Teletex was a type of terminal that could be used to send and receive text and graphics. As with Teletex, this attribute is rarely used anymore.

OID	2.5.4.22
Syntax	Teletex Terminal Identifier
Multivalued	Yes
User modify	Yes
Defined	RFC 2256

telexNumber

Used to store the number for a Teletex terminal. This attribute is almost never used.

OID	2.5.4.21
Syntax	Telex Number
Multivalued	Yes
User modify	Yes
Defined	RFC 2256

title

This attribute contains the title, such as `Vice President`, of a person in their organizational context. The `personalTitle` attribute is used for a person's title independent of their job function.

Superior	name
OID	2.5.4.12
Multivalued	Yes
User modify	Yes
Defined	RFC 2256

uniqueMember

This attribute is typically used to store the distinguished name of a group member. It may be used to store other unique membership information, but doing so probably will not make the membership information easily reusable; so, distinguished names are preferred.

OID	2.5.4.50
Syntax	Name And Optional UID
Equality	uniqueMemberMatch
Multivalued	Yes
User modify	Yes
Defined	RFC 2256

userCertificate

This attribute must be stored and requested in the binary form, as `userCertificate;binary`.

OID	2.5.4.36
Syntax	Certificate
Multivalued	Yes
User modify	Yes
Defined	RFC 2256

userPassword

This attribute is used to store passwords. Many directory implementations assume plain-text passwords unless the password value is prefixed by the mechanisms used to hide it.

OID	2.5.4.35
Syntax	Octet String{128}
Equality	`octetStringMatch`
Multivalued	Yes
User modify	Yes
Defined	RFC 2256

userPKCS12

PKCS #12 provides a format for exchange of personal identity information. When such information is stored in a directory service, the `userPKCS12` attribute should be used. This attribute must be stored and requested in binary form, as `userPKCS12;binary`.

OID	2.16.840.1.113730.3.1.216
Syntax	Binary
Multivalued	Yes
User modify	Yes
Defined	RFC 2798

userSMIMECertificate

This attribute is an S/MIME (RFC 1847) signed message with a zero-length body. It must be stored and requested in binary form, as `userSMIMECertificate;binary`. It contains the person's entire certificate chain and the signed attribute that describes his or her algorithm capabilities, stored as binary data. This attribute is preferred over the `userCertificate` attribute for S/MIME applications.

OID	2.16.840.1.113730.3.1.40
Syntax	Binary

Multivalued	Yes
User modify	Yes
Defined	RFC 2798

x121Address

X.121 is an addressing scheme used in X.25. This attribute can be used to store such an address.

OID	2.5.4.24
Syntax	Numeric String{15}
Equality	numericStringMatch
Substring	numericStringSubstringsMatch
Multivalued	Yes
User modify	Yes
Defined	RFC 2256

x500UniqueIdentifier

The x500uniqueIdentifier attribute is used to distinguish between objects when a distinguished name has been reused. This is a different attribute type from both the uid and uniqueIdentifier types.

OID	2.5.4.45
Syntax	Bit String
Equality	bitStringMatch
Multivalued	Yes
User modify	Yes
Defined	RFC 2256

PerLDAP

In part 2, we discussed a number of examples using the Net::LDAP module for Perl. However, many existing tools and scripts are written using PerLDAP, a module developed in 1998 by Netscape and the author of this book. This appendix gives a brief overview of PerLDAP and translates many of the key examples from part 2 from Net::LDAP to PerLDAP.

B.1   OVERVIEW OF PERLDAP

When discussing the differences between Net::LDAP and PerLDAP in chapter 6, we showed a diagram of PerLDAP's architecture with several components. In this section, we'll briefly review these components and the role they play.

B.1.1   The Conn class

The connection class, `Mozilla::LDAP::Conn`, manages the connection between the LDAP client and server. Every time you want to perform an LDAP operation, you use this class. These LDAP operations include bind, search, compare, add, delete, modify, and rename—all of which can be performed using the connection class.

B.1.2   The Entry class

The `Entry` class, `Mozilla::LDAP::Entry`, represents a single LDAP entry. It generally acts like a smart, named Perl hash. The `Entry` class is smart in the sense that it remembers all the changes that have been performed upon it since the last time it was retrieved from the LDAP server. By *named*, we mean that it is assigned a distinguished name corresponding to an entry in the directory.

B.1.3   LDAP messages

Certain tasks are commonly performed by applications accessing LDAP directories. The utilities class, `Mozilla::LDAP::Utils`, makes some of these tasks much easier. Among the tasks this component simplifies is the parsing of command-line arguments in a way that conforms with the de facto standard `ldapsearch` and `ldapmodify` command-line applications. Other simplified tasks include distinguished name manipulation.

B.1.4   LDIF

Because most existing LDAP-enabled applications and servers can use LDIF, PerLDAP's ability to create and parse files in this format is a real timesaver. This functionality is provided by the `Mozilla::LDAP::LDIF` component.

B.2   EXAMPLES FROM CHAPTER 7: ENTRY MANAGEMENT

Our first example mirrors the adduser.pl example from listing 7.1. It allows for the creation of new users with a web form. In listing B.1, the bolded lines indicate changes from the version in chapter 7 to allow the use of PerLDAP rather than Net::LDAP. Notice the use of `$ld->getErrorString()` to print an error message as opposed to the error handling provided by Net::LDAP.

Listing B.1   Adduser.pl

```perl
use CGI qw/:standard/;
use Mozilla::LDAP::Conn;

my $server = "localhost";
my $port = 389;
my $user = "cn=Administrator";
my $pass = "password";
my $org = "dc=domain,dc=com";

print header,
    start_html('Add User'),
    h1('Add User'),
    start_form,
    "First Name:",textfield('givenname'),p,
    "Last Name:",textfield('sn'),p,
    "UserID:",textfield('uid'),p,
    "Mail:",textfield('mail'),p,
    submit("Add"),end_form,hr;

if (param()) {
    my $ld = new Mozilla::LDAP::Conn($server,$port,$user,$pass);
    my $givenname = param('givenname');
    my $sn = param('sn');
    my $uid = param('uid');
    my $mail = param('mail');
```

```perl
    my $cn = "$givenname $sn";
    my $dn = "uid=$uid,$org";
    my $objectclass = "inetOrgPerson";

    print "Adding User: ",$dn,p;

    my $entry = new Mozilla::LDAP::Entry();

    $entry->setDN($dn);
    $entry->addValue("objectclass",$objectclass);
    $entry->addValue("givenname",$givenname);
    $entry->addValue("sn",$sn);
    $entry->addValue("uid",$uid);
    $entry->addValue("mail",$mail);
    $entry->addValue("cn",$cn);

    if (!$ld->add($entry)) {
        print "Failed: ",$ld->getErrorString();
        exit;
    }
    print "Okay!",p;
}
```

Our second example from chapter 7 (listing 7.2) provides a way to add a minimal amount of information using a web page and have that information be joined with other external information to create a full entry in the directory. The version of that example in listing B.2 uses the same web-handling techniques, but uses PerLDAP rather than Net::LDAP for directory access. Notice that when the entry is created, you set the objectclass using a standard Perl array reference.

Listing B.2   addimportuser.pl

```perl
use CGI qw/:standard/;
use Mozilla::LDAP::Conn;

my $server = "localhost";
my $port = 389;
my $user = "cn=Admin";
my $pass = "manager_password";
my $org = "dc=domain,dc=com";
my $maildomain = "domain.com";

print header,
    start_html('Sync User'),
    h1('Sync User'),
    start_form,
    "UserID: ",textfield('uid'),p,
    "Password: ",password_field('password'),p,
    submit("Sync"),end_form,hr;

if (param()) {
    my $ld = new Mozilla::LDAP::Conn($server,$port,$user,$pass);
```

```
        my $uid = param('uid');
        my $password = param('password');

        my ($login,$pass,$userid,$groupid,$quota,
            $comment,$gecos,$home,$shell,$expire) = getpwnam($uid);

        if (!$login || crypt($password,$pass) ne $pass) {
            print "Invalid Username or Password.",p;
            print "Crypt: $pass",p;
            exit;
        }
        $gecos =~ /(\w+)$/;
        my $sn = $1;
        my $dn = "uid=$uid,$org";
        my $entry = new Mozilla::LDAP::Entry();
        $entry->setDN($dn);
        $entry->{objectclass} = [ "top", "person", "inetOrgPerson" ];
        $entry->addValue("cn",$gecos);
        $entry->addValue("sn",$sn);
        $entry->addValue("userPassword","{crypt}$pass");
        $entry->addValue("uid",$uid);
        $entry->addValue("mail","$uid\@$maildomain");

        print "Adding $dn.",p;
        if (!$ld->add($entry)) {
            print "Failed: ",$ld->getErrorString();
            exit;
        }
        print "Okay!";
        exit;
}
```

In our final example in chapter 7 (listing 7.3), we offer a command-line tool that creates standard posixAccount entries in the directory that will be compliant with the various pluggable authentication modules (PAM) available for many Unix platforms. The version in listing B.3 changes the connection handling to use PerLDAP, but otherwise provides the same functionality.

Listing B.3   account_add.pl

```
use Mozilla::LDAP::Conn;

$conn = new Mozilla::LDAP::Conn("localhost",389,"cn=Admin",
    "password");

print "Username: ";
$username = <>;

print "Password: ";
$password = <>;

print "UID#: ";
$uid = <>;
```

```
print "GID#: ";
$gid = <>;

print "Full Name: ";
$gecos = <>;

print "Home Directory: ";
$home = <>;

print "Shell: ";
$shell = <>;

$entry = $conn->newEntry();
$entry->addValue("uid",$username);
$entry->addValue("uidNumber",$uid);
$entry->addValue("gidNumber",$gid);
$entry->addValue("gecos",$gecos);
$entry->addValue("homeDirectory",$home);
$entry->addValue("loginShell",$shell);
$entry->addValue("userPassword",$password);
$entry->addValue("objectclass","posixAccount");
$entry->copy("uid","cn");

$dn = "cn=" . $username .
    ", ou=Division A, ou=Accounts, dc=domain, dc=com";
$entry->setDN($dn);

if (!$conn->add(entry)) {
    print "An error occurred adding the account to the directory.\n";
    die $conn->getErrorString();
}
print "Account added successfully!\n";
```

B.3 EXAMPLES FROM CHAPTER 8: MIGRATION AND SYNCHRONIZATION

The first example in chapter 8 provides a way to migrate a comma-separated table into an LDAP directory. The version in listing B.4 mirrors listing 8.1, but changes the initial connection creation and subsequent entry creation to use the PerLDAP module. Note that although most of the entry creation is similar to Net::LDAP, the multi-valued objectclass attribute is populated using a traditional Perl tied hash rather than the addValue method. Either technique works.

> **Listing B.4   migrate_table.pl**

```
use Mozilla::LDAP::Conn;
use Mozilla::LDAP::Entry;

$conn = new Mozilla::LDAP::Conn("myserver",389,"cn=Admin",
    "admin-password");

while ($line = <>)
```

```
{
    chop $line; # remove the trailing linefeed
    ($last,$first,$telephone,$email) = split(/,/,$line);
    ($username,$domain) = split(/@/,$email);
    $dn = "uid=" . $username . ",dc=xyz,dc=com";
    $entry = new Mozilla::LDAP::Entry();
    $entry->setDN($dn);
    $entry->addValue("sn",$last);
    $entry->addValue("cn","$first $last");
    $entry->addValue("givenName",$first);
    $entry->addValue("uid",$username);
    $entry->addValue("mail",$email);
    $entry->addValue("telephoneNumber",$telephone);
    $entry->{objectclass} = [ "top","inetOrgPerson" ];
    $conn->add($entry);
}
```

In our second example from chapter 8, we migrate two tables from two different files into the directory. The structure of the code in listing B.5 is the same, but this example swaps out listing 8.2's Net::LDAP calls for PerLDAP calls.

Listing B.5 migrate_two.pl

```
use Mozilla::LDAP::Conn;
use Mozilla::LDAP::Entry;

$conn = new Mozilla::LDAP::Conn("myserver",389,"cn=Admin",
        "admin-password");

open(EMAILDB,"email.txt");
while ($line = <EMAILDB>)
{
    chop $line; # remove the trailing linefeed
    ($last,$first,$telephone,$email) = split(/,/,$line);
    ($username,$domain) = split(/@/,$email);
    $dn = "uid=" . $username . ",dc=xyz,dc=com";
    $entry = new Mozilla::LDAP::Entry();
    $entry->setDN($dn);
    $entry->addValue("sn",$last);
    $entry->addValue("cn","$first $last");
    $entry->addValue("givenName",$first);
    $entry->addValue("uid",$username);
    $entry->addValue("mail",$email);
    $entry->addValue("telephoneNumber",$telephone);
    $entry->{objectclass} = [ "top","inetOrgPerson" ];
    $entries{$username} = $entry;
}
close (EMAILDB);

open(PASSDB,"password.txt");
while ($line = <PASSDB>) {
```

```
    chop $line;
    ($uid,$password,$name) = split(/,/,$line);
    $entry = $entries{$uid};
    $entry->addValue("userPassword",$password);
    $conn->add($entry);
}
close(PASSDB);
```

Listing 8.3 provides a way to synchronize a user's password from a file. Listing B.6 does the same, but it uses PerLDAP instead of Net::LDAP. Notice the use of the update method on the connection class rather than an update method on the entry itself.

Listing B.6   update_password.pl

```
use Mozilla::LDAP::Conn;

$conn = new Mozilla::LDAP::Conn("myserver",389,"cn=Admin",
          "admin-password");

open (MYFILE,"inputfile");
while ($line = <MYFILE>)
{
    chop $line; # remove tailing linefeed
    ($userid,$name,$company,$password) = split(/,/,$line);
    $entry = $conn->search("dc=xyz,dc=com","sub","(uid=$userid)");
    if (!$entry)
    {
        print "Warning: Entry '$userid' was not found.\n";
    } else {
        $entry->replaceValue("userPassword",$password);
        $conn->update($entry);
        print "Updated Password for Entry '$userid'.\n";
    }
}
close (MYFILE);
```

In listing 8.4, we provide a way to use multiple criteria to try to identify the entry to update. Listing B.7 does the same thing, but it substitutes the PerLDAP connection handling, searching, and update techniques for the Net::LDAP routines used in chapter 8.

Listing B.7   fuzzy_update.pl

```
use Mozilla::LDAP::Conn;
use Mozilla::LDAP::Entry;

$conn = new Mozilla::LDAP::Conn("localhost",389,"cn=Admin",
    "admin-password") or die "Can not create LDAP connection.";

while($line = <>)
```

```
{
    chop $line;
    ($last,$first,$phone,$department) = split(/,/,$line);
    $entry = $conn->search("dc=xyz,dc=com","sub",
        "(&(department=$department)(cn=$first $last))");

if (!$entry) {
    $entry = new Mozilla::LDAP::Entry();
    $entry->setDN("cn=$first $last,dc=xyz,dc=com");
    $entry->addValue("objectClass","organizationalPerson");
    $entry->addValue("cn","$first $last");
    $entry->addValue("sn",$last);
    $entry->addValue("telephoneNumber",$phone);
    $entry->addValue("department",$department);
    $conn->add($entry);
} else {
    $entry->replaceValue("telephoneNumber",$phone);
    $conn->update($entry);
}
}
```

In the final example from chapter 8 (listing 8.5), we provide a way to synchronize
from LDAP to a file based on time stamps. Listing B.8 shows a slightly simpler version of that example—it doesn't do the time stamp generation. Notice that because
you are dealing with multiple entries from LDAP, you use the nextEntry()
method to advance to the next entry.

Listing B.8 sync_from_ldap.pl

```
use Mozilla::LDAP::Conn;

$conn = new Mozilla::LDAP::Conn("localhost",389,"cn=Admin",
        "admin-password") or die "Unable to open a connection.";

$lastrun = "199908150000";
$entry = $conn->search("dc=xyz,dc=com","sub",
        "modifyTimestamp>=$lastrun");

while ($entry)
{
    $cn = $entry->getValue("cn");
    ($first,$last) = split(/ /,$cn);
    $phone = $entry->getValue("telephoneNumber");
    $email = $entry->getValue("mail");
    $row{$email} = "$last,$first,$phone,$email";
    $entry = $entry->nextEntry();
}

while ($line = <>)
{
    chop $line;
    ($last,$first,$phone,$email) = split(/,/,$line);
    if ($row{$email})
```

```
    {
        print $row{$email} . "\n";
    } else {
        print $line . "\n";
    }
}
```

B.4 EXAMPLES FROM CHAPTER 9:
SERVER MANAGEMENT AND MONITORING

Listing 9.1 shows how to retrieve the root entry from an LDAPv3-compliant directory server. The version of the example in listing B.9 uses the LDIF printing capability of the PerLDAP Entry class to print the contents of the root entry.

Listing B.9   get_root.pl

```perl
use Mozilla::LDAP::Conn;

$conn = new Mozilla::LDAP::Conn("localhost", "389");
die "No LDAP connection" unless $conn;

$entry = $conn->search("", "base", "(objectclass=*)");

if ($entry)
{
    $entry->printLDIF();
}
$conn->close;
```

print_oclass_def.pl

The example in listing B.10 parallels listing 9.2, which shows how to extract information about object classes directly from an LDAP server. Most of the regular-expression code remains the same, but the initial code to retrieve the schema information is changed to use PerLDAP classes.

Listing B.10   print_oclass_def.pl

```perl
use Mozilla::LDAP::Conn;

my $conn = new Mozilla::LDAP::Conn("127.0.0.1",389,
    "cn=Admin","manager");
die "Unable to connect to LDAP server" unless $conn;

my $entry = $conn->search("cn=schema","base","(objectclass=*)");

if (! $entry)
{
    print "Sorry, this server doesn't support schema discovery.\n";
    exit;
```

```perl
}

my @objectclasses = @{$entry->{objectclasses}};

foreach my $oc (@objectclasses)
{
    my ($name, $desc, $sup, $must, $may, @must, @may, $match);

    if ($oc =~ /NAME '(.+)' DESC '(.*)'/)
    {
        $name = $1;
        if ($2 =~ /\w+/)
        {
            $desc = $2;
        }
    }

    if (grep (/^$name$/i,@ARGV))
    {
        $match = 1;

        if ($oc =~ /SUP (\w+)/)
        {
            $sup = $1;
        }

        if ($oc =~ /MUST [\(']+([$ \w]+)[\)']+/ || $oc =~
            /MUST (\w+)/)
        {
            $must = $1;
            $must =~ s/ //g;
            @must = split(/\$/,$must);
        }

        if ($oc =~ /MAY [\(']+([$ \w]+)[\)']+/ || $oc =~
            /MAY (\w+)/)
        {
            $may = $1;
            $may =~ s/ //g;
            @may = split(/\$/,$may);
        }
    }
    print "Name:\t$name\n" if ($match || $#ARGV < 0);
    print "Desc:\t$desc\n" if $desc;
    print "Sup:\t$sup\n" if $sup;
    print "Must:\t" . join("\n\t",@must) . "\n" if @must;
    print "May:\t" . join("\n\t",@may) . "\n" if @may;
    print "\n" if ($match);
}

$conn->close;
```

Listing 9.3 is similar to 9.2 from a directory access perspective, so we will not provide a PerLDAP version. To create a PerLDAP version of the example, simply perform almost the same substitutions as in listing B.10.

The get_monitor.pl example in listing 9.4 is also easy to translate by substituting the connection and search methods, as we've done in many of the previous examples. Listing B.11 shows that example with the appropriate substitutions.

Listing B.11 Get_monitor.pl

```perl
use Mozilla::LDAP::Conn;

my $conn = new Mozilla::LDAP::Conn("localhost",389);

my $entry = $conn->search("","base","objectclass=*");

my $monitordn;

if (!$entry) {
    $monitordn = "cn=monitor";
} else {
    $monitordn = $entry->{"monitor"}[0];
}
my $monitor_entry = $conn->search($monitordn,"base",
    "objectclass=*");

print "Connections: " . $monitor_entry->{"connections"} . "\n";

if ($monitor_entry->{"connections"}[0] > 100) {
    print "Warning: More than 100 concurrent connections.\n";
}
```

The final listing from chapter 9 (listing 9.5) offers a way to automatically test replication. Listing B.12 shows how you can write the same code using the PerLDAP module.

Listing B.12 test_replication.pl

```perl
use Mozilla::LDAP::Conn;
use Mozilla::LDAP::Entry;

@replicas = ("server-a","server-b","server-c");

$master = "masterhostname";

$conn = new Mozilla::LDAP::Conn($master_name,389,"cn=Admin",
    "password");

$testentry_name = "cn=Test Entry, ou=Test Branch, dc=domain,
    dc=com";

$master->delete($testentry_name);

$testentry = new Mozilla::LDAP::Entry();
$testentry->setDn($testentry_name);
$testentry->addValue("objectclass","inetOrgPerson");
```

```
$testentry->addValue("cn","Test Entry");
$testentry->addValue("sn","Entry");

$conn->add($testentry);

sleep 10;

for ( $i = 1; $i <= $#replicas; $i++) {
    $replica_name = $replicas[$i];
    $replica = new Mozilla::LDAP::Conn($replica_name);

    $entry = $replica->search($testentry_name,"base",
        "(objectclass=*)");
    if (!$entry) {
        print "$replica_name FAILED!\n";
    } else {
        print "$replica_name PASSED!\n";
    }
    $replica->unbind();
}

$conn->delete($testentry_name);

$conn->unbind();
```

B.5   *PERLDAP-ONLY FUNCTIONALITY*

Some functionality in PerLDAP is not available or not necessary in Net::LDAP. This section discusses some of this functionality and how to use it from the PerLDAP module.

B.5.1   Rebinding to another server

When you're following referrals, it is highly likely that the credentials that work for one server are not valid on another server. For that reason, in order for LDAP operations to automatically follow referrals, you need to create a callback that can tell the server what credentials to use when it needs to rebind to another server.

The setRebindProc() method on the Conn object takes a subroutine reference that can be used to return the proper information to authenticate successfully. Here is a simple subroutine that can act as a callback, and the call to setRebind-Proc() that activates it:

```
sub rebindsub
{
    return ("cn=Jeff Smith,dc=manning,dc=com","password",
            LDAP_AUTH_SIMPLE);
}

$conn->setRebindProc(\&rebindsub);
```

Rather than all this code, you can use the following method on the Conn object to accomplish the same result:

```
$conn->setDefaultRebindProc("cn=someone","password",
                LDAP_AUTH_SIMPLE);
```

The trick with rebinding is that it is possible for a server to refer the client to a server where the credentials currently being used are not valid. This is not usually the case when referral takes place to direct a client at a writable copy of an entry to be modified.

B.5.2 Adding and removing values with DN syntax

The addDNValue() method of the Entry class simplifies the addition of values to an attribute that has a DN syntax. For example, the uniqueMember attribute of a groupOfUniqueNames entry is defined to hold DN values of group members:

```
$entry->addDNValue("uniqueMember","cn=Jody Adams,dc=domain,dc=com");
```

By using the addDNValue() method, the uniqueMember attribute will first be checked to ensure that the value doesn't already exist. This is the same process used by the addValue() method, but it takes into account that the spacing between RDN components is irrelevant, and other DN construction rules.

A similar method, removeDNValue(), removes a DN-syntax value from a particular attribute:

```
$entry->removeDNValue("uniqueMember",
                "cn=Jody Adams,dc=domain,dc=com");
```

B.5.3 Copying and moving attributes

Directory-enabled applications do not always agree on the attribute type to use for a particular kind of value. One application may use postalAddress, and another may used registeredAddress. If the goal is to keep both attributes synchronized, you can do so by simply copying one attribute into another. The copy() method on the Entry class does this:

```
$entry->copy("postalAddress","registeredAddress");
```

This line copies the contents of the postalAddress attribute into the registeredAddress attribute. However, it will fail if registeredAddress already exists in the entry. You can add an additional flag to tell the copy() method to overwrite the destination attribute:

```
$entry->copy("postalAddress","registeredAddress",1);
```

You can use a zero (0) in the third argument to get the default behavior.

If you only want the values to exist in the destination attribute, call the move() method. This method takes the same arguments as the copy() method, but deletes the source attribute:

```
$entry->move("postalAddress","registeredAddress",1);
```

In this line, you place the current value or values of postalAddress into registeredAddress, while at the same time deleting those values from postalAddress.

B.5.4 Forcing a change

If you're familiar with Perl, you may wonder why you don't simply use the push and pop commands available in the Perl language to operate directly on the array references used to store values in the Entry objects. Unfortunately, these methods do not allow you to track changes to the Entry object. Because you only submit changes, not the entire entry, to the LDAP server when update is called, this change tracking is very important.

If an array is updated directly, perhaps by some existing code that is unfamiliar with PerLDAP, the attrModified() method can be called to tell PerLDAP to force a change on the specified attribute:

```
$vals = $entry->{"mail"};
push @$vals, "someone\@domain.com";
$entry->attrModified("mail");
```

In this example, you retrieve the array reference for the mail attribute and push an additional value into the array. Because PerLDAP will not detect this change, you need to tell it that the change has occurred by calling attrModified().

index

D

NO-USER-MODIFICATION
   in schema definition 207
Novell
   history in directories 6

O

o attribute 291
object classes 46
   defining 46
   inheritance 47
   listing information from
      server 170
   naming 46
   representing in DSML 100
   standard 38
   types 48
   writing as DSML 199
   writing in LDIF 95
Object IDentifiers 39
   for object classes 47
object modeling
   classes 51
   instances 53
   of LDAP schema 51
   relationships 51
objectClass attribute 36, 46,
   49, 291
   using to match any entry 77
objectclasses 46
   retrieving in Perl 172
   special schema attribute 95
OID 39
one-level scope
   using in Net::LDAP 114
Online Certificate Status
   Protocol 268
Open Database Connectivity
   (ODBC)
   performance vs. LDAP 7
opening a connection
   in Perl 175
OpenLDAP xx
operational attributes 87
OR (|) operator 85
ordering matches 83

Organization for the Advancement of Structured Information Standards (OASIS) 98
organization object class 38, 276
organizational boundaries
   crossing with DSML 196
organizationalPerson object
   class 38, 277
organizationalRole object
   class 277
organizationalUnit object
   class 278
ou attribute 292
owner
   attribute 292
   group attribute type 135

P

parentheses
   use in search filters 79
   when combining search
      filters 85
parse()
   method on PerlSAX 189
parser
   instantiating 195
parser handler
   for XML in Perl 186
passwd file 133
   See also Unix passwd file
passwords
   comparing 119
   handling over the
      network 119
   initializing via migration 157
people entries
   creating 126
performance
   for different filter types 81
   increasing for searches 88
   read vs. write 9
   substring searches 83
Perl
   comparing attribute types to
      variables 45

Perl modules
   getting xx
Perl XS
   and PerLDAP 108
PerLDAP 108, 302
   adding and removing DN
      values 314
   copying and moving
      attributes 314
   forcing changes 315
Perl-LDAP module
   getting xx
PerlSAX 186
   automatic error checking 189
   instantiating parser 189
person object class 38, 278
   definition 199
personalization 14
physicalDeliveryOfficeName
   attribute 292
policy information
   management in LDAP 142
polling the monitor entry 180
posixAccount
   object class 138
postalAddress attribute 293
postalCode attribute 293
postOfficeBox attribute 293
pre-existing data
   using to populate
      directory 126
preferredDeliveryMethod
   attribute 294
preferredLanguage attribute 294
presentationAddress
   attribute 294
printLDIF()
   method on Net 195
privacy 27, 254
private key 261
protocolInformation
   attribute 294
provisioning tools 125
public key cryptography
   256, 261